Gabriel Tarde

ON COMMUNICATION

AND SOCIAL INFLUENCE

THE HERITAGE OF SOCIOLOGY

A Series Edited by Morris Janowitz

Gabriel Tarde

ON COMMUNICATION
AND SOCIAL INFLUENCE

Selected Papers

Edited and with an Introduction by

TERRY N. CLARK

THE UNIVERSITY OF CHICAGO PRESS

CHICAGO AND LONDON

Library of Congress Catalog Card Number: 69-14824

THE UNIVERSITY OF CHICAGO PRESS, CHICAGO 60637
The University of Chicago Press, Ltd., London W.C. 1

Contents

v

Preface

SOME OF THE NEGLECT of Tarde in the English-speaking world is due to the fact that several of his more serious works have never been translated. Accordingly, to present a meaningful sampling of his many contributions, it has been necessary to translate for the first time more than three-quarters of the selections contained in the present volume.

The hackneyed dictum that there are no satisfactory translations must inevitably come to the mind of anyone attempting to render Tarde's work in English, for he was a a stylist who enjoyed manipulating language as much as he did ideas. One is tempted to simplify his complex verbal constructions by rewording them in more contemporary English prose, especially when he deals with technical questions. But this would be to destroy the poetic elements of his work. While this is by no means a poetic translation—for we are not poets—we have retained some of Tarde's stylistic gymnastics rather than force him into the idiom of contemporary social science. For his own set of technical concepts, which are only partially translatable into those currently in use, we have sought the closest English equivalents.

The translation was accomplished in three stages. N. Claire Ellis, a graduate student at the University of Chicago, prepared a first draft, which was then checked and edited line by line by Priscilla P. Clark, assistant professor of French at the University of Illinois at Chicago Circle. Finally, Terry N. Clark reviewed the translation once again, revising it and adding editorial comments in conjunction with Priscilla P. Clark.

Morris Janowitz, as colleague and general editor of the Heritage of Sociology Series, provided advice throughout the development of the volume. Peter M. Blau, Philip M. Hauser, Steven Lukes, Fred L. Strodbeck, and George W. Stocking offered useful suggestions for the Introduction. Fred E. Duffell served once again as a thoroughly professional typist. M. Guillaume de Tarde generously provided the photograph of his father which appears on the cover.

Introduction

GABRIEL TARDE ranks as one of the three most outstanding sociologists of nineteenth-century France, but, especially in recent years, he has been read less closely than either Auguste Comte or Emile Durkheim. Too often dismissed as a debator of Durkheim who lost, or the dated antecedent of Le Bon, Tarde has been stigmatized as an inchoate and imprecise philosophical or literary writer. Such misconceptions, magnified many times by distorted secondary accounts, have flourished. Remarkably few are those who have sufficiently penetrated Tarde's work to find more than support for their preconceived notions. This volume has been prepared to facilitate a more careful examination of Tarde.

Tarde contains much of value for the present-day social scientist. The famous debate with Durkheim did not in fact terminate with a clear victory for either side; each man contributed to a more sophisticated picture of the relationships between the individual and society, and in the debate one finds many issues clarified which later writers have seldom considered in such detail. Awareness of the problems raised in the debate—and the solutions of Tarde and Durkheim—heightens one's sensitivity to basic issues of the nature and scope of sociology, problems that plague sociologists even today.

One finds too, in Tarde, the elaboration of a general conceptual framework that serves to integrate middle-level theory and emipirical analysis. But the integration provided by this framework is not simply one of dry categorization: abstract formulations are skillfully combined to generate middle-level propositions which, in turn,

1

generally either are tested or the necessary evidence is indicated which would serve to confirm or reject them. One can observe, in Tarde's hands, how such a general framework—one which incorporates innovation, conflict, and change as central elements—can serve as a powerful beam to bring into focus and illuminate selected empirical problems.

The propositions concerning imitation and diffusion, which derive largely from this framework, are among the most stimulating of Tarde's ideas for contemporary research. Criminologists, too, find some some of their guiding concepts in Tarde's writings on deviance and social control. Tarde also scrutinized collective behavior, mass communication, and public opinion, not as isolated phenomena but as elements to be explained within the context of broader societal patterns. But unlike subsequent mass society theorists, Tarde integrated his discussion of macro-societal changes with those on the small group level. In this way, for example, he arrived at a two-step model of communication flow. In following Tarde through these and other problems, we can observe a versatile mind, always seeking, often reaching, the ideals that he set for the creative thinker. Finally, in presenting his thoughts Tarde offers a model of literary exposition that more contemporary writers would do well at least to consider if not to imitate.

I. *Life*

Jean-Gabriel Tarde was born in the small town of Sarlat, about one hundred miles east of Bordeaux, in 1843.[1] His father's family was practically as old as the town, and, since the eleventh century, Tardes, or de Tardes, had served as local officials of one sort or another. (The aristocratic particle, dropped by the family in 1789 but restored in 1885, was never used by Tarde in his writings.) These traditions intrigued Tarde, and he wrote several

[1]   On Tarde's life, see Gabriel Tarde, *Introduction et pages choisies par ses fils*, preface by Henri Bergson (Paris: Louis Michard, 1909); Alfred Espinas, "Notice sur la vie et les œuvres de M. Gabriel de Tarde," *Séances et Travaux de l'Académie des Sciences Morales et Politiques* 174 (1910), 309–422; Terry N. Clark, "Gabriel Tarde," *International Encyclopedia of the Social Sciences* (New York: Macmillan and Free Press, 1968).

short volumes on the family and the town, as well as editing and republishing the papers of outstanding family members.[2]

Tarde's own father (1797–1850) served as a military officer until his two brothers were killed in the wars of Napoleon, but then turned to law under family pressures and finished his life as a judge in Sarlat. At forty-four he married the nineteen-year-old daughter of another established Sarlat family, Anne-Aline Roux. Jean-Gabriel was their only child. His father died when he was only seven, and he was raised by his mother, to whom he remained exceptionally close throughout her life.

Tarde attended a school in Sarlat operated by Jesuit priests, who offered a rigorous classical training built largely on Latin, Greek, history, and mathematics. While always the first student in his classes, the sensitive young Tarde was pained by the Jesuit discipline, so much so that during his last three years, while a boarder at the school, he once even scaled the wall to escape temporarily. Although Tarde never failed to praise the classical training for binding together the leaders of nation with a common set of values, he retained a permanent distaste for socially imposed discipline whenever it limited individual freedom. The scholastic training also moved him toward a strong emphasis on the role of the intellect as well as an even more hierarchical conception of society than was held by many of his contemporaries.

Leaving school at seventeen, Tarde—like Karl Marx, Claude Bernard, and many other mid-nineteenth-century youths—first tried his hand at verse and dramatic pieces. Despite the encomiums of his sons,[3] however, it seems that the world did not lose a great poet when Tarde forsook his muse for more prosaic activities. But, again like Marx, Tarde's later works bore the stamp of these early literary endeavors.

Tarde was also fascinated by mathematics in his early years, and at one point he considered attending the Ecole Polytechnique. It was perhaps the applied, ordered training, combined with its regimented social life, that made him shun the Ecole. From nine-

2   See the Bibliography at the end of the volume for Tarde's publications.

3   ʹ *Introduction et pages choisies par ses fils.*

teen to twenty-five, however, he suffered from an eye disease which severely limited his reading. For these several reasons Tarde acceded to his mother's wishes and settled on the less demanding study of law. He passed his first law examinations at the nearby Toulouse Faculty of Law, and then spent one more year (1865) in Paris—accompanied by his mother—completing his legal studies.

From 1869 to 1894 he held a series of regional court posts in and around Sarlat, but from the outset he accepted these positions with the view that his many free hours could be spent at independent study and writing. Tarde developed the habit of walking the banks of the nearby Dordogne river, meditating about the works which he had read and elaborating his own thoughts. Cournot's many contributions, but particularly his *L'enchainement des idées fondamentales dans les sciences et l'histoire* (1861), served as a major source of inspiration for Tarde's thoughts on imitation. Here too, as in Spencer, was found the analogical thinking which sought to discern general principles underlying physical, biological, and social phenomena. From Hegel, particularly esteemed in France at this time, Tarde learned how conflicts and oppositions could in turn create new syntheses. John Stuart Mill provided a model of logic and science which Tarde always admired but which he felt compelled to transcend. Tarde would interrupt his walks to jot down the essentials of an insight, and by the time he was thirty, he had drafted a series of notes to himself containing the essentials of his "laws of imitation" as well as the outlines of the conceptual framework elaborated in his many later works.

In 1877, Tarde married Mlle Marthe Bardy-Delisle, daughter of a magistrate, who gave him three sons. They enjoyed the social life, such as existed, of the regional high society. As a recognized leader in conversation and wit, as well as more serious thought, Tarde was called upon to prepare poetry or comedies for various occasions. He thus penned some dozen comedies and vaudeville acts, several of which even found their way into print.

Although he liked to minimize the importance of his professional activities, these led him to an interest in the causes of crimes, which, in turn, brought him in contact with the work of Italian criminologists. The success of racial and geographic theories which Lombroso, Garofalo, Ferri and others had developed led Tarde to publish a series of articles criticizing the "new Italian school" and emphasizing the preponderance of social factors—especially socialization and imitation—behind crime. Several articles were collected for his first book, *La criminalité comparée*, which soon established him as a leading criminologist and a leading spokesman of what later came to be referred to as the "French school." He collaborated regularly with the *Archives d'Anthropologie Criminelle*, founded in 1886 by Dr. Lacassagne, and in 1893 he became codirector of the journal. His last major statement on criminology, however, was *La philosophie pénale*, and after it appeared in 1890 he published practically nothing in this area although he continued to attend criminological congresses and to serve as codirector of the *Archives* until his death in 1904.

Also in 1890 appeared what was to become his most famous sociological work, *Les lois de l'imitation*, sections of which had already circulated in the *Revue Philosophique* in the 1880's. In 1893 he brought out a short work, *Les transformations du droit*, examining general legal questions from a sociological perspective. Thus, by the 1890's Tarde was reasonably well established as a criminologist and sociologist, and as a "mere provincial magistrate" he stimulated numerous favorable comments on the quality of personnel in the French judicial system. He had made no efforts to advance his legal career—which would necessitate leaving Sarlat—so long as his mother was alive, but after her death in 1891 he began to consider moving. Two years later, the Minister of Justice, Antonin Dubost, invited Tarde to prepare a report on the organization of criminal statistics, and in 1894 Tarde was named director of criminal statistics at the Ministry of Justice in Paris. As in his positions at Sarlat, Tarde was not obliged to spend more than a limited portion of his time at the Ministry. He drafted annual reports for the government and served as the official representative to congresses of the International Statistical Institute in Saint Petersburg and Copenhagen, but in this last decade of his life, spent in Paris, he became involved in a wide range of other activities.[4]

[4]   The character of some of these statistical activities is examined in Terry N. Clark, "Social Research and Its Institutionalization in France: A Case Study," *Indian Sociological Bulletin* 4, no. 4 (July, 1967) : 235–54.

No sociology was taught in Paris inside the official university system until Durkheim was called from Bordeaux in 1902, but social questions drew enormous public attention throughout the 1890's. As perhaps the most eminent representative of the new science in the capital, Tarde was in constant demand to lecture— never at the university, for reasons that we shall examine presently, but in a whole array of newly created teaching and research institutions.[5] Initially, for such lectures, he drew on sections of two major volumes that filled out his general conceptual framework: *La logique sociale* (1894), and *L'opposition universelle* (1896). In the first he dealt more systematically with social institutions (especially religion and the economy) than he had in his *Laws of Imitation*, and in the second he developed more completely than in any other work the role of conflict as both a creative and a destructive social force. The Ecole Libre des Sciences Politiques asked him to present a course every two years, and in 1896 he applied his sociological perspective to political matters. The materials he presented there, combined with those for another course at the Collège Libre des Sciences Sociales, were later published as *Les transformations du pouvoir* (1899). He presented a summary outline of his general framework at the Collège Libre the following year, published in 1898 as *Les lois sociales*.[6] He offered a course at the Ecole Russe des Hautes Etudes Sociales, presented papers at the Société de Sociologie de Paris and the Institut International de Sociologie, and continued to publish widely in philosophical, so-

5   The teaching and research institutions, journals, and societies referred to here are discussed in more detail in Terry N. Clark, *Institutionalization of Innovations in Higher Education: Social Research in France, 1850–1914*, forthcoming.

6   In contrast to a scientific modesty shown in his more serious works, this small *œuvre de vulgarisation* was unexcelled in its bombast. As a summary of lectures to a general public, it carries the indelible stamp of simplification and overstatement. That many writers commenting on Tarde, especially Americans, refer to him as immodest suggests that they have not gone far beyond this work—the first to be translated into English, and one too often cited by English-speaking writers as an outstanding summary of his entire contribution. No doubt *Social Laws* has greater unity than his longer studies and brings together ideas that are scattered throughout the longer works; but it is too often content with superficiality. The serious reader should avoid it for anything other than a brief introduction.

ciological, and general intellectual journals. Two volumes of collected essays were also brought out in these same years, *Essais et mélanges sociologiques* (1895), and *Etudes de psychologie sociale* (1898).

Then, in 1899, when the chair in modern philosophy at the Collège de France was vacated with the death of the philosopher Nourrisson, some of Tarde's influential associates (Théodule Ribot and Louis Liard) encouraged him to present his candidacy. He asked that the faculty of the Collège change the title of the chair to sociology, but although they refused this request, they nevertheless appointed him to the chair (over Henri Bergson) in January, 1900, and implicitly left him complete freedom to teach as he pleased.[7]

In December, 1900, when he was elected to the Académie des Sciences Morales et Politiques, Tarde held virtually every leading position open to a French social scientist outside the university system.

In the last four years of his life he lectured at the Collège de France on the transformations of morality, on opinion and conversation, which was dealt with in his 1901 volume in this area (*L'opinion et la foule*), on the social-psychological foundations of economics, bringing out two volumes on the subject in 1902 (*La psychologie économique*), on the philosophy of Cournot, and on "intermental psychology" (the subject of an unfinished volume on deposit at the Collège de France). In the last year of his life he also planned to undertake a series of empirical social psychological studies on school children with Alfred Binet, but the eye disease of his youth returned once again, and in 1904 he died.

II. *Conflicting Intellectual Currents:*
Tarde, Durkheim, and Sociology

From 1902 to 1904, Tarde and Durkheim were both in Paris and thus were able to confront one another personally in a

[7]   A valuable collection of unpublished materials on Tarde, dealing with such matters as his nomination to the Collège de France and his relations with Bergson, is on file in the library of the Centre d'Etudes Sociologiques in Paris.

debate that they had carried on in journals for years. The debate represented more than a simple disagreement of personalities; in it, two conflicting traditions of thought, two opposing sectors of French society, two hostile sets of institutions did battle to defend what each adversary felt to be the proper perspective for the study of society.

The first cultural configuration—represented in the debate by Durkheim—was Cartesianism.[8] The legacy associated with the name of Descartes was identified with reason, order, and authority, and housed in the bureaucratic institutions exemplifying this *esprit de géometrie:* the church, the governmental administration, the army, and the state university system. In the aftermath of the Revolution and under Napoleon it was the bourgeoisie that began to raise this orientation to a quasi-official ideology, and at that time the basic lines were laid for many of the national bureaucratic structures, but it was the creation of the Third Republic after 1870 that assured the ascendancy of the Cartesian mentality for some time to come.

The basic cultural configuration opposed to Cartesianism was that of Spontaneity. It was a mentality of artistic creation, romantic subjectivism, and personal invention guided by an *esprit de finesse.* As the bourgeoisie and Cartesianism came to be more and more identified with the established institutions in the last part of the nineteenth century, their opponents grew increasingly antibourgeois, antiinstitutional, anticollective, and, occasionally, revolutionary. Aesthetic, political, and economic attacks were fused in antibourgeois ideologies put forth by the heirs of the traditional nobility, the rural peasantry, or the urban proletariat. Against bourgeois republican ideologues Renouvier and Littré, and parliamentary leaders Clemenceau and Combes, were the champions of Spontaneity of the left—the anarchists, anarcho-syndicalists, and certain socialists—complemented by the advocates of Spontaneity of the right—the romantic nationalists. Occasionally, when anti-

8   The traditions of Cartesianism and Spontaneity are elaborated with greater detail and supporting documentation in Clark, *Institutionalization of Innovations in Higher Education*, chap. 1, "Culture, Social Structure, and Intellectual Currents in Nineteenth-Century France."

bourgeois sentiments grew sufficiently strong, and social ties sufficiently weak, individuals could move from the Spontaneity of the
left to that of the right without excessive difficulty. The most outstanding example was the theoretician of orgiastic violence,
Georges Sorel, who, from an intellectual leader of anarcho-syndi-
calism, became an esteemed guide for the Action Française and
eventually for fascism.

The most important intellectual center of Cartesianism in the
first part of the nineteenth century was the Ecole Polytechnique.
Established under Napoleon to apply the best scientific knowledge
available to the solution of military and engineering problems, it
was not a large step to extend the application of these same methods to social questions. Inspired by the heady ideas of Saint-Simon
and Auguste Comte that prevailed at the Ecole, students "ventured to create a religion as one learns at the Ecole to build a bridge
or a road."[9] From the graduates of the school were recruited the
major disciples of Saint-Simon and Comte, and they suffused this
mentality throughout the bureaucratic institutions of the state and
the bourgeois-dominated sectors of society.

Frequently opposing the Ecole Polytechnique in the first part
of the century was the Sorbonne, which, for many, was an embodi-
ment of the outlook of Spontaneity. Its major spokesman was
Victor Cousin, whose creatively rhetorical style, and "supple,"
individualistic philosophy left a deep stamp on the institution
through much of the Second Empire.

But after the demise of the Second Empire, seen as a defeat for
loose living and unsystematic thinking, the partisans of Cartesianism remade the old educational system into the "new University."
Not for them the frivolous philosophy of Cousin; the reformers
sought their ideals in the positivism of Auguste Comte, the scien-
tism of Hippolyte Taine and Ernest Renan, and the precision of
Claude Bernard. And they patterned the new institutions after the
research-oriented universities of disciplined, protestant Germany.
Throughout the 1880's and 1890's, these men succeeded in placing their representatives in influential positions, and when the

[9]   Albert Thibaudet, quoted in F. A. Hayek, *The Counter-Revolution
of Science* (Glencoe, Ill.: Free Press, 1955), p. 113.

young Emile Durkheim came to their attention, they felt that they had found the man who could best extend the mentality and methods of Cartesianism to the study of society. Durkheim's works also perfectly suited the ideological demands of the Republican government: to the anticlericals he contributed a philosophical basis for a secular morality to replace the earlier Catholic dogmas; to the radical and radical socialist politicians of "solidarity," he offered a more systematic grounding for their political philosophy; for the Dreyfusards he provided coherent intellectual guidance. After the turn of the century, in the Sorbonne, in national university councils, and through his close contacts with the Ministry of Education, Durkheim became one the most powerful university politicians in France. He enjoyed enormous support from those sympathetic to his basic views, but was violently opposed by others. Some of his strongest opponents found their inspiration in the tradition of Spontaneity.

Although the affluence of certain aristocratic supporters facilitated the creation of a considerable number of ad hoc journals and teaching institutions around, and opposed to, the Sorbonne, partisans of Spontaneity enjoyed no secure institutional niche. Among the established institutions, the Faculties of Law, and to some degree the Collège de France, were perhaps the most hospitable.

Tarde, after his negative reaction to the Cartesian aspect of the Jesuits, had been exposed to a more Spontaneous tradition at the Toulouse and Paris Faculties of Law, for although they were officially part of the national university system, their students were not the Radicals who abounded at the Sorbonne, but the more socially prominent young men who maintained an institutional culture glorifying the ideology of Spontaneity. Then, later, when Tarde was considered by the Collège de France, he could find there such men as the philosophers Paul Janet, who had forced Durkheim to delete a chapter from his thesis that contained a complimentary reference to Auguste Comte, and Jean Izoulet, who penned the widely-quoted assertion that "the obligation of teaching the sociology of M. Durkheim in 200 Normal Schools in France is the gravest national peril that our country has known for some time."[10] Then, too, the successor of Tarde at the Collège was Henri Bergson, who was the apotheosis of the tradition of Spontaneity. Bergson, in turn, was a continuing source of inspiration for Georges Sorel and Charles Péguy, as well as one of Tarde's sons who was a law student, Alfred de Tarde. (The aristocratic particle, while ignored by the father, was insisted upon by the son.) Writing with another student under the *nom de guerre* of Agathon, Alfred de Tarde captured the antagonism toward Durkheim of those committed to Spontaneity. A short passage from a volume by Agathon, modestly entitled *L'esprit de la Nouvelle Sorbonne: la crise de la culture classique, la crise du français,*[11] suggests the temper of the period:

> Would it be M. Durkheim that M. Liard has charged with elaborating the new doctrine? The powers that he has conferred to him in the organization of the New Sorbonne leave us with some basis to fear that this is the case. He has made of him a sort of *préfet d'études.* . . . The case of Durkheim is a victory of the new spirit. Charged with university pomp, he is the regent of the Sorbonne, the all-powerful master, and it is known that the professors in the section of philosophy, reduced to the role of humble civil servants, follow his every order, oppressed by his command. . . . M. Durkheim has firmly established his intellectual despotism. He has made of his teaching an instrument of domination.

Given the passionate commitment to opposing philosophies of persons very close to Durkheim and Tarde, one is forced to admire the relative calm which they were able to assume in their confrontations with one another. Although neither was totally immersed in one or the other mentality—all such ideal typical formulations must be applied to concrete individuals only with qualification— they could not resist being swayed by the charged atmosphere which characterized their immediate surroundings. Readers habituated to a cooler intellectual climate should at least remain sympathetic when they take note of an occasional dogmatism in the debate between Durkheim and Tarde.

[10]   M. Goyau, *Comment juger la "sociologie" contemporaine* (Marseilles: Editions Publioror, 1934), p. 184.
[11]   (Paris: Mercure de France, 1911), pp. 98–100.

The disagreement between the two men raised in the debate should nevertheless not obscure a number of quite important underlying similarities. We will briefly consider some of these basic similarities before turning to the areas of disagreement.

Tarde and Durkheim both recognized—although differing in their interpretations of the relevance and significance of various contributors—the major historical antecedents of sociology in the works of Montesquieu, Comte, Quetelet and Spencer. Agreement on these common historical roots, despite disagreement on the inclusion of others, nevertheless distinguished Tarde and Durkheim from two major clusters of social researchers in France at the time that would not admit to these same antecedents: the social statisticians and most of the disciples of Le Play.[12]

In what might be called their taxonomies of sociological work, there was also substantial agreement between the two men.[13] On the lowest level were the activities associated with collecting the raw materials for sociological production. Here, unlike certain more dogmatic contemporaries, as well as certain later writers, Tarde and Durkheim agreed that ethnographic materials from preliterate societies, case studies of selected aspects of contemporary societies, personal documents, legal records, governmentally collected statistics, and researcher-collected data, among others, were all valid and valuable types of materials for the sociologist. Both men were eclectics in terms of the data with which they felt the sociologist should work. We might add, however, that neither was overly concerned with improving specific procedures of data collection.

Intellectually meaningful results, they also both held, could only derive from specialization of individuals on narrowly delimited topics. These specialists on various aspects of social life—religion, law, the family, the economy, and so forth—in working closely

[12]   See Clark, *Institutionalization of Innovations*, for discussion of these various clusters of researchers.

[13]   Cf., inter alia, Tarde, "Sociology," this volume; and Durkheim's prefaces to the early volumes of the *Année Sociologique*, reprinted in translation in *Emile Durkheim, 1858–1917*, ed. Kurt H. Wolff (Columbus: Ohio State University Press, 1960), pp. 341–353.

with raw empirical materials, would record their observations in the form of empirical generalizations and "partial syntheses." But these operations could not take place entirely from induction; to help guide empirical activities, and to provide some basis for integration of the specialists' work, a more general conceptual framework was mandatory. Such a framework should grow from the empirical findings of concrete studies and be consistent with their various results, but as there was no one-to-one correspondence between empirical studies—especially those available in the early stages of development of the science—and general propositions emerging from an ambitious conceptual framework, the most abstract sort of sociological theorizing was at least a partially autonomous activity. Both in presenting these ideas about the various types of sociological work and in carrying them out by developing compendia of empirical generalizations, "partial syntheses," and general theoretical principles, Tarde and Durkheim steered clear of excessive commitment to one or another type of these activities at the expense of the others. They avoided the dry and lifeless sort of categorizing which passed with certain German writers for theory; when they engaged in narrow empirical work, it was never as a self-contained activity but for purposes of illuminating more general issues. The successful weaving of their various contributions into meaningful wholes provides outstanding examples of the coherence among different types of sociological work.

A third area of concord between the two men was their logic of analysis. Both drew heavily on John Stuart Mill for certain basic rules of investigation, the most salient of which is the use of the comparative method.[14] Committed to the development of general principles, they were convinced, through the experiences of economics and other disciplines, of the necessity of comparison. The "special" sciences which they discussed—linguistics, moral statistics, history, and so forth—would become sociological only through the use of comparative methods. And the most fruitful comparisons were those between phenomena that were similar in

[14] Cf. Tarde, "Sociology," this volume; Emile Durkheim, prefaces to the *Année Sociologique* and *The Rules of Sociological Method* (Chicago: University of Chicago Press, 1938). (First published in 1894.)

certain basic respects but dissimilar in others. Only through such comparisons would it be possible to move beyond descriptive discussion of single instances to the elaboration of more general principles. If the dictum of "No sociology without comparison" had been observed more carefully by their successors, sociology might well have progressed further in the half-century since Tarde and Durkheim than it in fact has.

The two men also generally observed a similar rule of logic in evaluating the various proposed explanations for a given phenomenon at the outset of a study, extracting the valid elements from each competing explanation and then building a new coherent explanation, which would in turn be tested against a variety of empirical data. This type of procedure is valuable in that it forces one to consider systematically earlier alternatives, to provide an explanation that does better, and to marshall available evidence which shows that the proposed explanation is in fact superior. But the weakness is that, like any such organizing scheme, it can degenerate into ritualism. Then, too, there is the danger of considering that if competing explanations have been disproven, the new one must be correct. Both men occasionally committed this fallacy.

Although they did not always reach the same conclusions, Tarde and Durkheim were often in agreement in the arguments which they dismissed. In evaluating the positions of various critics of sociology, they opposed those who were against sociology on the grounds that it conflicted with the doctrine of free will. They pointed out that, while concrete individuals could exercise individual discretion in their selection of alternatives, the statistical aggregates of these choices across individuals were nevertheless subject to general laws. To critics who held that a generalizing sociology was irresponsible and premature until the results of the "special sciences" were more thoroughly confirmed, they replied that astronomy and biology were possible before physics and chemistry had become developed disciplines.

They both also rejected many aspects of utilitarian theory. They denied the basic utilitarian assumption that society consisted of an aggregate of atomistic individuals. Whether it was John

Stuart Mill, who went from this assumption to conclude that sociology could develop from the law of association combined with the basic principles of logic,[15] or the contract theorists, who presented society as a collection of formal dyadic relationships,[16] Tarde and Durkheim forcefully opposed these conclusions. In dismissing the contact theorists' assumption that men could solve their basic needs through elaborating a series of contractual relationships, Tarde and Durkheim both emphasized the necessity of including the normative framework imposed by the broader society for any meaningful social analysis. But they did not go so far as some who chose to view society as a great organic whole. While not necessarily allied with utilitarianism—although it happened to be in the work of Herbert Spencer—the organismic analogy provided another popular basis for elaborating much of what passed for sociological theory in the second half of the nineteenth century. It was largely under the combined attacks of Tarde and Durkheim that the organismic analogy largely disappeared from informed sociological discourse after the turn of the century in France.

Thus, in terms of their definition of historical antecedents of sociology, their taxonomy of sociological work, their general logic of analysis, and common opposition to certain competing currents of thought, Tarde and Durkheim overlapped significantly. But after this point, as each man began actually to lay down the essentials of his system of thought, a number of divergencies appeared.[17]

Tarde held that a prerequisite for any science was the repetition of some basic measurable phenomenon. The arts were concerned with the examination and portrayal of unique, individual

15   Tarde, *Social Laws* (New York and London: Macmillan, 1899), pp. 30ff.
16   Tarde, Preface to *La logique sociale;* Émile Durkheim, *The Division of Labor in Society* (New York: Macmillan, 1933). (First edition published in 1893.)
17   These were articulated, among other places, in the four selections in Part I of the present volume; in Durkheim's *Rules of Sociological Method*; and in the exchange on "Crime et santé sociale," *Revue Philosophique* 39 (1895).

phenomena; science, based on generalization from a large number of cases, could only begin through observing some kind of repetition. As the object of study for sociology is man, but man in a social context, sociology must find its basic focus of inquiry, its fundamental "social fact," in some aspect of man which is characteristically social. The aspects of man thus open to the sociologist must be distinguished from his physical and biological, as well as his "intra-mental," or psychological, aspects. What remains are the "inter-mental" aspects of men, or man insofar as he is influenced by other men. The basic process by which this inter-mental influence takes place, and the basic social fact for sociology, Tarde holds, is imitation. Social relations are essentially imitative relationships. But sociology need be concerned with only those aspects of the psyche which are transmitted between minds. Here, the two basic psychic units, the two elementary particles of imitation, are what Tarde isolated in an early essay as "belief" and "desire," the one cognitive, the other emotive. The final result of imitation for the individual is a "mental imprint," an impression on the mind similar to the imprint on a photographic plate. Thus, psychology cannot be excluded from sociology as social processes consist, in the final analysis, of inter-mental relations.

It was precisely at this point that Tarde and Durkheim found themselves in radical disagreement. Durkheim posited as the essentially social fact not that which was imitated, but that which was exterior to the individual and imposed on him through a sort of constraint. Firmly committed to the position elaborated by his professor, Boutroux, that sciences developed on successive emergent levels, and that the basic principles of a science must be found distinctly on its "own level," Durkheim refused to accept that sociological principles should be grounded in psychology. Sociology as a distinctive science, he held, must take as its object of study social facts; and these social facts must find their causes as well as their consequences in other distinctly social facts. An apparently logical extension of this reasoning, which Tarde as well as Durkheim occasionally drew, was that the subject matter of sociology, being exterior to each individual, was consequently outside of all members comprising a given social group. But such a conclusion was absurd: take away all individual members of a group, and the essential sociological characteristics remain. This was, Tarde held, the necessary consequence of Durkheim's postulates, and it generated nothing more than the "scholastic ontology" of the medieval philosophical realists. In opposition to the doctrine that the whole is more than the sum of its parts, Tarde held that the whole is equal to no more than the sum of its parts; he labeled himself, when forced to do so, a philosophical nominalist.

As a rigorous thinker who chose to drive his postluates to their extreme logical conclusions, Durkheim more than once espoused the realistic position that Tarde referred to as his "ontological Phasmagoria." Insofar as he did so, Durkheim must be judged by subsequent sociologists as being simply wrong, and Tarde as being right. With time, however, whether as a consequence of continued empirical observation[18] or through being convinced by Tarde and others of the logical absurdity of his position, or both, Durkheim moved away from the extreme realism. This was most clearly the case in his empirical studies,[19] however, for Durkheim never explicitly contradicted his earlier pronouncements on this issue. This was unfortunate, for in subsequent years ardent disciples adhered to what had come to be defined as Durkheimian gospel, with near disastrous consequences for the development of both sociology and psychology in France.[20]

Tarde, however, went so far in asserting that society was composed of no more than its individual members that he in turn underestimated the importance of certain collective influences. Nevertheless, he presented a more sophisticated view of the relationships between the individual and society than did Durkheim. Much social action, Tarde pointed out, was based not on constraint from the external imposition of social norms, but grew out of spon-

[18]   As Parsons has suggested. See Talcott Parsons, *The Structure of Social Action* (New York: McGraw-Hill, 1937), still the best single secondary account of Durkheim.

[19]   Especially in his *Education and Sociology*, *The Moral Education*, and *The Elementary Forms of Religious Life*. See also Harry Alpert, *Émile Durkheim and His Sociology* (New York: Columbia University Press, 1939) on this point.

[20]   See section *x*, below.

taneous imitation of beliefs and desires that subsequently became internalized by the individual and, through a process of learning, continued to structure his behavior.

Growing largely from the commitment of Tarde to an emphasis on the autonomy of the individual and a grounding of his behavior in Spontaneity, and of Durkheim to the predominance of the collectivity and a Cartesian striving for order, the difference between the two men was reflected in several other issues. In discussing the general bases for social change, Tarde stressed the centrality of the creative individual in suggesting new lines of development which the collectivity would subsequently adopt. Durkheim preferred to emphasize the structural conditions which predisposed a given collectivity to change, minimizing the importance of individual factors.[21]

To explain processes of norm formation, Tarde presented an interactionist theory similar in many ways to that associated with the name of George Herbert Mead. Durkheim, on the other hand, relied on such group conditions as heightened collective activity, but he was much less precise in this area than was Tarde (see section *vii* below).

Tarde elaborated a theory of social control that grew out of social interaction, and was extended through larger social groupings with such developments as extensive mass communications (see section *ix*). Durkheim, to explain social control, focused more on the constraining influences of values and norms.

Durkheim maintained at some points that the elementary social unit was the horde, to which Tarde retorted that it was the individual, or at least the household; but both men recognized that this was not a point to be resolved a priori, but through more extended study.[22]

For us today, many of these positions appear more complementary than contradictory; but such was not always the case for Tarde and Durkheim. Nevertheless, their debates have helped clarify the vision of subsequent sociologists.

[21]   Tarde, "Two Elements of Sociology," this volume; Durkheim, *The Division of Labor in Society*.
[22]   Tarde, "Two Elements of Sociology."

III. *The Structure of Tarde's Thought: Invention, Imitation, and Opposition*

Turning to a more careful examination of Tarde's basic theoretical principles, we must stress at outset an underlying similarity with the work of Durkheim as well as with several other writers who converged near the end of the nineteenth century on what Parsons has termed the voluntaristic theory of action.[23] The convergence was in the direction of a social theory which included as central elements, and as analytically independent variables, all five of the following: an *actor*, directed toward specific *goals*, restricted by certain fixed *conditions* in his environment but free to utilize other *means* toward the attainment of his goals, acting in a social framework defined by institutionalized *norms*.[24]

France, we might note in passing, was particularly well placed for fostering a synthesis of the various traditions of thought that converged in the voluntaristic theory of action, which in turn, laid the essential base for much of contemporary sociological theory. In eighteenth- and nineteenth-century social thought, the most extreme positions—those which were forced to make the most radical modifications in order to achieve the voluntaristic synthesis—were found in traditions established most firmly not in France, but in England and Germany. The very strong tradition of British utilitarianism,[25] in laying undue emphasis on the actor's conditions and means, correspondingly neglected the goals toward which actors were directed, and the norms which structured their behavior. In Germany, on the other hand, it was the idealistic tradition that dominated much of social thought—the tradition which erred significantly in the opposite direction from that of utilitarianism by focusing predominantly on the norms and goals of actors while neglecting their means and conditions. When deviations from

23   Parsons, *The Structure of Social Action.*
24   *Ibid.*, chap. 2.
25   J. W. Burrow, *Education and Society, A Study in Victorian Social Theory* (Cambridge: At the University Press, 1966) particularly stresses the utilitarian tradition in British social thought.

these "national" traditions did take place in England or Germany, they often consisted more of importations from the opposing tradition than of genuinely creative ideas. French social thought, while it may have moved toward excessive rationality in the work of the positivists, remained markedly eclectic by contrast with England or Germany throughout most of the nineteenth century.[26] General philosophical circles were open to the extent that it was considered necessary to be familiar with both utilitarian and idealistic traditions. As a consequnce, throughout the last part of the nineteenth century, numerous attempts could be found in France to merge together these disparate elements into a coherent system of thought. Tarde and Durkheim were placed in an advantaged position in this respect; because they could build on earlier efforts their own tasks of integration were correspondingly facilitated. Despite their roots in the conflicting French traditions of Spontaneity and Cartesianism, they each were successful in working the five basic analytical elements into their conceptual frameworks.

In dealing with social *actors*, Tarde was more careful than Durkheim in attending to such factors as individual differences and their consequences for social behavior. In his discussion of invention, the general *goals* toward which inventors strive—wealth, religious ideals, adventure—are considered in the ways they direct activity toward various types of discoveries.[27] A careful examination of the relations between *conditions* restricting social action, such as the technology of transportation and communication, and the *means* available to achieve particular goals, especially the mass media, is found in Tarde's work on public opinion and mass communication.[28] If Tarde underemphasized any one of the five basic elements, it was probably that of *norms*. As we pointed out, reacting to Durkheim's emphasis on the external, constraining aspects of social norms, Tarde stressed the possibility of their spontaneous internalization; but this of course was not to denigate their impor-

[26]   See D. G. Charlton, *Positivist Thought in France During the Second Empire, 1852–1870* (Oxford: Oxford University Press, 1959).
[27]   Part II, 5, below; and Gabriel Tarde, *Social Laws* (New York and London: Macmillan, 1899), pp. 30ff.
[28]   Part IX, 17, below.

tance. Then, in his discussion of the susceptibility of various social groups to imitation, Tarde pointed to the importance of an alternation between more traditional or more innovative norms.[29] At other points, however, he would take pains to stress that norms, insofar as they exist, represent a residue of inventions handed down from earlier periods.[30] The tradition of Spontaneity generally led Tarde to stress the freedom of the individual and the degree to which norms were the creations of social behavior as well as the causes.

Although we can point to a theoretical articulation between the five elements of the voluntaristic action scheme and Tarde's basic ideas, this does not, of course, imply that he made explicit use of these categories. On the contrary, Tarde elaborated his thought largely through the imaginative manipulation of three central concepts: *invention, imitation,* and *opposition.* Inventions, the creations of talented individuals, are disseminated throughout social systems by the process of imitation. These imitations spread—to use one of Tarde's favorite analogies—like the ripples on the surface of a pond, regularly progressing toward the limits of the system until they come into contact with some obstacle. The obstacle, however, is likely to be the imitation of some earlier invention, and when the two collide, from their opposition is likely to emerge a new product—that is, a new invention—which in turn is imitated until it too meets further obstacles, and so on, ad infinitum. The three processes thus form an interdependent whole, continuing to generate and influence one another in a multitude of ways. Examining these three basic processes again and again, focusing on their operation in personalities, in small groups, in the economy, in the polity, in international relations, and other areas, Tarde distills a number of generalizations characterizing their operation. To these generalizations he occasionally applied the term "law," and, although recognizing that their tentative character made the term "a slight misuse of vocabulary," he pointed out that it nevertheless was a misuse sanctioned by "the convenience of monosyllables."[31]

29   Part III, 9, below.
30   Part III, 10, below; Tarde, *Social Laws*, pp. 51ff.
31   Part II, 5, below.

A basic principle that held for all three processes was the "law of progressive enlargement."[32] This law held that as inventions are imitated throughout increasingly broad areas of social life, they generate correspondingly increasing numbers of oppositions, which in turn create increasing numbers of subsequent inventions. The limits of a particular system do not necessarily restrict the operation of these processes, as most imitations are likely to collide with innumerable others before they reach the system's limits and to be redirected from these collisions toward further innovations and imitations.

Invention.—As each of the three processes leads to the next, the analysis of the overall circular pattern may logically begin with any one of the three. Invention, as the ultimate source of all human innovation and progress for Tarde, is a convenient point of departure. The rate of development of a particular sector of society—for example, the economy, science, literature—depends on the number and quality of innovative ideas generated in that sector, and as a society as a whole advances with the developments in its many sectors, the creation of significant inventions is of greatest importance for vigorous social change. Despite the central social role played in his system by invention, and the continual attention it received in his works, Tarde admitted that his formulations on the subject never attained the precision of those on imitation—the process for which he developed the most elaborate explanatory principles. This was in part because of the paucity of literature on invention in contrast to that relevant to imitation; correspondingly, Tarde's own work significantly advanced the level of thinking on the social foundations of invention.[33]

The ultimate source for all invention is found in creative asso-

[32]   *Ibid.*

[33]   The importance of his contribution is suggested by a reference to it more than half a century later: "Not since Gabriel Tarde . . . has there been any real attempt to formulate a theoretical explanation of the innovative process and of the individual and social circumstances involved therein." R. T. La Piere, "Editor's Introduction," in H. G. Barnett, *Innovation: The Basis of Cultural Change* (New York: McGraw-Hill, 1953), p. v.

ciations originating in the minds of gifted individuals.[34] Limits
are placed ultimately on the inventive abilities of a social sector or
a total society by the intellectual capacities— biological and psychological—of its members. Citing Galton's *Hereditary Genius*,
Tarde stressed the importance of a few highly gifted individuals for
the development of inventions in a particular area. He generally
emphasized the rational and conscious aspects of invention and, at
some points, its "essentially deductive character."[35] Inventions
derive largely from conscious volition of the inventor, and occasionally may even follow, he suggested, from a syllogistic sort of
reasoning: (1) the inventor recognizes a particular goal as desirable; (2) he seeks to achieve the goal with existing means, but if
these are for some reason insufficient, he (3) affirms the necessity
for such action as can generate a new means by which the goal can
be attained. To generate sufficient means, he seeks to create an
appropriate invention.

But while this conscious, goal-seeking model offered a partial
explanation of invention, Tarde was quick to assert the necessity

---

[34]   An example of difficulties emerging from Tarde's imprecise application of central concepts concerns the essentially interchangeable use
he made of the terms "invention" and "discovery." At many points Tarde
needed a term that would generally cover all new ideas; although the term
invention in common parlance (in both French and English) is slightly
more restricted than this meaning, it is a defensible extrapolation from
standard usage. But all "discoveries" are not the creations of individual
minds. The term implies a more passive role on the part of the "discoverer,"
and suggests that the "discovery" existed prior to the activities of any particular individuals seeking it. To "invent" a new means of transportation
demands a more actively creative role than to "discover" a previously unknown territory. In seeking to develop a truly general conceptual framework, Tarde necessarily ignored a number of distinctions such as this one;
the most frequent result was greater generality. But in cases such as the
propositions about factors contributing to invention, the results were
simply not applicable, or at least less applicable, to some instances of
discovery. Greater precision than Tarde generally demonstrated would
have helped clarify matters such as this.
[35]   Part II, 6, below.

of additional factors, for example, the creative inspiration of various emotions and moods which an inventor would experience at different times. And in contrast to the more rational bent of certain late nineteenth-century sociologists like Weber or Durkheim (here, once again, his indebtedness to the tradition of Spontaneity was apparent), he felt that the unconscious part of the mind, or the "sub-self," could break through into consciousness as a source of creative inspiration.

Bordering on the physiological, Tarde further pointed out an apparent overlap between the ages of greatest intellectual as well as sexual creativity: the years from about twenty-five to thirty-five. Many of his examples supporting this generalization were drawn from the natural sciences, and, indeed, subsequent more systematic studies have shown these years to be the period of greatest creativity for many of the natural sciences—although this is not the case for all fields.[36]

While stressing the "external" factors producing invention, Tarde nevertheless was more careful than many social scientists of his time in calling attention to the "internal" factors of intellectual development.[37] He formulated two basic principles in this area. The first, the principle of accumulation, emphasized the essentially cumulative character of all knowledge: new discoveries do not simply replace older ones (although they may in terms of technological use, they do not from the standpoint of intellectual development); there is continual addition to the legacy of *la connaissance humaine*. Knowledge may grow at different rates in varying periods and societies, but the overall tendency is toward progressive accumulation of knowledge in virtually all areas. Related to the principle of accumulation is that of *irreversibility*. The growth of some types of knowledge may take place in essentially random order; there is no logical necessity, for example, to explore one part of an uncharted territory before other parts. But in other cases, certain

[36]   Harvey C. Lehman, *Age and Achievement* (Princeton: Princeton University Press, 1953).
[37]   On this debate in the history of science, see A. Rupert Hall, "Merton Revisited," *History of Science*, vol. 2 (1963).

inventions presuppose certain others: a cart, for example, can be created only after wheels are available. Knowledge, Tarde stressed, advances in small increments, and even the most creative discoveries are heavily dependent on antecedent ideas. The most outstanding inventions are those which recombine already acquired bits of knowledge into highly original syntheses. But although the general lines of intellectual development are governed by the dual principles of accumulation and irreversibility, the specific directions as well as the rate of advance are heavily dependent on psychological and social factors.

Social stratification, in Tarde's eyes, was functional to invention because it produced greater leisure time for the upper classes, thereby allowing greater communication and social interaction within the elite; and with this increasing density of stimulating contacts and increasing exchange of ideas, correspondingly greater numbers of creative discoveries would emerge. A certain minimal rigidity of class lines also insulates the elite from the inhibiting ideas of the populace; if leaders are forced to submit to opinions of the majority at every turn—and here Tarde cited the dysfunctional consequences of democracy as detailed by de Tocqueville—they will not be free to invent. Social stratification can thus favor discovery in the same way that university structures guarantee a certain minimum of academic freedom for those working inside them.

In addition to class differences, national differences in inventiveness are also evident, Tarde stressed. But in contrast to certain of his contemporaries—most especially the English followers of Galton—Tarde did not have recourse to racial explanations for national differences. The most striking variations across countries were the result of different combinations of educational and intellectual structures that facilitated or hampered inventiveness. On a methodological level he pointed out that to measure national differences appropriately it was essential not to compare gross indicators reflecting the diffusion of inventions, such as economic output, or the large-scale production of recent inventions. One should compare indicators directly tapping inventiveness, such as patent licenses or the inventions exhibited at an international fair.[38]

The factors generating national differences in inventiveness are many and complex, but in isolation we find one structural factor which neatly arose from Tarde's general system with its stress on communication as an antecedent to invention: the greater the isolation, ceteris paribus, the lower the inventiveness.[39] Such ancient preliterate societies as those in Oceania, Tarde reasoned, had been held back because of their extreme geographical and social isolation, while in the same years the societies bordering on Mesopotamia rapidly developed inventions through a more dense network of communications. The same principle of social isolation is thus applicable both to individuals and to social groups.

Different cultural values, Tarde pointed out, also predispose societies toward different rates and types of inventiveness. The values structure the goals of individual actors within each society, emphasizing some types of activities over others. Due to their higher cultural evaluation, certain types of activities attract more and better qualified persons, with the inevitable result of greater inventiveness in these culturally preferred areas. At first glance it might appear that societies with a greater stress on economic advancement would generate more inventions than other societies where the satisfaction of immediate desires represent a higher cul-

[38]   In the last part of the nineteenth century, international fairs were much more important for international competition on a reasonably high intellectual level than they have become in more recent decades. That Frédéric Le Play organized several World's Fairs under the Second Empire suggests the esteem with which the fairs were regarded by intellectuals no less than the general public. A few years later, the unveiling of the impressive Eiffel Tower at the 1889 World's Fair was widely regarded as a spectacular device for establishing the engineering and metallurgical skills of the French to help them recapture international markets for heavy steel and machine products from the Germans.

[39]   Some of the patterns by which isolation can nevertheless contribute to innovation are taken up in Terry N. Clark, "Marginality, Eclecticism, and Innovation," *Revue Internationale de Sociologie*, 2d ser., vol. 3, no. 1–3 (December, 1967) : 12–27; and Clark, "Institutionalization of Innovations in Higher Education: Four Models," *Administrative Science Quarterly* 13, no. 1 (June, 1968) : 1–25.

tural goal. But the same invention, Tarde emphasized, can sometimes result from quite diverse goals. The Spanish and Portuguese,
for example, were often successful discoverers of new lands, not because they sought simply commercial gain or religious conversion
—the major goals of British and Dutch exploration—but also because they were motivated by a spirit of lusty and passionate conquest. As a consequence, their discoveries were often more spectacular. A cultural propensity toward immediate gratification,
combined with adventurousness, can generate invention by leaving
a greater role to chance—not entirely random chance, which always has some role, but a more structured sort of calculated risk,
which, in some cases, has an enormous pay-off, such as in the
discovery of America.

Imitation.—Some inventions or discoveries—such as America
—are more easily accepted than others. Tarde, given the structure
of his system, preferred to think in terms of the "imitation" instead
of the "acceptance" of inventions. As one of the three central processes of his system, imitation implied a much broader concept
than mere acceptance. In his volume *The Laws of Imitation*, Tarde
offered no explicit definition of the term, and when in the preface
to the second edition he stated that he referred to a "quasi-photo-
graphic reproduction of a cerebral image," he did not greatly
clarify matters.[40] But here, as in many other instances, we can
best learn from Tarde not by criticizing his lack of precision but
by seeking out his insights.

One of the most fundamental "laws of imitation" was that the
more similar are inventions to those already imitated and hence institutionalized in a particular social system, the more likely they
are to be imitated. Restated as what Tarde referred to as a "logical
law of imitation"—in which the rational-logical aspects of imitation were emphasized—this general idea led to the principle that
the closer a particular invention is to the most advanced technological aspects of a society, the more likely it is to be imitated.[41] A new
type of horsedrawn cart is not likely to be imitated by a society that
has not yet invented the wheel, any more than by another which

[40]   *The Laws of Imitation* (New York: Henry Holt, 1903), p. xiv.
[41]   Part III, 8, below.

makes widespread use of automobiles and railroad trains. The "extra-logical" form of the same law—the more an invention meets the predominant cultural emphasis, the more likely it is to be imitated—calls attention to such nontechnological factors as the relative cultural emphasis on novelty as opposed to tradition.[42]

Attention to these two contrasting emphases—the logical or the extra-logical—resulted in two corresponding types of laws. Concern with the logical aspects of invention and imitation moved Tarde to distinguish inventions that could be used as substitutes for one another from those that could be accumulated without displacing others. When two substitutable inventions compete—contrasting linguistic expressions, or forms of dress—the result is a "logical duel"; when two complementary inventions are brought together, the result is "logical union"—for example, the wheel and the domesticated animal in the horsedrawn cart. But even logically opposed inventions will not be forced into overt opposition with one another unless observers in the society around them point out their incompatibility; in the absence of such criticism, relatively incompatible inventions may very well coexist for some time. Eventually, however, their presence tends to generate what Tarde referred to, in a discussion in many ways similar to more recent ones dealing with "cognitive dissonance,"[43] as one of two basic types of "logical strain." The second source of strain is in the absolute advance of knowledge, which would lead to increasing numbers of logical unions. To explain the source of this strain, Tarde does not rely on what more culturally-oriented social scientists might have posited—the incomplete attainment of a basic value favoring the increase of knowledge. On the contrary, his preference for "intermental" explanation becomes apparent. Both types of strains originate in a common source: the intensive interaction of minds, which leads to rapid circulation of ideas and to greater consistency of thought as well as a tendency toward the expansion of knowledge.[44] Thus, stated in propositional form, the more frequent the interac-

42 Part III, 9, below.

43 For a survey of research in this area, see J. W. Brehm and A. R. Cohen, *Explorations in Cognitive Dissonance* (New York: Wiley, 1962).

44 Part III, 8, below.

tion in a society, the greater the strain toward consistency of thought, and the more rapid the growth of knowledge.

But Tarde recognized that such a formulation is too simple. Ignoring cultural variables at outset he introduced them later. Societies, as well as historical periods, vary, he pointed out, in the relative emphasis that they place on consistency as opposed to inventiveness. He even suggests a cyclical pattern according to which societies would alternate between an emphasis first on inventiveness and then on consistency; when large numbers of inventions are being created, consistency is difficult to maintain, but over time efforts toward rationalization become increasingly essential. The nineteenth century, he suggests, was a century of massive invention, and perhaps the twentieth century would have to be devoted to rationalizing the discoveries of the nineteenth. As far as social thought is concerned, there seems to have been more than a grain of truth in this prediction, at least for the first half of the twentieth century.

Turning to the "extra-logical" laws of imitation, we find one general principle underlying much of Tarde's discussion: initially inventions tend to be imitated by those parts of man and society that are closest to the source of invention, from which they subsequently radiate outward to more distant parts.[45] While not explicitly stated, this principle lies behind Tarde's otherwise less than obvious law that imitations spread "from the inner to the outer man." Nowhere is his general preference for intellectual over material causes more apparent than in the propositions deriving from this law.[46] Tarde posits that ideas are communicated before their material expressions; religious dogmas are transmitted before the associated rites; ends are disseminated before the means to their attainment; general ideas are accepted before they receive juridical or legislative support. In this series of propositions, Tarde seized on one lines of causation which is unquestionably valid in some instances. But in his associated discussion, he characteris-

---

[45]   Part III, 9, below.
[46]   Espinas emphasizes the Christian glorification of the "inner man" behind Tarde's intellectualism here. See "Notice sur la vie et les œuvres de M Gabriel de Tarde," pp. 316ff.

tically devoted far too much space to supporting examples and not enough to establishing the limiting conditions under which the propositions were in fact valid.

The second basic extra-logical law is that imitation is channeled by status: it descends from social superior to social inferior. An elite functions not merely to ferment invention; it also provides the guiding model for the rest of society and thereby diffuses new discoveries. It is not always easy to separate invention from the first stages of imitation, particularly in the case of less logical or scientific inventions, such as life style. But there is often a significant overlap: as soon as a particular elite ceases to supply leadership in invention and merely preserves established custom, its decline is imminent.[47] A reasonably unified elite serves as the basic source of imitation for a society and also ensures a fundamental unity of belief throughout the society. The role played by the Roman Catholic Church in rationalizing and diffusing belief in the Middle Ages is the outstanding example cited by Tarde.

In democratic periods, the functions performed earlier by nobilities tend to be taken over by capital cities. This transformation was particularly striking in France, where so much of the intellectual, economic, and political life of the country was (and is) centered in Paris. Capital cities provide leadership because in them are found those members of society who are most qualified to generate and diffuse inventions: disproportionately large numbers of males, adults, and the "most active brains" of a society.

Tarde held, somewhat tautologically, that the more hierarchical a society, the greater the social distance traveled by an imitation. Social distance, in turn, may be measured operationally by the number of social strata an imitation must cross before reaching a society's lowest sectors. Introducing the principle that people imitate the socially "closest" models, Tarde could then define a society as democratic when its lowest members could directly imitate the highest stratum without waiting for intermediary strata to transmit imitations.

47 This same proposition has been discussed by Toynbee and Deutsch among others. See Karl Deutsch, *The Nerves of Government* (New York: Free Press of Glencoe, 1963), p. 160.

This view of democracy was at odds with the conception of writers like de Tocqueville, who preferred to view democracies as societies where nobilities and cities of more stratified periods are replaced by the majority of the population. As each man grows less sure of his own superiority, he will be increasingly influenced by the force of numbers in arriving at a decision. "Eighty thousand Frenchmen can't be wrong," was the logical conclusion to be drawn from such reasoning. But Tarde, reflecting his own aristocratic background and his emphasis on the utility of the concept of imitation, stressed that any belief held by such a large number of individuals as the majority in any society must be the inevitable product of massive imitation. Even the cherished democratic concept of equality, as Tarde delighted to recall, was of aristocratic origin: it developed with the continual interaction among members of the royal court despite opposition there by some who vehemently repulsed the pretensions of the lower nobility.[48]

Thus it was virtually impossible for Tarde to conceive of a nonstratified society. Even while recognizing that social superiors might imitate social inferiors, he maintained that this was the exception; the law of imitation from superior to inferior generally held. Nevertheless, this law did not contradict another holding that logically superior inventions replaced inferior ones, regardless of the social origins of the inventor. Tarde's reconciliation of these two laws took the form of a principle that has since had wide currency: when introduced by social inferiors, the best new ideas may not be imitated immediately, but if the leading strata merit their position, they will soon espouse them. Whereupon, having been legitimated by the elite, the new ideas will be imitated throughout the society. This same basic principle, which might be tagged the "pump priming effect," has been reported as operating for the institutionalization of innovations inside university systems,[49] for

---

[48] Part III, 9, below, and *L'opinion et la foule* (Paris: Alcan, 1902).
[49] David Riesman, *Constraint and Variety in American Education* (Garden City, N.Y.: Doubleday Anchor Books, 1958). Diffusion models for higher education are reviewed and criticized in Clark, "Institutionalization of Innovations."

the recognition of ideas by scientists,[50] and for the acceptance of new drugs by practicing physicians.[51]

Seeking to capture long-term trends in imitative patterns, Tarde suggested a movement away from unilateral toward reciprocal imitation. As societies develop, he suggested they move from relationships based on authoritarian submission, where superior unilaterally dominates inferior, to more egalitarian relationships, where reciprocal exchange and imitation take place among all parties. Working relationships based on domination by the superior give way to mutually agreed upon labor contracts; social patterns of extreme deference yield to egalitarian discussion; choice by parents cedes to voluntary selection as a basis for marriage; and so on in other institutional realms. The explanation proffered by Tarde for this fundamental "transformation" was, once again, familiar: imitation. Inferiors, continually exposed to ideas from their superiors, seek in turn to be imitated by others. Continued social interaction erodes the hierarchical differences between actors.

An extension of this unilinear to reciprocal imitation principle to the direction followed by history predicted a trend away "from the reversible to the irreversible." This formula encompassed changes only with respect to hierarchical relationships, however. Tarde referred here to a tendency away from a highly stratified pattern of social relationships toward an eventual state of general equality. And, once equality prevails, it will be impossible to return to the earlier hierarchical state. Tarde's explanation behind this principle is that although imitation is continuous, invention becomes ever more rare. And as the rate of invention declines, and the rate of imitation remains constant, imitators progressively resemble their models.

But postulating *in abstracto* that imitation generates equality leaves too much too vague: what particular forms of imitation, with what frequency, under what conditions, with what specific effects, remain unanswered questions. Why such a transformation as that

50   Robert K. Merton, "The Matthew Effect in Science," *Science* 159, no. 3810 (January 5, 1968) : 56–63.
51   James S. Coleman, Elihu Katz, and Herbert Menzel, *Medical Innovation* (Indianapolis: Bobbs-Merrill, 1966).

from unilateral to reciprocal imitation should take place more rapidly in some periods than others, and why invention should decline, and when—these are precisely the sorts of questions that need to be raised. In a period when grandiose historical speculation still was held by some as synonymous with sociology, Tarde's philosophy of history was not seen as incongruous with the rest of his work. We, today, must judge it as one of the weaker parts of his contribution.

Opposition.—With the publication of *l'Opposition universelle* in 1897, Tarde explicitly added to the concepts of invention and imitation that of opposition as the third basic element of his system. In his earlier writings, opposition had, somewhat implicitly, played a role similar to that which he formulated in *l'Opposition universelle*, but the full development awaited this work.

His characteristic penchant for physical and biological analogy suggested to Tarde that the opposition of social forces generated results similar in some cases to the outcome described by a vector of forces in mechanics. But in other cases such an analogy was literally and inevitably too "mechanical." Following Darwin, Tarde suggested that social conflict resulted in more successful adaptation and consequently progress and human advancement. He further emphasized, however, that besides destroying inferior elements, conflict also generated more successful adaptations to changing social conditions. Focusing on the intellectual aspects of opposition, he posited that social conflict arises out of the clash of antagonistic ideas held by various social carriers, a clash which occurs when these carriers meet. Reverting to the analogy of physical waves, Tarde suggested that if two waves (or ideas in the form of imitations) which clashed were exactly equal in force, they would necessarily annihilate one another. If one were much larger than the other, the smaller would be engulfed with minimal impact on the larger. But if the differences fell somewhere between these two extremes, the result would be a new invention, an "adaptat."[52] And Tarde's principal interest in opposition lay precisely in such creation of further inventions. How creation arose from the conjunction of opposing impulses was something that Tarde never

[52]   Part II, 5, below.

satisfactorily explained, however; he asserted, simply, that it did in fact occur.

Starting from the somewhat unique definition of opposition not as the maximum difference between two entities but as a special sort of repetition—that of "two similar things that are mutually destructive by virtue of their very similarity"—Tarde introduced a threefold typology of oppositions. First are oppositions of "series," where opposition is qualitative and irreversible, leading to a series of discrete stages such as those of a chemical transformation. Contrary to the first, the second opposition is quantitative and reversible; these are the oppositions of "degree," under which are subsumed the opposition of such forces as those which generate the fluctuations recorded by stock markets or crime statistics. Third are the oppositions of "sign," the diametrical opposites to which positive or negative signs may be attached, such as positive or negative attitudes toward a particular matter. Too much of *l'Opposition universelle* was devoted simply to enumerating countless examples of these varying types of oppositions in the physical, biological, psychic, and social worlds. There are, however, a number of interesting observations interspersed between cases exemplifying the typology, although they are not always directly relevant to opposition or conflict. (One of our two selections on "Methodology, Methods, and Quantification" is taken from *l'Opposition universelle*.)

Dealing with the consequences of centralized versus decentralized conflict is one particularly penetrating discussion which grew out of Tarde's concern with the interrelations between individual and social phenomena. When conflict within an individual is greatest, and he is barely able to reconcile the powerful internal oppositions, social conflict is minimal as individuals remain too divided to commit themselves to action.[53] As oppositions become externalized, psychic strains are considerably reduced, but the level of social conflict is correspondingly increased. Thus, the greater the

[53]   Here, Tarde's discussion contains the basic ideas behind the concept of "cross pressure" as used in voting behavior studies. See Bernard R. Berelson, Paul F. Lazarsfeld, and William N. McPhee, *Voting* (Chicago: University of Chicago Press, 1954).

social conflict, the lesser the psychic strain, and vice versa. "Integrating" the individual psyche pushes conflict into surrounding social groups; integrating smaller social groups pushes conflict out to larger groups; integrating all social groups in a society may imply national unity, but also probable international conflict. Thus, Which is preferable, individual tranquility or social peace? Tarde asks, intimating that the two are largely incompatible. But, he observes, the question may pose a false dilemma. His optimism led him to seek a solution which would permit peace, both individual and social. And once he had found what seemed to be a solution, he suggested that the drift of history was in its direction—at least this is the impression one retains from his work. His deus ex machina was that if one more step is taken beyond international conflicts, and an attempt is made to integrate nation states into blocs, inside each bloc relations will be relatively pacific, even if conflict among blocs is increased. But the final and decisive stage is reached when a genuine coalition among all nations of the world is achieved, for then both internal and external sources of conflict will be eliminated. One cannot but recall Marx's discussion of the increasing unity of the proletariat, which, by expanding the basis of class struggle, finally terminates it in an apocalyptic revolution and initiates a new era of peace and freedom. But if one overlooks the extrapolations, one finds in Tarde's analysis the central insights of certain recent discussions on the expansion of conflict.[54] Less precise than more recent conflict theorists, Tarde merits our attention for the breadth of his vision, if not for the depth of his analysis.

Tarde also contended that the same pattern of expanding scope of opposition may be discerned in the field of economic competition, where competition between individuals is replaced by competition between small merchants, then cartels. But the ultimate result is not necessarily monopoly in the sense of domination by a single all powerful corporation in each industry. It may just as well assume the form of a national or international association among numerous small and middle-sized companies, each of which retains some individual autonomy within the larger complex.

[54]   See James S. Coleman, *Community Conflict* (Glencoe, Ill.: Free Press, 1957).

A third area of opposition where a similar transformation takes place is in discussion. Discussion is implied in the first two areas, but under this heading Tarde focuses more specifically on the exchange of intellectual content in such matters as science, religion, and law. Verbal discussions between two men tend to be replaced by coteries, later by major schools, and finally by nationally integrated communities. What may have been a general tendency for certain intellectual currents in France—especially pronounced there because of the centralized and monolithic university, administrative, and ecclesiastical systems—was elevated by Tarde into universal principle. Once again, he exceeded the limits of plausibility even while calling attention to an important pattern.

In numerous discussions, such as the one dealing with changing patterns of conflict, Tarde sought to elaborate certain general principles to describe these "transformations." The term was used consciously to distinguish it from the simplistic universal theories of "evolution" so current at the time he wrote. Tarde's conception of transformation was perhaps more ambitious than more recent social scientists would like, but he was much more supple and sensitive in isolating patterns of transformation than many others of the period.[55] He stressed the voluntaristic element of individual action which would influence the directions and rates of particular transformations, and in conceiving of alternative branching patterns of development, he served as a basic source of inspiration for the anti-evolutionary theories later elaborated by such anthropologists as Boas.[56] With the renewed interest in evolutionary thought among sociologists in recent years,[57] after several decades of avoiding the topic, Tarde's transformistic propositions are both relevant and timely.

[55] J. W. Burrow, *Evolution and Society.*
[56] Robert H. Lowie, *History of Ethnological Theory* (New York: Farrar and Rinehart, 1937), p. 137.
[57] See, for example, Talcott Parsons, *Societies: Evolutionary and Comparative Perspectives* (Englewood Cliffs, N.J.: Prentice-Hall, 1966) and Robert M. Marsh, *Comparative Sociology* (New York: Harcourt, Brace, and World, 1967).

IV. *Personality, Culture, and Social Structure: Belief and Desire*

Tarde's contributions to the study of personality per se were less than outstanding; but he did see what many others did not: that close ties bound the structure of personality to culture and social structure in the broader society. As a psychologist, Tarde was a social psychologist par excellence. In all fairness, however, it must be recalled that his major paper on personality, "Belief and Desire," was published in 1880, a time when personality theory was as yet a nascent area of study. Tarde never seriously reopened the subject in later years, for his basic ideas, as expounded in "Belief and Desire," provided a sufficiently coherent basis for the elaboration of his general system that he felt no need to revise them.

The two fundamental elements of personality,[58] for Tarde, provided the title of his classic paper: belief and desire. Belief referred to the cognitive component of personality, and desire to the affectual; in this respect Tarde's thought maintained a distinction that could be found as early as the Greeks, but he did little to sharpen the general dichotomy. He even confessed, in attempting some small minimum of precision, that in response to the question that "one might ask in passing, just what is belief, what is desire?" he was forced to reply, "I admit my inability to define them." His only consolation was that, prior to him, "others have failed at it," such as Hume and J. S. Mill. He did, however, reject the simple associationistic thesis, maintaining that "belief, no more than desire, is neither logically nor psychologically subsequent to sensation; that, far from arising out of an aggregation of sensations, belief is indispensable both to their formation and their arrangement; that no one knows what remains of sensation once judgment is removed; and that in the most elementary sound, in the most

---

[58]   Tarde did not use the term personality as an analytic concept, nor were his general substitutes—spirit, soul, character, etc.—developed with precision. The only two related concepts he elaborated systematically were belief and desire.

indivisible colored point, there is already a duration and a succession, a multiplicity of points and contiguous moments whose integration is an enigma."[59] Thus, Tarde was at least entirely candid in admitting the limits of his and others' knowledge on central questions of personality.

In his discussion of personality structure he was careful to avoid the extremes both of empiricism and of a prioristic thinking. But a basic weakness of his discussion stems from the fact that he did not include any specific internal mechanisms for changes in personality. Over time, additional beliefs and desires are internalized by individuals through the ever present process of imitation, he tells us, but beyond statements on this general level, he says very little. Had he focused more specifically on socialization and developmental processes, he might have been led to resolve some of the difficulties he experienced. Social psychologists concerned with personality development and learning theory—from Cooley to Miller and Dollard—have rightly identified the absence of a truly dynamic concept of personality as a particularly unfortunate weakness in Tarde's thought.[60] Here, as with most other aspects of his work on personality, we should nevertheless not be too hard on Tarde; he was certainly no more at fault than most other writers of his time. Freud's great contribution did not come until a generation later, and it was well into the twentieth century before more satisfactory social psychological theories of socialization began to take shape.

But if Tarde's considerations of socialization and personality change are wanting, his conception of the close articulation between the individual personality, patterns of imitation, and social structure and culture still deserves our attention. The beliefs and desires of each individual personality are to some extent a result of probabilistic conditions that Tarde referred to as "credibility" and "desirability." In some cases the external conditions impose general limits on the types of beliefs that individuals are likely to have—for example, the knowledge that there are ten tickets in an urn leads us to believe with a high degree of probability that any

59   Part IV, 11, below.
60   See section x, below.

one drawn will bear a number between one and ten. These external conditions influence patterns of internal belief. But while he pointed to some general limits on the type of belief and desire that were likely in an individual in the presence of certain external conditions, Tarde posited no systematic pattern of causality.

Probabilistic Conditions	*Personality Characteristics*	*Social Imitation Patterns*	*Social Beliefs*	*Basic Cultural Elements*
Credibility	Belief	Credulity	Public Opinion	Truth
Desirability	Desire	Docility	General Will	Value

More valuable than his treatment of the origins of belief and desire was Tarde's discussion of the institutionalization of elements corresponding to them (see the figure above). When particular beliefs or desires begin to diffuse through social imitation, they generate the corresponding states of "credulity" or "docility"[61] as they gradually become institutionalized. When beliefs about a particular matter, or desire for a given object, spread further to become generalized throughout a society, they result in "public opinion," on the one hand, and the "general will," on the other.[62] Over time, certain beliefs and desires become so firmly embedded in society that they come to define, in turn, what shall be recognized as "truth" or "value."[63] Tarde occasionally uses these particular terms in his works without making clear their systemic origins: the distinctions he draws between certain aspects of social belief or basic cultural elements may only be understood as an elaboration of the basic concepts of belief and desire.

V. *Methodology, Methods, and Quantification*

If one strength of Tarde's formulations with regard to personality lies in demonstrating its close interdependence with social structure and culture, a second is found in his astute remarks regarding quantification and measurement. Central to Tarde's work

---

61   *Social Laws*, p. 197.
62   Part III, 10, below.
63   Part V, 12, below.

on personality was the belief that thinking would best advance if more attention were devoted to quantification. The opening sentence of his "Belief and Desire" asserted a basic thesis of the article: "Among many continuous dimensions that the soul seems to present us with . . . it would be scientifically desirable to isolate one or two real quantities which, while everywhere mixed with the qualitative elements of sensations, would lend themselves in theory or in practice to measurement."[64] As core materials of personality, and as the basic elements diffusing throughout societies via the process of imitation, belief and desire, Tarde held, were the fundamental elements for social scientists to measure.

Reviewing alternative methodologies for this program, Tarde finds fault with the assumptions of Bentham's "hedonistic calculus" as well as with approaches based on probability theory. They all err, says Tarde, for the same basic reason: not only do they assume a completely logical model of attitude formation, wherein all objective advantages and disadvantages of a given course of action are rationally calculated, but they also go so far as to claim that the net result of this rational calculus is equal to a person's attitudes. A procedure derived from these assumptions can provide the "mathematical reasons for believing," from which point one can compute the probability that an individual will hold a certain belief. But Tarde stressed that calculating these "credibilities" or "desirabilities" behind certain beliefs or desires is by no means an adequate substitute for directly measuring them.

Tarde was fascinated by the suggestive methodology of the psychophysicians for computing a mathematical relationship between the size of an objective stimulus (analogous to the "credibility" of the logicians above), and the objective response to that stimulus.[65] He did not, however, think it possible to establish a

64   Part IV, 11, below.
65   On early psychophysics, see Edwin C. Boring, *A History of Experimental Psychology*, 2d ed. (New York: Appleton-Century-Crofts, 1950), pp. 27–49, 275–96; and Roger Daval, François Bourricaud, Yves Delamotte, and Roland Doron, *Traité de psychologie sociale* (Paris: Presses Universitaires de France, 1963, 1964), vol. 1, chap. 3.

constant relationship between objective probabilities and subjective attitudes in the same way that the Fechner and Weber laws expressed the relationship between the size of an objective stimulus and a subjective response—and in this matter his position was consistent with contemporary thought on attitude measurement.[66]

How, then, is one to measure attitudes? One solution is to adopt a behavoristic perspective and to observe—and count—the muscular movements and other observable behaviors manifested by a person. Tarde was plainly dissatisfied with the grossness of such a solution and lamented the absence of a more precise method for measuring internal attitudes. Still, it should be stressed that unlike many of his French,[67] and particularly his German, contemporaries,[68] Tarde saw as the primary obstacles to the development of such techniques a lack of general societal interest and a paucity of research; at no point did he question the validity of such efforts on epistemological grounds. And this holds not only for the difficulties in measuring individual attitudes but also for the

[66]   Part IV, 11, below; and Tarde, *La criminalité comparée*, 8th ed. (Paris: Félix Alcan, 1924), p. 79.

    Boudon has stressed the modernity of Tarde's formulations on attitude measurement and the similarity of his conceptions to much contemporary work on trace characteristics. Raymond Boudon, "La 'statistique psychologique' de Tarde," *Annales Internationales de Criminologie* 2 (1964): 342–57.

    See Paul F. Lazarsfeld, "The Logic and Mathematical Foundation of Latent Structure Analysis," in Samuel Stouffer *et al.*, *Measurement and Prediction* (Princeton: Princeton University Press, 1950), pp. 362–412, for an influential discussion of "traces" as an attribute of attitudes; and Bert F. Green, "Attitude Measurement," in *Handbook of Social Psychology*, ed. Gardner Lindzey (Cambridge, Mass.: Addison-Wesley, 1954), 1:335–69, and Daval *et al.*, *Traité de psychologie sociale*, 1:191–342, on more contemporary attitude measurement and scaling.

[67]   For example, René Worms, *Philosophie des sciences sociales*, 2d ed. (Paris: Giard & Brière, 1918), 2:98.

[68]   See Talcott Parsons, *The Structure of Social Action* (Glencoe, Ill.: Free Press, 1949), esp. chaps. 13, 16, 18, 19; and Paul F. Lazarsfeld and Anthony R. Oberschall, "Max Weber and Empirical Social Research," *American Sociological Review* 30 (April, 1965): 185–98.

legitimacy of aggregating them in order to derive a measure of general public opinion.[69]

The practical individual is too fascinated with action and concrete behavior to investigate systematically the *degrees* of certainty or conviction with which people carry out a particular activity. "A desire, like an opinion, can be used to manage public or private business, by vote or notarized act, only if it is considered absolute and not relative. The man of action appears to give himself completely to everything he undertakes and indeed believes he does so."[70]

On the other hand, some writers, including such eminent philosophers and *littérateurs* as Cournot, Renan, and Sainte-Beuve, have continually stressed the importance of the distinction between concrete behavior and subjective beliefs. But they were never interested enough in the empirical measurement of human behavior to examine the possibilities for quantifying or measuring some of their general concepts.

Thus, one finds Tarde pointing out the theoretical utility and practical feasibility of measuring individual attitudes for an indicator of public opinion.[71] But, as no workable method had yet been discovered, he suggested several alternatives, among them the use of large-scale, readily available "social bookkeeping" sta-

[69]   We must note, however, that Tarde's conception of society as an aggregate of individuals led him to neglect group characteristics that were not the measurable consequence of such an aggreation. He ignored what have subsequently been identified as "structural" and "global" characteristics. See the articles by Lazarsfeld and Menzel, and by Coleman in *Complex Organizations*, ed. Amitai Etzioni (New York: Holt, Rinehart, and Winston, 1961).

[70]   Part IV, 11, below.

[71]   On early developments in measurement leading to attitude scales, see Daval *et al.*, *Traité de psychologie sociale*, 1: 191–342; Theodore M. Newcomb, Ralph H. Turner and Philip E. Converse, *Social Psychology* (New York: Holt, Rinehart and Winston, 1965), pp. 496–534; and Dorothy C. Adkins, "Louis Leon Thurstone: Creative Thinker, Dedicated Teacher, Eminent Psychologist," in *Contributions to Mathematical Psychology*, ed. Norman Frederiksen and Harold Gulliksen (New York: Holt, Rinehart and Winston, 1964), pp. 1–40.

tistics, such as figures on population movements, industrial production, commercial activities, strikes, crime rates, and so forth. Ingenious analysis, he argued, can yield a broad spectrum of useful information from materials of this sort.[72]

Still, there are a number of weaknesses inherent in "social bookkeeping" materials that he identified. An elementary problem is inaccuracy resulting from insufficient precision in data collection. The extent of this particular weakness depends on the phenomenon classified and counted; births and deaths, for instance, are relatively easy to classify but, because they are not always legally registered, they are not so easy to count. More problems arise when one must depend upon a rather crude classification applied by a lower-level civil servant, as with most criminal statistics, where all types of robberies, for example, are classified together irrespective of the particular type of theft, the motives of the criminal, the underlying circumstances, and so forth. (Durkheim pointed to the same weakness in the official classification of the motives for suicide.)[73]

A perhaps more serious drawback to social bookkeeping data, Tarde held, is that such statistics embrace an entire spectrum of attitudes leading to the performance of a single act; acts are classified, not the attitudes behind them.

In looking over the work of statisticians, it is most important to remember that the things which are under calculation are essentially subjective qualities, desires and beliefs, and that very often the acts which they enumerate, although equal in number, give expression to very different weights among these things.[74]

[72]   See Part V, below.
[73]   Emile Durkheim, *Suicide* (Glencoe, Ill.: Free Press, 1951), p. 148. It may be remarked that in the preface of *Suicide* (p. 39) Durkheim comments apropos of the originally computed tables included in the text that his nephew, Marcel Mauss, carried out the tabulations, and that "these tables have been drawn up from documents of the Ministry of Justice not appearing in the annual reports. They have been most kindly submitted to us by M. Tarde, Chief of the Bureau of Legal Statistics. His assistance is most gratefully acknowledged."
[74]   Tarde, *The Laws of Imitation*, p. 106.

For example, the number of persons attending church or voting for a politician may remain constant while the level of religiosity or degree of support for the politician may vary greatly.[75]

Third, a methodologically elementary but substantively crucial weakness, statistics are simply not collected for many phenomena of interest to the social scientist. In several different works Tarde repeatedly pointed up the utility of regularly collecting varied statistical information as indicators for public opinion. Time series on donation figures and legacies to the clergy[76] and on the number of persons entering churches and attending confessions and communions could help chart shifts in religiosity.[77] He also advocated keeping statistics on the quantity and type of books and newspapers sold, and on "virtuous acts" such as donations to charity.[78] The distribution and extent of cross-national linguistic interpenetration (likely to be particularly strong in border areas) could be measured through diffusion of various foreign words and phrases.[79]

Much of this information could be regularly collected by governmental agencies like most other large-scale statistics, or alternatively by some sort of special research agency. Other types of measures for public opinion that Tarde discussed involved methods more suitable to smaller research organizations. For example, at one point he came close to outlining a program for content analysis when, in addition to recommending a statistical count of the

[75]   In *Les transformations du pouvoir* (Paris: Félix Alcan, 1899), p. 18, Tarde suggests the desirability of creating "bourses politiques"— literally "political stock markets"—for different political personalities and national governments analogous to financial stock markets, in order to measure their bases of power over time. But he outlines no specific research methods for carrying out this program.

[76]   Part IV, 11, below.

[77]   Tarde, *L'opposition universelle* (Paris: Félix Alcan, 1897), p. 344.

[78]   *Ibid.*

[79]   *Ibid.*, pp. 345–46. The degree to which the provinces of Alsace and Lorraine, ceded to Germany after the 1870 war, were actually becoming Germanized was a subject of a great deal of public concern and debate near the turn of the century in France. See Claude Digeon, *La crise allemande de la pensée française (1870–1914)* (Paris: Presses Universitaires de France, 1959), pp. 255ff.

absolute number of letters sent in different areas and time periods, he noted the desirability of data on the lengths as well as the contents of letters.

Letters have just about the same format, the same type of envelope and seal, the same type of address. . . . But open the letters and what characteristic differences, profound and substantial, you find, despite the constant element of the ritual formulas at the beginning and the end! Adding up such heterogeneous things is therefore not doing very much. We know their number but not even their length. It would be interesting to find out, at any rate, if as they become more numerous they become shorter, which seems likely, and more prosaic [plus sèches] as well.[80]

In his study on conversation, where he develops many of his ideas on the importance of personal influence, Tarde comments on the desirability of a *statistique des conversations*. Recorded accounts of the congresses of learned societies provide a first step in this direction, as would extensive personal diaries if they were kept accurately enough.[81] A first type of interesting analysis for a "statistics of conversation" would be the measurement of the speeds at which different types of conversations take place:

The average walking speed of pedestrians in various capitals of the world has been measured, and the statistics that were published showed rather large differences in speeds, as well as steadiness, from one to the next. I am persuaded that, if it were considered worthwhile, it would be possible to measure the speed of conversation in each city as well, and that it would differ a great deal from one city to another as well as from one sex to another. It seems that as people become more civilized, they walk and talk more rapidly. . . . Many travelers have also commented on the slow speed at which Arabs and other primitive peoples converse. Does the future belong to peoples that speak slowly or rapidly? To those that speak rapidly, probably, but it would be worth the trouble, I believe, to examine this side of the question with numerical precision; the study could develop into a sort of social psychophysics. The elements, for the moment, are lacking.[82]

[80]   *L'opinion et la foule*, pp. 152–53.
[81]   *Ibid.*, pp. 152–54.
[82]   *Ibid.*, p. 86.

A final source of empirical information that Tarde discussed was archaeology. Although it may appear rather unusual to contemporary sociologists, archaeology was one of two methods (with statistics) discussed in detail in a methodological chapter of the *Laws of Imitation*. The concern with archaeology was understandable given Tarde's historical and comparative interests. Its value, he held, lay in its ability to force historians—"those poor carvers-up of reality who have been unable to perceive the true dividing line between vital and social facts"[83]—to become more abstract and to focus on the essential details of human existence. It is, then, the "archaeologists [who] stand out as makers of pure sociology because, as the personality of those they unearth is impenetrable . . . they hear, in a certain way, like the Wagnerian ideal, the music without seeing the orchestra of the past."[84]

With the methods and procedures of archaeology it is possible to document the historical periods and geographical locations of particular discoveries. And with the same evidence one can also trace the paths of imitation followed by discoveries as they spread from one time and place to the next. Here, Tarde's concerns stimulated those of cultural anthropologists working on analogous topics.[85]

But although archaeology yields valuable information for extinct societies, the sorts of data it provides are far less rich than those of statistics. At least this is true in so far as data regarding imitations are concerned: for information on invention archaeology may yield valuable information whereas most statistics are virtually worthless.

A particularly appealing aspect of statistics for Tarde was the possibility it offered of subjecting changes in particular phenomena to precise examination over time: such data would enable an investigator to refine and extend the laws of imitation. His general procedure for examining time series was to seek out progressions, the slopes of which could be expressed in equations and thus compared with others. Progression is the "natural" tendency of a

83   *Laws of Imitation*, p. 101.
84   *Ibid.*
85   See section *x*, below.

time series, in Tarde's view, since it represents cumulative imitation of a particular invention throughout a social system. Regression, on the other hand, is not a "natural" process but occurs because of the displacement of one innovation by another.[86] Thus, to explain the decline in use of horses, the increasing series of trains and automobiles should be examined. Tarde remained singularly vague, however, about how it could legitimately be inferred that regression in one particular series was the consequence of progression in another. Durkheim's discussion of Mill's procedure of concomitant variations as well as his uses of it, among other places, in *Suicide* were more precise than Tarde's contributions in this respect.

Tarde's use of statistical information affords an interesting contrast with Durkheim's procedure. Tarde's theoretical orientation, we have observed, led him to consider time series as the basic form of statistic for social analysis. In this respect, he differed with Quételet "and his school" no less than with Durkheim.[87] Quételet had held that the type of statistical result that should be sought by the social scientist was not the increasing but the constant time series. Indeed, for Quételet these "statistical plateaus" represented the basic "laws of nature." To focus on such social constants was to emphasize, like Durkheim, structural causation, the significance of which Tarde minimized. Basic constants could be found, Tarde held, in biological and geographical factors—sex, age, climate, time of year, and so forth—and by recognizing the interplay of these factors with social forces he demonstrated less dogmatism than Durkheim. But Tarde's systematic orientation nevertheless prejudiced him against the analysis of data involving differences between social groups at one point in time.

In his general discussions of statistical analysis one finds the particular cognitive set induced by Tarde's conceptual framework unusually narrowing. And if in certain of his close empirical analyses, such as in "Social Control and Deviance,"[88] he began to break out of these limiting methodological precepts, nevertheless

---

[86] Cf. part V, this volume.
[87] *Laws of Imitation*, p. 114.
[88] Part VII, 15, below.

he remained handicapped by them. To recall that Durkheim, even in such a sophisticated work as *Suicide*, was perhaps still more confined by his particular theoretical orientation does not excuse Tarde, but it highlights the degree to which empirical investigation was structured for each man by a definite theoretical outlook. Despite its obvious limitations, such a conception as Tarde's of the use of statistical data guarded against the lifeless reporting of uninterpreted tables so frequent in the work of the social statisticians of the period, as well as against the too facile elaboration of "social laws" from the simple isolation of a few similar statistical curves.[89]

VI. *The Origins and Functions of Elites*

From his conceptual framework Tarde elaborated a series of ideas on social stratification that for the period were unusually sophisticated. Because his thoughts on stratification were so intimately related to his overall system, we have necessarily touched on them at several points above. Correspondingly, propositions dealing with stratification are found throughout the selections below, but one particularly stimulating discussion of "nobilities" is translated from *Les transformations du pouvoir*.[90]

As used by Tarde, the term nobility was a shorthand designation for elite: his conception was essentially one of functional leadership. He was close to the views later associated with the names of Davis and Moore and Parsons[91] when he pointed out

[89]   Physical scientists who turn a hand to social analysis seem particularly prone to this last fallacy. See, for example, T. J. Rainoff, "Wavelike Fluctuations of Creative Productivity in the Development of West-European Physics," *Isis* 12 (1929) : 287–88. Even as sophisticated an observer as Derek Price is not immune to such difficulties, for example in *Science since Babylon* (New Haven: Yale University Press, 1962).

[90]   See "The Origins and Functions of Elites," this volume.

[91]   Kingsley Davis and Wilbert E. Moore, "Some Principles of Stratification," *American Sociological Review* 10, no. 2 (1945) : 242–49; Talcott Parsons, "A Revised Analytical Approach to the Theory of Social Stratification," in Parsons, *Essays in Sociological Theory*, rev. ed. (Glencoe, Ill.: Free Press, 1954), pp. 386–439. See also Suzanne Keller, *Beyond the Ruling Class* (New York: Random House, 1963).

that the definition of a social superior depends on the "social goods . . . pursued . . . by the majority of men of a given epoch and country," and that the qualities which make a man superior are his abilities to interpret the most important inventions of his period.[92] In this way, the elite reflects the central values of the society even while leading it by innovating changes in the value system.

Societies based on few inventions, according to Tarde's deductions from his system, will in turn be characterized by an elite narrowly skilled in these particular inventions. When increasingly numerous and complex inventions are developed, several more sophisticated elites emerge, each of which is skilled in a particular invention. An elite may thus achieve its eminence from success in war, attainment of great wealth, demonstration of saintliness or superior morality, or mastery of an aesthetic and civilized culture.

Tarde, with this interpretation of social leadership, provided a more integrated theoretical underpinning for the structural and functional differentiation of elites than did, for example, even that brilliant commentator on social stratification, Max Weber. In his threefold distinction of class, status, and party, Weber helped advance thinking on social stratification far beyond the monolithic conception of a unitary elite atop a single vertical hierarchy, as found in so many writers of the period.[93] But Tarde, by systematically relating leadership patterns to the broader structures of a society, moved social thinking even further toward an integrated theory of leadership and social stratification.

VII. *Social Control and Deviance*

Tarde elaborated his ideas on social control and deviance in a number of different contexts, including the discussions of imitation and mass communications, but his 1897 article on juvenile delinquency is especially interesting in this area, as its analysis does not grow directly out of his general conceptual framework.[94]

[92]   See part III, 9, below; and *Laws*, p. 234.
[93]   Max Weber, "Class, Status, Party," in *Essays in Sociology* (New York: Oxford University Press, 1946), pp. 180–95.
[94]   See part VII, below.

Noting that misdemeanors had increased in several European countries as well as in France over a period of several decades, Tarde attempted to unravel the underlying causes. The increasing crime rate was a phenomenon that had concerned him ever since his early years as a provincial judge; the attention Tarde devoted to this social problem was similar in many ways to his concern, shared by Jacques Bertillon, Leroy-Beaulieu, and Durkheim, among others, about the problem of depopulation.[95] It is interesting that both Tarde and Durkheim, when occupied with these empirical problems instead of more general theoretical issues, came to strikingly similar conclusions.

Tarde distinguished five major factors, all related to one another but each somewhat distinct, which he felt lay behind both the increasing crime rate and the declining birth rate. First was the breakdown of traditional morality based on a Christian system of ethics. Numerous moral doctrines had contributed to the destruction of Christian ethics, and in the process had weakened the moral strength of the family without replacing these previously established beliefs with any firm alternatives.

In part as a consequence of this first factor, there developed among the middle and lower social sectors of society an increased desire for social advancement as well as greater demand for new luxury commodities. Partially released from the moral nexus of the family, rural farm workers and small land owners were attracted to urban industrializing areas offering a higher standard of living than that available in the rural areas. This geographical mobility, in turn, further weakened traditional family ties.

But third, Tarde argued, despite the rising standard of living possible for the general population, the proximity of recent urban migrants to far greater affluence than they had previously witnessed generated demands that exceeded the possibilities offered by legitimate employment.

Out of these background factors emerges a deviant subculture, strengthened by alcohol, popular newspapers, and the breakdown of traditional cultural patterns. "The little newspaper, supplement-

[95]   Clark, *Institutionalization of Innovations in Higher Education.*

ing the little drink, alcoholizes the heart."[96] The weakening of moral certainty in the lower and middle sectors renders them increasingly unfit to resist the attractions of such a deviant subculture; furthermore this malaise is increased by the shifting cultural patterns of the upper classes.[97]

Attuned to unorthodox intellectual currents, the upper classes become less sure of themselves as a model of social behavior for the lower sectors. Comtean positivism Tarde singled out along with social Darwinism as especially unsettling. And social Darwinism in particular supports a competitive mentality that may easily be extended to criminal behavior. Associated with this competition among social doctrines were the disagreements and contradictions among various theories of jurisprudence. Such moral anarchy, especially as it emerged in the confused beliefs presented to students in the schools, offered more support to deviance than would a fixed socialization into any one set of beliefs, whether based on the Bible, the Koran, or modern philosophical systems. Among recent attempts at moral synthesis of which Tarde was especially critical was the one offered by Emile Durkheim. He parodied Durkheim's solution: "When a star of the first magnitude rises before the little, nervous, discouraged, broken-down Frenchman, the energy of the great days will reappear, the law of Duty will be known again, and all the difficulties of Reason will vanish."[98] Seeking moral unity and social integration in an ideology of Duty and Patriotism, Tarde conceded, might have been appropriate for a small city state, but it was thoroughly unrealistic for a large industrial society. (The version of Durkheim's thought to which Tarde was reacting here was the one that became diffused as the new principles of national pedagogy, and not the

96   Part VII, below.
97   It is remarkable to note how many elements of the theory of deviance developed by Merton and Cloward and Ohlin are contained in Tarde's observations. See Robert K. Merton, "Anomie, Anomia, and Social Interaction: Contexts of Deviant Behavior," in *Anomie and Deviant Behavior*, ed. Marshall B. Clinard (New York: Free Press of Glencoe, 1964), pp. 213–42.
98   Part VII, below.

corporatism developed in the 1902 preface to the second edition
of *The Division of Labor in Society*.)

Tarde's own preferred solution for these moral problems was,
for the short term, a renewed strengthening of family ties, the
same solution that had been favored by conservative critics of industrialism both before and after Le Play developed his ideological theories supporting stronger family integration.[99] But Tarde's
peculiar affinity for conservative as well as futuristic solutions to
social problems is evident in his feeling that a long-term cohesive
moral order could not be founded except on internationalistic
sentiments. The bases for such a new order, he felt, were being
laid by developments in industrial technology and the expansive
influences of the mass media. It is these ideas, which emerged
from his discussions of publics, crowds, and mass communications,
to which we turn next.

VIII. *Publics and Crowds*

Tarde's basic article on crowds appeared in 1893,[100] and
when, five years later, he discussed publics and conversation, it
was initially conceived as a comparison with his remarks on
crowds.[101] The concept of a public was more appealing to Tarde
than that of a crowd; dealing by preference with the more civilized
aspects of human behavior, he left the topic of crowds to more
popular writers such as Le Bon. Nevertheless his treatment of
publics is only comprehensible in conjunction with the work on
crowds.

To be sharply distinguished from the crowd, "a collection of
psychic connections produced essentially by physical contact," is
the public,[102] at once its extension and antithesis. Publics may
originate in groups characterized by physical proximity—for

[99]   Cf. Terry N. Clark, "Henri de Tourville," *International Encyclopedia of the Social Sciences* (New York: Macmillan and Free Press, 1968).
[100]   "Foules et sectes au point de vue criminel," *Revue des Deux
Mondes* 332 (1893): 349ff.
[101]   "The Public and the Crowd," this volume.
[102]   *Ibid.*

example, a theatrical public—but this is only a restricted meaning of the term. For Tarde, the public is best conceived as a "purely spiritual collectivity, a dispersion of individuals who are physically separated and whose cohesion is entirely mental."[103] Further, "their bond lies in their simultaneous conviction or passion and in their awareness of sharing at the same time an idea or a wish with a great number of men."[104] But how does such a "spiritual collectivity" arise if not from social interaction, which is in turn dependent on physical proximity? Tarde's answer is that the public cannot exist without certain technological requisites, some means of communication that serve to bind the members of a public together. The most basic means to this end is provided by the newspaper. And as the modern, large-circulation newspaper in turn was dependent on such inventions as the printing press, the telegraph, and the railroad, the modern public could only emerge with the nineteenth century. That century might be characterized, Tarde asserts, not the era of the crowd, as Le Bon would have it, but the time of the public. Crowds have existed from time immemorial and are, with the family and the horde, the most ancient of social groups.

Publics are incomparably more complex forms of social groupings and generate quite different consequences for their members. An individual can belong to several publics simultaneously, Tarde observes, but only to a single crowd. Because of the restriction of physical proximity, definite limits are fixed on the maximum size a crowd may attain. Publics, on the other hand, are not circumscribed in this manner. From these dual factors of overlapping membership and size—for size implies in turn greater heterogeneity of membership—it follows that publics tend to be more tolerant than crowds. Correspondingly, nations dominated by crowds tend to be more intolerant than those dominated by publics. Tarde went on to elaborate a series of interesting observations about the orientations and styles of publics and crowds which result from various compositional characteristics: sex, age, religion, and so forth.

103   *Ibid.*
104   *Ibid.*

But probably the most important single aspect of a public is the opinion to which it gives rise. "Opinion," Tarde writes, "is to the modern public what the soul is to the body." More precisely, it is "a momentary, more or less logical cluster of judgments which, responding to current problems, is reproduced many times over in people of the same country, at the same time, in the same society."[105] In order that this "cluster of judgments" may become true public opinion, however, the members of the public must develop a consciousness of sharing certain fundamental beliefs. As mass communications both diffuse beliefs throughout a public and generate a consciousness among its members that these beliefs are shared, they deserve, Tarde asserts, careful attention. Tarde was one of the most perceptive commentators in the practically untouched field of mass communications and their effects, and precisely because of the wide sweep of his remarks in this area they assume additional interest for contemporary students who are once again seeking to understand media in their broadest context.

IX. *Mass Communication, Social Interaction, and Personal Influence*

Examining the impact of technological developments on social relations, Tarde discusses the role of the telegraph, the telephone, mass-produced books, and even printed invitations and announcements; but to him the most important single medium was unquestionably the modern mass-circulation newspaper. Still, the modern newspaper depends on rapid means of communication (the telegraph and telephone) as well as rapid means of transportation (the railroad) in order to receive news and to speed distribution of newspapers over a large territory. The newspaper depends, then, on a complex of technological innovations which are present only in a relatively highly industrialized society; it is difficult if not impossible to isolate completely the impact of the newspaper from that of innumerable developments associated with industrialization.

[105]   Part IX, below.

A case in point is the shift in the locus of social control. Prior to industrialization and the associated development of communication media, integration and social control were functions that accrued to traditional, fixed social units: the village, the occupational group, the family.

> In feudal states such as medieval England or France, each city, each village had its internal dissensions, its own politics and currents of ideas. . . . There was no general "opinion" but thousands of separate opinions with no continuing ties between them.
>
> This tie was only provided by the book, first of all, and later, with far greater efficacity, by the newspaper. The daily or periodic press permitted these primary groups of highly similar individuals to form secondary and higher aggregations whose members were closely associated without ever seeing or knowing one another.[106]

Tarde views the creation of intermediate-level organizations and extended patterns of loyalties as a doubly liberating phenomenon; like Simmel, he shows that corresponding to an increase in the size of a group is a decrease in the integration of individual members, hence an increase in personal freedom.[107] Moreover, as the number of groups with overlapping memberships increases, the extended and conflicting loyalties of members enable groups to shift ideological perspectives, form coalitions, and even make international alliances with greater flexibility.

As mentioned in the discussion on opposition, Tarde analyzed the processes through which conflict originating in the mind of a single person can precipitate social conflict among families, communities, regional groups, and even national societies, possibly terminating in international conflagration. A functional prerequisite for the eruption of violent conflict beyond the intercommunity level, however, is an effective communication system. For although international wars may have existed practically as long as nations themselves, in preindustrial societies wars were actually quite narrowly limited; officially, entire nation-states declared war on one

---

[106]   Tarde, *L'opinion et la foule*, pp. 70–71.
[107]   See Georg Simmel, *The Web of Group-Affiliations* (Glencoe, Ill.: Free Press, 1955) ; and Kurt H. Wolff, ed., *The Sociology of Georg Simmel* (Glencoe, Ill.: Free Press, 1950), esp. pp. 87–180.

another, but the widely-observed rules of chivalry effectively re-stricted the actual hostilities. In order for international conflict to grow to the extent of arousing the passions of entire populations and mobilizing national economies, it was imperative to establish communication and transportation networks connecting all sectors of a nation.

But although the social transformations associated with the newspaper increase the potential threat of large-scale conflicts, other modifications, to Tarde, tip the balance toward peace: in the long run, he felt, the outstanding contribution of the newspaper would be its civilizing and rationalizing influences.[108]

If we conceive of the set of changes just discussed primarily as modifications on a social structural level, we may view a second set of developments as predominantly cultural. Tarde envisaged a constant interweaving of influences between these two levels: tech-nological developments make newspapers possible, newspapers promote the formation of broader publics, and they, by broadening the loyalties of their members, create an extensive network of overlapping and shifting groupings. These groupings facilitate the formation of broader ideological perspectives; rationality, toler-ance, international peace, and understanding are the eventual results.

Thus, mass media can work for good and for ill, the former perhaps neutralizing or minimizing the latter. But Tarde was sor-rowfully imprecise in these matters. Neither rationality nor civil-ization are given any more precise meanings than those of general conversational usage. And just how influential a role newspapers actually play in the overall process varies from one presentation to the next.

In some places, newspapers are treated as a primordial factor effecting the transformation of societies into aggregates of in-creasingly broad and overlapping publics. And, occasionally,

---

[108]   See Raymond Aron, *La société industrielle et la guerre* (Paris: Plon, 1959), for a discussion of Comte, Veblen, and Schumpeter which stresses that like Tarde they shared the nineteenth century's optimistic view that war was a barbarous anachronism that would disappear with advancing industrialization.

civilization and rationality (the cultural changes) flow almost automatically from the subsequent reorganization of social groupings (the social structural changes).[109] Thus, although the tendency of his analysis is in the same general direction as that, for example, of Tönnies, Simmel, Weber, or Durkheim in pointing out the fundamental movement in industrializing societies from smaller, more intimate, and highly integrated social groupings toward broader, more distant, and more complex networks of relationships, Tarde differs from the German writers, and to some degree from Durkheim as well, in several respects. He is, for one, less systematic than they in analyzing the dynamics of the overall process. He also does not share their pessimistic view—a partial carry-over from German romanticism—that with further industrialization men will become cold, calculating, and "dehumanized." Quite on the contrary, Tarde enthusiastically greeted the developments he observed, and held that with increased communication men would become progressively more urbane and civilized.[110]

Tarde's optimism, in contrast to the qualified pessimism of many others, may in part have been a consequence of his emphasis on the importance of personal relationships in tempering the effects of broader structural modifications. His stress on face-to-face human contacts places Tarde much closer than most of his contemporaries to more recent thought on analogous problems.

Perhaps the simplest way to summarize Tarde's views in this area for the contemporary reader is to say that he offered a nineteenth-century French version of what has since become known as "the two-step flow of communication."[111] But Tarde, in contrast to Lazarsfeld, used the *mondain* Parisian conversationalists of

---

109   Cf. Tarde, *L'opinion et la foule*, pp. 15, 16, 20, 61, 76.

110   In addition to his pronouncements in *L'opinion et la foule*, Tarde went beyond the limits of his scholarly work in a fanciful discussion of a utopia founded to support continual conversation among highly educated and socially sophisticated individuals. See *Fragments d'histoire future* (Paris: Félix Alcan, 1905), translated as *Underground Man*, preface by H. G. Wells (London: Duckworth, 1905).

111   For an overview, see Elihu Katz, "The Two-Step Flow of Communication: An Up-to-Date Report on an Hypothesis," *Public Opinion Quarterly* 22 (1957): 61–78.

Proustian salons as his principal empirical material rather than middle-class Ohio housewives.

Thus, while Tarde emphasizes the power of newspapers in restructuring modern society, their influence, he stresses, can only be exerted in concert with direct personal influence. "If people did not talk," he writes, "it would be futile to publish newspapers . . . they would exercise no durable or profound influence on people, they would be like a vibrating string without a sounding board."[112]

Tarde certainly gives due credit to the press as a molder of public opinion in modern times, but he also emphasizes the significance of conversation both in the past and at present:

But the press is only one source of opinion, and one of the most recent. If we have studied the press before any other source, it is because it is the most obvious. But it is now advisable to study, and on a wider scale because it is an unexplored field, the formative agent of opinion that we have already recognized as being the most continuous and the most universal—the little invisible spring that flows, albeit irregularly, at all times and in all places: conversation.[113]

As a well-to-do French intellectual with a humanistic streak, Tarde was fascinated with conversation as a subject in itself. At one point in his essay on the subject[114] he offers a rebuttal against attacks (particularly from Taine) on conversation and the literary salon which saw these as causes of conservativism and superficiality in French intellectual life. Here, in particular, Tarde reveals his love for conversation as a sparkling, exhilarating exercise—a pure joy in and of itself.[115] In addition, within the framework of

112 "Opinion and Conversation," this volume.
113 "L'opinion et la conversation," in *L'opinion et la foule*, pp. 82–83.
114 In commenting on American sociologists' ignorance of Tarde's *Psychologie économique*, Everett C. Hughes remarks that the same is true of his essay on conversation. Hughes, "Tarde's *Psychologie Economique:* An Unknown Classic by a Forgotten Sociologist," *American Journal of Sociology* 66 (May, 1961): 553–59.
115 At different points Tarde refers thus to conversation: "cette fleur esthétique des civilisations," *L'opinion et la foule*, p. 84. ". . . occupons-nous plus à loisir de la conversation cultivée comme un art spécial et un plaisir exquis," *ibid.*, p. 110. "La conversation est mère de la politesse," *ibid.*, p. 141. "La conversation a été le berceau de la critique littéraire," *ibid.*, p. 146.

his general system, conversation stands as the source of creative invention: in fiery, brilliant conversations, proponents of opposing inventions rub against one another, and the resulting sparks touch off new inventions; these in turn are disseminated throughout entire social networks largely through other, generally shorter, less intense conversations.

Basic to Tarde's analysis of conversation is a central sociological proposition: social intraction leads to the development and affirmation of common norms shared by a community of actors in a social system. Indeed, much of Tarde's discussion consists of elaborations and refinements of this central theme. Because every social system depends for its very existence upon the maintenance of norms, interaction is a functional imperative.

A further imperative for the maintenance of a large social system is a hierarchy of authority. But to maintain itself, such a hierarchy must be founded on the legitimacy deriving from a set of common symbols and shared normative beliefs. Both a national press and continuous social interaction diffuse these basic symbols and beliefs through a society. Of course, Tarde did not go so far as to say that national integration arose solely from the rise of the newspaper; rather he cites a whole complex of developments—a central postal service, a national road system, the formation of a permanent army, and the development of a court around the king —as contributing to the same end. "But it remained above all for the printing press to bring about this great work."[116]

Early steps in the development of collective interests and a national identity were taken in the formation of parliamentary-type structures in several European countries. Before a national press came into existence and made possible the mobilization of voters in strong national party organizations, parliaments were more assemblies of regional interest groupings than meetings of citizens with common loyalties to a national society. Tarde did not discount the effects of such electoral reforms as expanded suffrage in facilitating this change; but he particularly stressed the contributions of newspapers.

[116]   "Opinion and Conversation."

The political system is not alone in needing a normative consensus in order to function, however; the operation of the economy depends upon an analogous foundation: lacking certain basic agreements among large numbers of persons, it would be clearly impossible to set prices or work out exchanges.[117] In the earliest markets, there were no fixed prices; only through extensive bargaining between buyer and seller could a price be reached. With broadening normative consensus, and despite temporal and geographical differences, prices could be relatively standardized from one market to the next. Extended negotiations were no longer necessary between producer and consumer. Through advertising, producers attempt to compensate for the loss of direct personal influence, although personal influence retains its importance in certain situations.

Conversations among family members and friends lead to the establishment of certain hierarchies of needs and desires, according to which values are assigned to commodities. And in the actual buying situation adept salesmanship is not to be discounted.[118] Further, in major transactions on the wholesale level, the role of personal influence remains crucial in settling prices.[119] The entire system of markets, prices, and retail and wholesale transactions is thus held together, Tarde stressed, by the complementary influences of newspapers and personal influence.

Focusing on political authority and economic transactions, Tarde gives a detailed demonstration of the ways in which newspapers, complemented by personal influence, disseminate and reinforce the norms of a social system.

The next logical step is, of course, to formulate some general principles through which these phenomena operate. One basic principle was that the more distant the source of communication, the less strong is its influence. Highly centralized France, where geographical, psychological, and sociological distance overlap more than in most other countries, is, appropriately, the perfect illustration of this assertion; ever since the late sixteenth century,

[117]   See Tarde, *Psychologie économique* (Paris: Félix Alcan, 1902), 2:30 and *L'opinion et la foule*, pp. 126–27, 137–38.
[118]   *Psychologie économique*, 2:30–31.
[119]   *Ibid.*, p. 34.

Paris has been the undisputed educational, cultural, and industrial apex of French society. In several discussions Tarde illustrates this principle by showing that the impact of Parisian models on the geographically and socially outlying sectors of French society is relatively weak.[120]

There are exceptions, however, and the general rule should not blind the observer to deviations: for example, within the very shadow of modern industrial capitals can still be found "villages . . . where old needs and old ideas remain, where people order their cloth from the weaver, like to eat brown bread, speak only in dialect, believe in sorcerers and magic."[121]

From the general distance principle is derived the proposition that imitation descends from social superior to social inferior. In discussing, for example, the French peasantry, Tarde tells us how much originality to expect at this lowest level of society:

Go into the dwelling of a peasant and examine his belongings: from his fork and his glass down to his shirt . . . there is not one article of clothing, not one tool which, before descending as far as his cottage, did not *begin by being a luxury item used by kings, or warrior chieftains, or ecclesiastics, then by noblemen, then by bourgeois, then by the neighboring landowners.* Have a peasant speak: you will not find in him a notion of law, agriculture, politics or arithmetic, not a family sentiment or a patriotic thought, not a hope or a desire, which was not originally a discovery or an innovation propagated from social heights, and gradually sank down to his depths.[122]

Influence is not, however, always transmitted from social superior to social inferior; the most noble prince living in the country with only his servants will tend to adopt their vulgar accents and even their expressions. On the other hand, it sometimes happens— as with certain conquered peoples who continue to oppose their new rulers—that social inferiors may stubbornly refuse to imitate their superiors. Still, Tarde considers the great majority of social influences and imitations to travel downward, to the extent, he maintains, that it is possible "frequently to neglect, even most of the time, in our societies, the impressive action exercised by

120   "Opinion and Conversation."
121   Tarde, *La Philosophie pénale* (Paris: Masson, 1890), p. 328.
122   *Ibid.*, pp. 330–31. Emphases added.

slaves on their master, children on adults . . . inferiors on superiors, and only take account of the inverse type of action, the true explanation of history."[123]

Because he applied this general principle to the exercise of personal influence in virtually all subject matters, Tarde failed to conceive of the pattern of multiple-opinion leadership as documented in more recent studies on the diffusion of influence.[124] He also neglected personal influence among relative equals, or from inferior to superior in terms of social standing. Of course, in this respect Tarde was no different from many writers on the same subject, even in later years. Then, too, there may well have been an increase in imitation among social equals since the time that Tarde wrote. As a dedicated scientist, Tarde was fully aware that his formulations would in time be surpassed. It is, however, ample testimony to his stature that so many generations of work were necessary before this could happen.[125]

X. *Continuities: The Diffusion of Tarde's Thought*

As Tarde himself aptly observed, the optimal conditions for the creation of new ideas are not the same as those for their propagation. Tarde created many ideas; in France, at least, he propagated few.[126] Unquestionably the most efficient machine in

123   *Ibid.*, p. 329.
124   See Robert K. Merton, "Patterns of Influence: Local and Cosmopolitan Influentials," *Social Theory and Social Structure* (Glencoe, Ill.: Free Press, 1957), pp. 387–420; Elihu Katz and Paul F. Lazarsfeld, *Personal Influence* (Glencoe, Ill.: Free Press, 1955); Everett M. Rogers, *Diffusion of Innovations* (New York: Free Press of Glencoe, 1962). Rogers, incidentally, opens his study with a quotation from Tarde.
125   On the architectonics of intellectual stature, see Robert K. Merton, *On the Shoulders of Giants* (New York: Free Press of Glencoe, 1965).
126   A framework for analyzing "discontinuities" as well as "continuities" of intellectual currents is presented in Terry N. Clark, "Discontinuities in Social Research: The Case of the *Cours élémentaire de statistique administrative,*" *Journal of the History of the Behavioral Sciences* 3, no. 1 (January, 1967): 3–16.

France for propagating ideas was the national university system. Those at its center controlled (and largely control) the content of courses, examinations, degree requirements, teaching and research appointments, research grants, and to some extent journal and book publication outlets. And the stratification of academic prestige was so great that the university, and especially the Ecole Normale Supérieure, attracted many brilliant scholars and most of the outstanding students. To have Durkheim, one of the two or three most influential *universitaires* of his day, as an arch rival was not propitious for the continuing success of one's ideas. As Tarde offered courses at half a dozen teaching institutions, one might nevertheless expect that his ideas would have spread, especially as these institutions attracted no little public attention at the time. But their success and esteem were short-lived; they soon collapsed whereas the university endured.

Tarde and Durkheim, as well as those around them, deservedly were heady with breaking virgin intellectual territory. After World War I, however, for a variety of complex reasons, the quality of French social scientific work dropped appreciably. Innovation, inside and outside the university, declined in favor of servile imitation of ideas from earlier years. The Durkheimians tended to mention Tarde's name simply as that of an early adversary of the master who had lost several debates. And in their own debates with psychologists, they grew, with time, not more sophisticated but more rigid in reaffirming the slogans which Durkheim had expounded in his debates with Tarde. Most psychologists, too, carried on these debates with equal vacuity, defending an extremely narrow conception of the individual psyche as independent of the impact of social factors. The results were devastating for the development of social psychology in France.[127] Remarkably little progress in the discipline was made from the time of Tarde's work until after World War II, when the American version of the new field was imported into France.[128]

[127]   Daniel Essertier, *Psychologie et sociologie* (Paris: Félix Alcan, 1927).

[128]   Jean Maissonneuve, *Psychologie sociale* (Paris: Presses Universitaires de France, 1960).

Still, Tarde was not entirely without followers in France. At the peripheral institutions where he taught, as well as at the eminent Collège de France, no doctoral dissertations were prepared. So, directing neither dissertations nor a laboratory, he never developed a cluster of disciples in the usual sense of the term. Where he did have a more enthusiastic following was among a middle-aged group of lawyers, lycée professors, government officials, and freelance writers of various sorts who were associated with the institutions created by René Worms: principally the Société de Sociologie de Paris, the Institut International de Sociologie, and the *Revue Internationale de Sociologie*.[129] Tarde was one of the leading intellectual lights of these organizations, and while he found in them few true disciples, his influence was noticeable on the thoughts of many. His early battles to exclude biology from sociology were continued in spirited discussions held in these institutions where he attacked social Darwinists, racial criminologists, and partisans of organismic analogies.

René Worms radically modified his sociology from his first major synthesis, *Organisme et société*, to his later *Philosophie des sciences sociales* largely under the influence of Tarde's criticisms.[130] Gaston Richard, a disciple of Durkheim until he was appointed to a Bordeaux professorship, was one of several who found respite from the Durkheimians in the Tarde-Worms cluster of institutions. Throughout the interwar years, he led attacks on the sociologism of the Durkheimians.[131] Raoul de la Grassière, particularly active with the *Revue*, found much inspiration in Tarde's work. The same was true of G. L. Duprat, who, working closely with Worms in Paris, later became professor at the University of Geneva, thus underlining the international orientations of the cluster. Both Richard and Duprat were subsequently editors of the *Revue Internationale de Sociologie*. Near the end of the interwar years the

[129]   Clark, *Institutionalization of Innovations in Higher Education.*

[130]   Terry N. Clark, "René Worms," *International Encyclopedia of the Social Sciences* (New York: Macmillan-Free Press, 1968).

[131]   See, for example, Gaston Richard, "Nouvelles tendances sociologiques en France et en Allemagne," *Revue Internationale de Sociologie* 36 (1928) : 647–69.

efforts of such men as Daniel Essertier and Charles Blondel to reconcile the warring camps and establish the bases for a mutually
productive merging between the disciplines of psychology and
sociology gradually began to succeed. But it is notable that it was
not until nearly World War II that a consensus began to emerge,
influenced by such younger men as Georges Gurvitch and Jean
Stoetzel, who helped develop social psychology in France after the
war.[132] In working out an acceptable statement of the relations between the individual and society, and in undertaking social psychological research after the war, the French drew on the experience
of the Americans who had been less hampered by ideological
debate.

American social scientists, at an earlier stage, had learned much
from Tarde. Among his leading American contemporaries Tarde
was widely acclaimed. For Baldwin he was "one of the most authoritative and distinguished living writers in sociology and social
psychology."[133] Albion Small considered him "very prominent,
perhaps the most prominent, figure just at present among the
founders of the new science" of sociology.[134] Lester Ward praised
Tarde as "one of the leading thinkers of our time."[135] Giddings
wrote an adulatory introduction to the English translation of *The
Laws of Imitation.*

Equally enthusiastic, and more intellectually indebted to Tarde,
was E. A. Ross, whose 1908 *Social Psychology* served as probably

[132]   See Georges Gurvitch, *La vocation actuelle de la sociologie* (Paris:
Presses Universitaires de France, 1963), 1: 31–118; Gurvitch, *Détermin-
ismes sociaux et liberté humaine* (Paris: Presses Universitaires de France,
1963) ; Jean Stoetzel, "Sociology in France: An Empirical View," in *Modern Sociological Theory*, ed. Howard Becker and Alvin Boskoff (New York:
Holt, Rinehart and Winston, 1957), pp. 623–57.
[133]   James Mark Baldwin, "Editor's Preface," to Tarde, *Social Laws*,
p. vii. For some of Tarde's favorable remarks about Baldwin, see *ibid.*, pp.
42ff. Through independent discovery as well as borrowing of ideas, Baldwin's work was similar enough to Tarde's that he felt obliged at one point
to point out precisely where it in fact differed.
[134]   Small, Review of *Les lois sociales*, *American Journal of Sociology*
4 (1898-99) : 395.
[135]   Ward, Review of *Social Laws*, *Science* 11 (1900) : 260.

the most important single vehicle for the diffusion of Tarde's thought in America.[136] With Baldwin, Ross, and others, Tarde became identified as one of the proponents of imitation as a basic principle of explanation of human behavior, the major alternative of which was represented as instinct in one form or another. The rivalry between these more social or psychological approaches, associated, respectively, with the competing volumes by Ross and McDougal, is well known.[137] In the 1920's, the simple version of the instinct theory was largely dismissed, but imitation was also criticized as at once too simple and too general.[138] C. H. Cooley and G. H. Mead started with the same proposition that Tarde had used in so many different ways—social interaction leads to the formation of common norms—but they went beyond Tarde to examine in more detail the processes by which interaction leads in turn to changes in personality.[139] Most subsequent social psychologists have moved in the same direction, fusing the general idea of imitation with various conceptions of personality to generate theories of socialization and learning.[140]

Anthropologists were likewise indebted to Tarde's work on imitation when they formulated various models of cultural diffusion. The *Laws of Imitation* was recognized as one of the most outstanding works in the area, and it "profoundly impressed" the first dean of American anthropologists, Franz Boas, "and, through

---

[136]   New York: Macmillan, 1908. On Ross's indebtedness to Tarde, see the "Preface" to *Social Psychology* as well as "The Ward-Ross Correspondence, II: 1897–1901, III: 1902–1903," ed. Bernard J. Stern, *American Sociological Review* 11, no. 6 (December, 1946): 743–48, and 12, no. 6 (December, 1947): 703–20.

[137]   Fay Berger Karpf, *American Social Psychology* (New York: McGraw-Hill, 1932); Gordon W. Allport, "The Historical Background of Modern Social Psychology," in *Handbook of Social Psychology*, ed. Gardner Lindzey (Cambridge: Addison-Wesley, 1954), 1: 3–56.

[138]   Ellsworth Faris, *The Nature of Human Nature* (New York: McGraw-Hill, 1937), pp. 73–83.

[139]   Charles Horton Cooley, *Social Organization* (New York: Schocken Books, 1962), pp. 327ff; Cooley, *Social Process* (Carbondale: Southern Illinois University Press, 1966), pp. 371ff; George Herbert Mead, *Mind, Self, and Society* (Chicago: University of Chicago Press, 1934), pp. 53ff.

[140]   Neal E. Miller and John Dollard, *Social Learning and Imitation* (New Haven: Yale University Press, 1941); Allport, *op. cit.*

him, dozens of anthropologists in the United States."[141] The spread of cultural elements through different societies could be interpreted with the principles developed by Tarde; Boas drew on them to help explain such phenomena as the patterns of growth of secret societies on the coast of British Columbia.[142] Paradoxically, however, Tarde could provide stimulation both for partisans of cultural diffusion and those of independent invention in the debate that so divided anthropologists between the wars, since he had formulated basic principles about both phenomena.[143]

Tarde was equally stimulating for sociologists concerned with diffusion in contemporary societies. As a student under Giddings, Ogburn apparently was influenced by ideas deriving from Tarde, and in his *Social Change*,[144] as well as many subsequent studies,[145] he went on to refine precisely the sort of analysis of inventions, social trends, and diffusion that Tarde had initiated. Chapin's well-known study of diffusion of the city manager form of government formulated the idea of an "S-curve" of adoption of innovations,[146] which subsequently became refined by many others.[147] A number of disparate traditions of research on diffusion developed in anthropology, sociology, rural sociology, education, and other substantive areas throughout the first half of the twentieth century, and only quite recently have systematic attempts been made to synthesize the findings emerging from these several areas and to isolate empirically validated principles.[148]

[141]   Robert H. Lowie, *History of Ethnological Theory* (New York: Farrar and Rinehart, 1937), p. 106.
[142]   *Ibid.*, p. 109.
[143]   H. G. Barnett, *Innovation: The Basis of Cultural Change* (New York: McGraw-Hill, 1953).
[144]   New York: Huebsch, 1922.
[145]   See Otis Dudley Duncan, ed., *William F. Ogburn on Culture and Social Change*, Heritage of Sociology Series (Chicago: University of Chicago Press, 1964).
[146]   F. Stuart Chapin, *Cultural Change* (New York: Century, 1928).
[147]   See Everett M. Rodgers, *Diffusion of Innovation* (New York: Free Press of Glencoe, 1962).
[148]   *Ibid.*; Elihu Katz et al., "Research on the Diffusion of Innovation," *American Sociological Review* 28 (April, 1963): 237–52; Herbert F. Lionberger, *Adoption of New Ideas and Practices* (Ames, Iowa: Iowa State University Press, 1960).

Tarde's writings were used by such contemporaries as A. Lawrence Lowell in treating questions of public opinion and by Scipio Sighele, Gustave Le Bon, and Robert Park[149] in their works on publics and crowds. It was largely through Park that the Chicago sociologists of the interwar years became acquainted with Tarde. Although, as Everett Hughes points out,[150] not one single excerpt from Tarde's work was republished in "Park and Burgess," the Bible of interwar year Chicago sociologists, it nevertheless contained more references to Tarde than to Comte, Cooley, Durkheim, Simmel, Thomas, or Weber.[151] Through Park one can find the stamp of Tarde's ideas on such later writers on publics, collective behavior, and mass communications as Herbert Blumer, Morris Janowitz, Ralph H. Turner and Lewis M. Killian, and Kurt and Gladys Engel Lang.[152] Edward Shils's writings on center and periphery would have delighted Tarde.[153]

One might expect that studies on mass communications and public opinion at Columbia University in the 1940's and '50's, which did so much to stress the role of personal influence,[154] might

[149]   Lowell, *Public Opinion and Popular Government* (New York: Longmans, Green, 1913) ; Le Bon, *The Crowd* (New York: Viking Press, 1960), Intro. by Robert K. Merton. Tarde's works were profusely cited in Robert E. Park, *Masse und Publikum* (Bern: Lack and Grunau, 1904), Park's Hiedelberg thesis, but less often in later works.

[150]   Hughes, "Tarde's *Psychologie Economique:* An Unknown Classic by a Forgotten Sociologist," *American Journal of Sociology* 66, no. 6 (May, 1961) : 553–59.

[151]   Robert E. Park and Ernest W. Burgess, *Introduction to the Science of Sociology* (Chicago: University of Chicago Press, 1921).

[152]   Blumer, "The Mass, the Public, and Public Opinion," in *Public Opinion and Communication*, ed. Bernard Berelson and Morris Janowitz, 2d ed. (New York: Free Press of Glencoe, 1966), pp. 43–50; Janowitz, *The Community Press in an Urban Setting*, 2d ed. (Chicago: University of Chicago Press, 1967) ; Turner and Killian, *Collective Behavior* (Englewood Cliffs, N.J.: Prentice-Hall, 1957) ; Lang and Lang, *Collective Dynamics* (New York: Crowell, 1961).

[153]   Shils, "Centre and Periphery," *The Logic of Personal Knowledge*, Essays presented to Michael Polanyi (London: Routledge and Kegan Paul, 1961), pp. 117–31.

[154]   See Joseph T. Klapper, *The Effects of Mass Communications* (Glencoe, Ill.: Free Press, 1960).

have drawn on Tarde's insights, but Lazarsfeld and most of his associates were unfamiliar with Tarde's work in this area at the time.[155]

In part because lawyers, judges, and criminological theorists in France were generally trained not at the Durkheimian dominated Sorbonne but at the Faculties of Law, it has been they rather than professional sociologists who have kept the legacy of Tarde alive. One of the most influential criminological treatises in France today draws heavily on Tarde's work,[156] and he continues to be an important source of ideas for basic research on deviance and social control.[157] Studies by Davidovitch and Boudon have combined analysis of the sort of time series that Tarde used so often with mathematical models and computer simulation techniques.[158] Such work as theirs, by adapting and refining Tarde's basic ideas and methodological precepts in particularly sophisticated fashion, demonstrates the continuing relevance to contemporary sociologists of the work of Gabriel Tarde.

[155] Personal communication, Paul F. Lazarsfeld.
[156] Pierre Bouzat and Jean Pinatel, *Traité de droit pénal et de criminologie*, vol. 3, *Criminologie*, by Jean Pinatel (Paris: Dalloz, 1963).
[157] André Davidovitch, "Criminalité et répression en France depuis un siècle (1851–1952)," *Revue Française de Sociologie* 2 (1961): 30–49.
[158] Raymond Boudon, "La 'statistique psychologique' de Tarde," *Annales Internationales de Criminologie* 2 (1964): 342–57; A. Davidovitch and R. Boudon, "Les méchanismes sociaux des abandons de poursuites, analyse expérimentale par simulation," *Année sociologique*, 3d series (1964), pp. 111–246; Raymond Boudon, *L'analyse mathématique des faits sociaux* (Paris: Plon, 1967), esp. pp. 324ff.

I. The Nature and Scope
of Sociology

1

SOCIOLOGY

1898

AT THE MOMENT sociology is in vogue, succeeding in the
predilections and preoccupations—be they spontaneous or suggested—of the serious public and indeed even the ordinary public.
This attraction should not displease those who, like the author of
this article, think of sociology simply as collective psychology, if
it really is all that simple. But if this vogue, this allegedly unexpected success ought not surprise them, perhaps it should concern
them. It is not difficult to forsee that the adventuresome spirits, the
conquistadors of this new world, who are more fit to ravage than
to explore, will jump into this new and already rather clamorous
science, whose very name was proscribed until just recently but
now is found on covers of so many books and journals. And there
are still other dangers to be feared: its obvious complexity and
indetermination, the hopes and fears that it raises, a danger too
in those who expect it to solve their most urgent social problems;
and also, for some of its most disinterested theoreticians, those
most indifferent to practical consequences, the excess of faith which
sometimes leads them to raise sociology so high that they cause
t to lose contact with reality. It seems then that the time has come
o circumscribe this new field of study with exactitude, to show
how it has been cultivated until now and how it should be devel-
ped, what has been sought and what has been found, and what
ruits we may expect to gather from its cultivation.

In the stories of our ancestors, when a child was born, all the

From "La sociologie," in *Etudes de psychologie sociale* (Paris: Giard &
Brière, 1898), pp. 1–62.

fairies assembled around its cradle and each gave it a talisman with which it could perform miracles. At present when a science is born or even begins to announce its arrival, a certain number of philosophers encircle it, each bringing his own method for it to follow with the assurance of the greatest success if its rules are applied promptly and with perseverance, as if it were a method or program of discoveries of which a nascent science is most in need! It is in discovering things and as they are discovered that a science learns its own best way to discover; if this is not the last thing a science discovers, it is certainly not among the first. Or rather, each researcher has his own method, individual and almost intransmissible, and the science advances as a result of the conjunction of these diverse methods and often of their conflict. What a new branch of knowledge most needs to grow is a bud which, for some unknown reason, sprouts somewhere; in other words a *good idea*, which will be the seed of new knowledge and will continue its development according to a hidden logic. But a single idea does not suffice; it is necessary to have several ideas in succession and in combination. The first idea in the case of sociology was born in Florence or Venice as far back as the Middle Ages. It consisted in counting and measuring social facts, though only a few of them at first. The first sociologist, without knowing it and without wishing it, was the first statistician, who set the example of looking at societies from the wrong side, so to speak, from their quantitative and measurable side and not from the right side, the qualitative and incomparable side. The essential subject of a science consists in quantities, similar things which repeat themselves, and the relationships of these quantities (which are themselves repeated) whose quantitative variations correlate.

Men must have begun by numbering in this way things whose similarity was most evident, such as the same type of merchandise or pieces of silver or gold. Thus was formed, by degrees and for the economists' use, the idea of Value, which had great advantage over the jurists' idea of Right, over the moralists' idea of Good, over the aestheticians' idea of Beauty, even over the idea of Truth espoused by the theologians and the authoritarian philosophers, who see Truth as something which either is or is not, having no intermediary degrees; over all these ideas Value had the advantage of being a true social quantity whose rise and fall are a matter of daily observation and have a special measure—money. Such was, along with many obvious inferiorities (palliated in vain), the superiority of the economic point of view over the juridical, artistic, moral, theological, and metaphysical points of view for the scientific observation of the social world. In vain does political economy now look askance at its daughter sociology; the latter will not have the ingratitude to forget that it is the economists who, gaining acceptance in the long run for their way of thinking despite the obstinate resistance of jurists and moralists in particular, prepared the ground for the sociologists' constructions. They had the great merit of indicating the true path to the sociologists, who were usually wrong to deviate from it. They discovered, or thought they had discovered, the laws of value, the laws of production, exchange and distribution of various values, and spoke of them as the physicist speaks of laws of production and communication of motor forces, as laws applicable in all countries and at all times, in every society, whether real or just possible. These pretensions were eminently scientific, since no science exists except by formulating laws of this scope. They founded a sort of social physics, narrow and precise like the social physiology which others, long afterward, tried to establish, but the success of the latter was shorter lived, and although its apparent breadth was greater, it had less true depth. But let us not get ahead of ourselves. As the economists conceived it, society was not an organism but, what is clearer, an astronomical system whose freely linked elements, each gravitating separately in its individual sphere, only influenced each other externally and at a distance. The insufficiency of this conception could have been concealed even longer if it had not been uselessly limited to being a static model of society. Then, without abdicating its mechanical character, it could have tried sketching social evolution. Nothing prevented reconciling the very sound idea of constant and universal laws with the no less necessary idea of succession of stages. This is an idea which the jurists, those great enemies of the economists, took from the historical development of Roman law and which they could have

taught the political economists long before the Darwinian trans-
formists.

Political economy was not born just from the idea of introducing numeration and measurement into social facts, but even more
from the idea of bringing the comparative method to them. The
conjunction of these two good ideas in this new field made it the
most fruitful of all the other so-called "moral and political" sciences. One could define it as comparative industry, and in this
respect it takes its place among a group of sister sciences: comparative grammar, comparative mythology, comparative legislation,
comparative art, comparative politics. But it should be noted that,
although the degree varies, in these sciences or half-sciences the
truly scientific character is much less marked than in political
economy. This is because the stamp of numerical precision which
distinguishes political economy is missing, and because the rules
that the others confusedly draw from facts are not clear like those
of political economy but remain enslaved to these facts, which they
summarize rather than explain. However, since this imperfection
is without doubt only temporary, these various disciplines, like the
economic gymnastics of thought, have all concurred in the advent
of social science. And among its distinct sources social science
must count all the successive good ideas by which, between languages, religions, bodies of law, arts, and governments until then
considered heterogeneous, successful *rapprochements* were tried
and inaugurated.

Another good idea, despite the abuse that has been and is still
made of it, is to use the tales of those who have traveled among
the barbarians and savages either to extend the area of previous
comparisons or especially to inform us about the prehistory of
civilized peoples. The starting point in this case is the frequently
(though not always) verified hypothesis, supported by archaeological excavations, that the stages of development at which many
savages have become fixed are the stages which have been tra-
versed by advanced peoples. It is well known with what fury the
hasty "pre"-sociologists of the eighteenth century, Montesquieu in
the lead, pounced on the anecdotes and even the nonsense tales
of travelers, but primarily as a change from the classical historians

and to extend their idea of humanity in space rather than to push human history back in time. It was left to our century to attempt, with an unhoped-for success, this jump back in time.

II

As early as the beginning of the century, everyone felt that the time had come to condense into a living synthesis the scattered fragments of social science grouped under the vague name of "moral and political sciences," which were alien to each other and even more alien to the harmonious group of the natural sciences. It was necessary to end their double incoherence by coordinating them and incorporating them into universal science. The attempts made in this direction were to remain sterile until the appearance of a master idea which would bind the scattered straws into a single sheaf. Shall we say that this idea came to light the day Auguste Comte formulated his famous law of the three stages—theological, metaphysical, and positivist—which, from whatever point of view one chooses, human development is compelled to traverse? A polemic on this subject arose between John Stuart Mill and Littré. Mill denied that the great founder of positivism had brought sociology to the point at which one can say that a science is truly constituted. For Littré, Comte's constituting of sociology resulted from the law in question. Who was right? I am afraid it was Mill. Can it be said that biology existed from the time, certainly long ago, when it was discovered that all living beings are subject to the "law of ages" and without exception pass through the successive stages of childhood, youth, maturity, and old age, unless a violent death interrupts this course? And this law of ages is general and profound in quite a different way from the law of the three stages.

On the other hand, insofar as it is valid, the law of the three stages was infinitely more difficult to discover. If our life, compared to that of other animals, was so short that we could not see these others one after another come to life, grow, age, and die, the sage who, from induction based on observation and intelligent research, first discovered the frequency and universality of this succession of stages in the animal world would be rightly admired as the author of a great and fruitful generalization. Would not his law of ages be reputed one of the fundamentals of physiology? In relation to human society, we individual humans are what in my hypothesis man is to the lives of animals. Hence we would readily concede that Comte's principle is one of the basic social laws if its scope were as general and its truth as certain as its author believed. Unfortunately, its application is limited to the intellectual development of societies. But even in this area it is not without exception and extends, moreover, neither to their economic nor to their aesthetic development.

Nor are the transformations of languages explained, or those of religion, all of whose phases remain in the first of the three stages. How then could Littré claim that by forming such a vague and incomplete law Comte did for sociology what Bichat did for biology in discovering the elementary properties of living tissue? As Mill pointed out, it is just these elementary properties of social tissue that are missing from the work, otherwise so substantial, of the Master of the positivist school.

Was Mr. Spencer more successful when he picked up an ancient metaphor, developed and enlarged it, pushed it to its extreme (until even he recognized its inadequacy) and in so doing classed social bodies among living bodies? Would we say that this thesis concerning the social organism is one of those good ideas which the new science could not do without and that, as a basis at least, it has had a certain fruitfulness? I believe it was simply a deceptive last resource, a life-saving but rotten branch clung to by those who believed it was impossible to bridge the gap between *nature* and *history* without it. It must therefore disappear as soon as some other conception appears which is able, as it were, to naturalize humanity. Social science was established not by comparing societies to organisms, but by comparing them to each other from their many linguistic, religious, political aspects. At the last International Sociological Congress, which took place in Paris in July 1897, this question was treated in depth and ended with the complete rout of the social *organism*. No one was able to show a single advance in social science stimulated by this way of thinking and it is easy to see the errors in social science that it introduced or suggested: the tendency to empty rhetoric, to substitute entities for realities, such as "the soul of crowds"; the need to subject social development to a single tyrannical series of phases comparable to the embryonic series; finally the lack of intelligence about the most truly social sides of societies, language and religion, for which there are no analogues in the organic being—hence the tendency either to belittle them or to eliminate them from sociology altogether. Thus we may explain the somewhat scornful protest of the racial historians, even the philosophical ones, against the new science presented to them in this guise.

Let us therefore consider this so-called theory as no more than an abortive attempt, an unsuccessful attempt at classification. At the very most, one may grant Mr. Espinas that, the social organism aside, there is still room for a certain social *vitalism*, or rather for a certain national realism, and that the reality of "social life" is not in doubt. To be sure, but the problem is its meaning; is not this "social life" only a resultant of individual lives related socially, or is it something else? In the first sense it is only a poetic expression; in the second, a mystical idea.

Auguste Comte set forth a law concerning the hierarchy of sciences which, if it were true without exception, would fully justify the support sociology asks of biology. In his view, all the sciences from arithmetic to social science, passing via mechanics, physics, chemistry, and the science of living things, are ranked by the decreasing simplicity and generality of their subjects, the lowest ranks having the simplest and most general subjects. It follows that each science must lean on the one immediately below it, and not vice versa, since the lower science studies those elementary realities whose more complex groupings are encompassed by the higher one. For example, a knowledge of chemistry is indispensable to the physiologist, whereas the chemist, even one concerned with organic substances, can do without a knowledge of natural history. Now all this is true, but on one condition: that the successive realities—the subjects of the successive sciences—be superimposed like geological formations of which the highest is most recent and could have been formed only through a transformation

or a combination of lower preceding layers. Let us suppose, however, that at a certain level of this scientific stratification there appear entirely new facts comparable to the hot springs of high
mountains, which, cutting through all the lower layers, rise up
from beneath even the lowest solid layer of earth. And grant
that the appearance of consciousness, of the self, on the highest
levels of the living world is a marvelous spring of this sort: can the
science concerned with this phenomenon, which is not reducible to
surrounding or preceding ones and is, though the highest, only
conditioned but not engendered by them, can this science be regarded as having a more complex and more special subject than
all the others? On the contrary, it may be highly probable that,
revealing a hidden reality, perhaps the simplest and most lofty of
all sciences, psychology, has more to teach its lower sisters than
vice versa. And this would also be the case for sociology if there
were any reason to think that the social phenomenon—which is
essentially psychological—is itself more general than it seems.

Are there not, in fact, some rather specious reasons for this
view? Was it not by assimilating organisms to society and not society to organisms that the clearest (or least obscure) light was
thrown on the great secret of life? Conceived of as an association
of cells or as a federation of cellular societies or colonies, the living
body becomes for the first time penetrable to man's probing. Much
more than natural selection, the cellular theory puts us on the road
to an explanation of the vital enigma. Natural selection is now regarded as one of the keys to life, but no one any longer considers
it the master key. Its mainly negative efficacity, its quality of eliminating harmful varieties and purifying the species, is no longer
contested, but less and less is it credited with a truly creative
power. The successful attempts to interpret historical progress by
social selection exposed the insufficiency of this principle and its
negative character. Neither in its bellicose form nor even in its
commercial or industrial form has social competition sufficed to
create a single one of those fundamental inventions which are the
necessary condition for human renewal. Is the discovery of gunpowder or dynamite due to the age-old furor about battles? Is the
discovery of the compass due to the greed for profit of the Phoe-

nician and Venetian merchant fleets who over the years battled for control of the seas? Is the discovery of the steam engine due to the unrestrained rivalry of competing industries? Not in the least. Warriors, merchants, and industrialists could have continued to battle for thousands of years, and all their efforts would have been in vain as far as invention is concerned, had there not been here and there a few seekers, the least warlike of men—from the chemists or alchemists of ancient Egypt to our Lavoisiers and Pasteurs, from Archimedes to Papin and Watt, from the Chaldean shepherds to Newton and Lavoisier—curious and empassioned men who little by little extracted from nature some of its secrets and at intervals communicated them to each other. There is not one industrial or even military advance that has arisen directly from a battle or a commercial rivalry and which does not have as its father someone outside the world of hate and war, someone who remained unknown until the day he furnished decisive arms to the combatants . . . and to the competitors. Undoubtedly wars, battles of all sorts, venomous conflicts of passions or interests call the spirit of invention to their aid when it has already come to life somewhere else and has proved itself. These calls stimulate invention, but it is not they that engender the invention itself. How much more often does it happen that they kill the germ of an idea! Invention had peace, love, family, or professional fraternity for a cradle, the disinterested cult of truth and beauty for a soul; and its motivation was genius served by luck, which favored the encounter of different ideas in a mind sufficiently gifted to guess their fitness, to make them reciprocally fruitful, to serve, so to speak, as the go-between for their mutual love. And to verify this idea in the very study which presently concerns us, is it not clear that sociologists ought to turn not to the daily polemics in the press on social questions for the basic ideas of their science, but rather to solitary meditations?

An excellent idea, not to be confused with the metaphor of the social organism, was the study of *animal societies* from the standpoint of their similarities to and differences from human societies.

This study was done well by Mr. Espinas. It is unfortunate only that his book, which opened so productive a route, did not have a successor. If he redid his work today he would probably indicate more clearly the distinction between the pseudosocieties of the lower species of animals, in which the solidarity of individuals, if indeed they are individuals, is entirely physiological, as in the polyp, and the true societies of a psychological nature like ours, which are the privilege of the vertebrates and the higher insects. A polyp is no more a society than a synanthous flower. There is in fact no vegetable society; why not? Not because a plant, taken separately, cannot be a society if we suppose—a hypothesis like any other—that its cells are animated by a sensitivity allowing them to recognize each other and to cling together. But once again we face the mystery of life, and, moreover, even from this point of view the vegetable would be like a state that had no international relations with its neighbors. It is precisely these international or interorganic relations that are the subject of social science.

III

Now the problem is to use all the good ideas just enumerated to make them interlock and illuminate each other, to set fire, as it were, to this immense faggot of documents that travelers and historians, statisticians and archaeologists, naturalists and psychologists, have brought from all sides and assembled for the use of the sociologists. This must be done and soon, for the need, today so general and so intense, to become aware of the laws of social life instead of being limited to obeying them as in the past, reveals another need, no less profound, for conscious and thoughtful collective action. Before *deliberately* reforming and remolding itself, society seeks to understand itself. Before progressing, and in order to be certain of progressing by self-transformation, must it not possess a "measurement of progress?" The misfortune is that the nascent science, in addition to the seeds of discord carried within itself, runs into all kinds of outside arguments. It has three types of adversaries: some deny that there is any scientific matter in social facts, which are an area of free choice; others see materials not just for a single science which, due to its precision and generality and despite its highly distinctive nature, is worthy of taking its place among the natural sciences, but rather material for several vague sciences with nothing natural about them but which are (they claim) very advanced and which until now have been designated "moral and political sciences"; and finally others, the only ones to whom we shall reply, who concede that there is a science to be constructed one day, but much later, when history, archaeology, and prehistory have achieved their goals, excavated the historical and prehistorical ground and underground, and have had "their last word."

At this rate what science would ever have seen the light of day? Before venturing forth, did astronomy, for example, wait until the universe had been scrutinized to its farthest extent by the most perfected telescope? Fortunately not. Perfecting instruments and methods of observation more and more, even accumulating more and more observations, is after a certain point so far from being the surest means of advancing a science that if Newton's law had not been discovered before the latest telescopic advances, the latter might have impeded rather than facilitated the appearance of this fundamental principle. In fact, when, owing to the multiple and bizarre perturbations which decorate the paths of planets in an excessively ornate, lacy pattern, it became possible to plot their periodic movements more exactly, it became more difficult to surmise that all these ellipses and perturbations, these rules and exceptions, were the effects of the same cause, the repetition of a single and unique fact. If someone had set forth this conjecture, it would have been rejected in the name of the most elementary scientific method. And likewise for sociology. To persuade oneself that before daring to express a theory that could be a basis for sociology it is necessary to wait until scholars have made their last probe of the past, the Schliemanns their last excavations in Greece or elsewhere— this is the same as saying that Kepler, Galileo, Newton, and all the theoretical astronomers of their time and their unknown collaborators were in too much of a hurry to establish astronomy. Here we find confused two very distinct things: the laws of societies and the "laws of history," a confusion facilitated by the elastic acceptance of the word *law*, which everyone misuses. There are, if you will, two sorts of laws, the laws of production, or rather the reproduction of phenomena, and the laws of their evolution. The first, the laws of reproduction, are, for example, the laws of mechanics, chemistry and general physiology. The second, the laws of evolution, govern or are supposed to govern the execution of the laws of reproduction under certain determined circumstances: such are La Place's theories of nebulas or the evolutionism of Hoeckel. The second group of laws is more complicated than the first, which it must therefore follow rather than precede. In astronomy the laws of rational mechanics and Newton's law came before the theory of the nebulas. In biology nothing has been found which is comparable to the law of universal attraction, but many laws of causation, under the name of properties of tissues, were discovered long before the law of natural selection. And the law of natural selection itself is not a pure law of evolution but rather a new law of causation. For the laws of biological *history*, if there are any, one must ask the successors of Darwin.

Unfortunately the Darwins and the Haeckels of sociology came before its Bichats. From Bossuet to Auguste Comte, via Vico, Montesquieu, and Hegel, we have nothing but celebrated geniuses attempting to encompass in a single glance and to confine in a single formula the entire course of history, with no apparent concern for first studying its *hydrostatics*. This pretension is already risky, but it is nothing next to the undertaking of Mr. Spencer and all the new evolutionists like him who, before seeking the general laws applicable to the elementary facts of social life, believed they had formulated the explanatory principles of the most complicated of these phenomena and had traced the course not only of real history, or rather of all the real histories (since they rightly distinguish several great independent historical series), but also of all possible histories. For such is the target of the sociologists of this school; and far from reproaching them for it, I praise them for having implicitly recognized (explicitly would be better) the essentially universal character of every scientific law, be it causative or evolutionary. When the master subjects social transformations to his general law of integrative differentiation, of the gain of matter and the loss of movement; when the disciples control more rigorously and in detail the transformations of language, religion, law, politics, art, and morals, and decree, for example, that idioms are compelled to pass from monosyllabism to agglutination, then to flexion, and finally to analytics, or that the family goes from promiscuity to matriarchy, then to patriarchy, and so forth—by these formulas or others do they not seek to express both what has happened in all known and unknown societies and also what would happen in all societies? (I do not mean all imaginable societies but all possible ones.) So conceived, and whether they deal with changes in the external universe or with the vicissitudes of the human world, the laws of evolution differ profoundly from the *philosophy of nature* or the *philosophy of history* as understood by Schelling or Hegel, by Condorcet, or by Auguste Comte himself, each of whom redid Bossuet's universal history in his own way. For them, as for the great episcopal transformist of the seventeenth century, natural or human history is a single and unique drama whose actors are successive species or nations and which follows a predetermined route from a marvelous or mysterious first scene to a common ending. This drama must not and cannot be played more than once. For the evolutionists of our own time, natural history is a multiplicity of dramas, but basically similar dramas capable of many performances.

From this point of view the laws of evolution cease to be in opposition to the laws of causation; both govern the reproduction of phenomena, although those controlled by the laws of evolution are complex in a different way. Thus it becomes clear that to claim to regulate composite facts when elementary ones have not yet been ruled upon is a dangerous error. And this error supposes another, the greatest that can be made: thinking that if no law of historical evolution (conceived of as universally applicable) succeeded in resisting the refutation of facts, if every rule of this type came to be gnawed and pulverized by exceptions or was reduced to expressing no more than greater or lesser probabilities, sociology would be no more than an empty word. Practically all the sociological publications seem created to give credence to this erroneous opinion, against which it is important to protest immediately. It is a question of knowing if, when they begin to advance (most of them are stationary), and despite the diversity of accidental circumstances or native tendencies, societies follow approximately parallel routes, routes which repeat themselves as do the steps on them; and if this question can perhaps be resolved in the negative (I do not in the least affirm that such is the case) without our having to deduce that social science is impossible. It could as well be said that astronomy and mechanics would no longer be possible because it had been shown that La Place's theory of nebulas is not generalizable and that the formations of stars observed in different parts of the sky appear to be thrown into divergent paths which cannot be reduced to a single formula. I admit that the spectacle of the starry sky would in no way be spoiled for me by the belief that the firmament is not an immense display of despairing monotony. For the same reason I should not be displeased, in reading history, to see in it the unexpected perpetually springing forth from the complication of regular causalities, liberty born from order, fantasy from rhythm, embroidery from the canvas.

It was therefore an error to think that in order to establish the new science it was necessary to trace all human histories to their point of departure, not omitting a single phase, and that if a single link on this chain were skipped, everything would be lost. From this idea came the exaggerated importance sometimes accorded the stories of travelers or the excavations of archaeologists, which do merit the sociologist's attention but never to the point of letting him think the future of the science depends on their results. Without agreeing with John Stuart Mill that, as a precondition for becoming a sociologist, it suffices to be a psychologist and a logician, we may say that the first thing to accomplish is a very careful analysis of one's own particular social state in order to discover hypotheses which, later verified or rectified by sufficiently extensive comparisons with foreign societies, will finally appear as the elementary principles of sociology.

Only the economists, I repeat, were aware of this methodical necessity. Their great merit has been to seek laws of causation applicable to their area—the law of least effort, for example, of supply and demand, or the theory of rent—and through them to create an abstract political economy, superior and necessarily anterior to concrete political economies. Auguste Comte was correct in noting that in every order of things there exist two types of science, one abstract and the other concrete—as for example an abstract astronomy which governs all possible stars and a concrete astronomy which applies the abstract laws to real stars. He added that the same distinction is applicable to sociology, but in this all he did was generalize what the economists had already put into practice in their own area. Their example was followed in varying degrees, and the religious, linguistic, juridical aspects of society, its moral, political, and aesthetic aspects, were studied in turn according to the comparative method by scholars who, from their multiple comparisons, succeeded in extracting many comments of very general importance, some of which certainly merit the title of laws. It is the condensation, the reciprocal interpenetration of all these partial sciences that we may call abstract sociology. It would have been for Comte to lay its foundations, but belying his remark that abstract science is anterior to its corresponding concrete science, his own works, so teeming with penetrating insights, sketch out a concrete sociology. Now, what would be the theory about the moon or Mars if Newton's law of attraction were still unknown? And how can there be a theory of Roman history or Arabian civilization without a key of universal sociological explanation? Montesquieu wrote a masterpiece of sociological anticipation in his *Grandeur et décadence des Romains*, but to tell the truth it is a barrage of penetrating insights without connection, a brilliant and multicolored barrage that he threw into the eyes of the spellbound reader.

It is necessary, therefore, to condense and synthesize the partial enlightenment derived from comparative grammar, comparative mythology, political economy, and the other social sciences; for each on its own set forth or stuttered out some laws, which, it must be admitted, were usually imperfect and must all be recast by the very reason of this synthesis. But the first condition of a good synthesis is a good analysis. Analyzing these laws, we shall see first of all and without difficulty that their common trait is a bearing on general facts, on similar facts which repeat themselves or are considered capable of indefinite repetition. In this they resemble all natural laws and differ from historical narratives, which, whether the individual biography of a man or the collective biography of a nation, group, or series of nations, always depend on what is singular, sui generis, and unique. In vain is the subject of these histories composed of general facts; it is in the singularity of its combination, never to be seen again, that history thinks of its subject. Quite to the contrary, when something singular appears in the social sciences as well as in the natural sciences, it is considered to result from the encounter of general facts, for example, similarities and repetitions.

The verbal roots, the inflexions, the grammatical forms, and the combination of these elements, which preoccupy the linguists, are things that have been repeated millions of times by millions of mouths with an exactness that is truly marvelous if we compare the perennial state of language with the rapid flight, the continual changing of the generations that have spoken it; it is their very transience that has maintained its permanence, their diversity that has sustained its identity. The myths, the rites, the dogmas with which the science of religion is concerned are no less abundantly, no less regularly repeated and transmitted across the ages and races. Jurisprudence deals with legal relationships which are reproduced every day and which remain the same for centuries. It has been said that no two trials are exactly alike; this is true but only in the way that no two families resemble each other, and it in no way prevents the questions of law raised by a case or the legal relationships implied by it, when taken one by one and separately, from being identical to the same type of questions or relationships raised and implied in a host of other cases. Political economy deals with production and consumption, that is, with acts that are continually repeated, often with time-honored fidelity. The subject of aesthetics is the artist's and the writer's creative use of rhythms and procedures, of artistic formulas, of strokes of the violin, or brush strokes —all of which have been repeated identically for centuries.

Considered from this point of view, in this minute but essential detail, societies, no less than the biological world or even the physical world, present precise repetitions, regular and identical series of acts and facts. Consequently, for the same reason as with these last two aspects of reality, societies lend themselves to numbering and measurement, and these enable general considerations to attain the level of scientific laws. And let us point out that the advantage thus obtained of being able to treat social as well as natural phenomena scientifically is not purchased at the cost of any confusion between these two orders of facts, which continue to be divided by a very clear line of demarcation, nor by the sacrifice of human personality to the exigencies of a completely naturalist conception of societies. Seeing things from this angle we can leave aside the vexing question of free choice, since, determinist or not, one cannot deny social man's necessary conformity in each one of the elementary acts of his behavior, no matter how original may be the combination of these acts. Nor can one deny that at every moment he imitates his peers, contemporary or past, and one is forced to accept the regular series, the regular radiation of successive examples which flow from this situation. Until now—and not without reason—sociology has clashed with moral conscience, which repulsed the despotism of its formulas and felt suffocated in the progression of uniformly linked and rigid phases through which most sociologists have condemned human evolution to pass. But it is because these philosophers did not perceive the elementary order, the basic repetitiveness of social facts, a repetition considered essentially imitative, that they felt obliged to construct a complex and arbitrary order, a supposed constraint on large, collective, vague, and confused phenomena to repeat themselves identically according to a supremely regulated order but with no knowledge of why or by whom. They had to imagine this, since it is not possible to create a science or formulate laws without accepting facts which repeat themselves and which in so doing give rise to generalizations. And without real and precise generalizations the only recourse is to confused and imaginary ones.

But however imprecise, it is these very laws of uniform evolution that fatally impair the individual character and particular reality of human personality, whereas, despite their relative precision, the formulas of imitation let this individuality breathe freely and develop within broad horizons. But we shall see that even in this regard social facts do not appear in complete isolation and that through their characteristic variations and characteristic repetitions they can be compared to the special variations and repetitions of the other stages of universal reality.

IV

There is in every order of events a first primordial distinction to be made and, at least provisionally, accepted: *that between things which repeat themselves and things which do not.* It is not only in human societies—by what we call the action of human liberty, though that matters little—that diversity, individuality, the unexpected constantly spring forth from the monotonous rotation of uniformities, but also in the biological and the physical worlds. Furthermore, here as there, diversity appears to be the result, the raison d'être, the final flowering of the uniformity. The most original invention is never more than the synthesis of previous inventions, and its propagation is only possible because it appears as a felicitous response to questions that have already been posed, to needs already born. But it is a strain and falsification of this truth to express it by saying that a genius is simply the result of the aspirations or the needs of a people and that he always comes at the hour of need. . . . [For in fact] genius often comes without being called, and then what happens? Either it goes unrecognized, and, buried off in some library, the germ of discovery is left to be unearthed at some future date, unless indeed it remains buried forever; or, although summoned by no one, this man by his mere appearance has the faculty of provoking that very summons to which he is presumed to respond, and this satisfaction awakens or stimulates that very need which it is supposed to fulfill. For example, the tyrannical and universal need at the present time to read the papers: where does it come from if not from the invention of printing, which little by little aroused the need in order to satisfy it more and more? As Mr. Boissier has shown, during the Roman Empire there existed certain types of manuscript newspapers, but because this journalism, lacking mechanical means of rapid publication, was not capable of development, public curiosity did not demand anything of the sort and turned elsewhere. In this case is it correct to say that the man of genius came just at the right moment? It would be more accurate to say that he moved the clock hand forward or backward and that, at least to a certain degree, he chose the hour at will. Certainly even the most artificial needs for luxuries are viable and durable and count socially only insofar as they are founded on the primitive needs of the organism. These primitive needs constitute a fertile stream of which any particular need is only a small channel, directed here or there and raised to hgher levels by a series of *chain pumps*, as it were, elevators propelled by the force of education and culture. This kind of channeling and sublimation, of specification and refinement of fundamental needs is capable of thousands of different directions and levels, and it is the inventors of the past or the present who have been the engineers in charge of this age-old job of irrigation. Within the limits imposed by organic necessities, racial characteristics, and physical resources, these engineers enjoyed considerable freedom, and if this liberty is restricted for each new inventor, it is because the older, forgotten inventors, whose good ideas have become public domain, created a general impulse with which their successors must reckon if they wish to succeed. Why did the need to drink become the need to drink beer in one place, wine elsewhere, or maté, or cider, so that a brewer who tried to introduce a new and better means of making beer in a country accustomed to drinking tea or wine, or a wine-grower who discovered a new and improved vine in a country accustomed to beer but which could nevertheless adapt to vini-culture, would have no success? Seek the cause of such failures not just in the climate, which circumscribed various rather indefinite boundaries for the cultivation of different things, but also and especially in the traditional influence of certain distant ancestors, regional Noahs or Bacchuses. It is because America had no Noah or Bacchus before the arrival of the Europeans that wine was absolutely unknown even in the numerous areas where vines grew wild. . . .

What we have just said about the inventors, artists, industrialists, men of state who have manipulated, used, and channeled the great stream of Desire even while following it, can also be said of the inventors, or rather the discoverers, scholars, theologians, and

philosophers who have exercised a similar action or channeled another great stream, partially independent of the first, the river of
Belief. When a discovery is brought before a fairly intelligent people and, despite its plausibility and supporting evidence, is not
taken up, that is, believed by anyone, it would be infantile to explain this refusal by the brain conformation of these people or by
the nature of their surroundings; the refusal is due simply to the
fact that this new idea is deemed contradictory to those beliefs
already established and consolidated in the minds of these people.
But why are these ideas there? Because at a more or less distant
era they were sown by a few illustrious founders of religions, or
apostles, mystical discoverers, and manipulators of belief. Christendom's long resistance to the discoveries of Kepler and Galileo
was basically no more than the battle of these new discoverers with
older ones, the fathers of the Greek and Latin church who founded
and coordinated Christian dogma. In the same way, when even
firmly based new theories have difficulty finding acceptance among
scholars or educated men, it is because their authors are in disagreement with earlier authors of accredited theories.

V

These examples could be multiplied infinitely, but those
above suffice to show the true relationships between the individual
and the general, between the variations and the repetitions in
societies. We can see clearly that these relations are the same here
as in the rest of nature: on the one hand, not everything that is
singular and individual, a new combination, succeeds in being
propagated or generalized; but on the other hand, everything that
is widespread and generalized at a given time began as a singular
fact, comparable to an invention. Let us add that in the social
world, as in the biological and physical ones, we see that only the
repeated variations become the proper domain of science, whereas
variations which are not repeated—the fugitive element, unique
and gone forever in the changing physionomy of things and beings, of landscapes, portraits, historical scenes—are the most
precious domain of art, whose gift it is to change this waste into

gold, to eternalize these ephemera. As for philosophy, the conflux of both science and art, it embraces in its sovereign complexity these two faces of reality. From this point of view, then, sociology is reintegrated without any difficulty into the other sciences; and at the same time it is freed from all servitude to the other sciences and preserved from any attack on its own originality. Sociology need no longer be subjugated to biology, giving itself scientific airs by borrowing the methods and framework, even the vocabulary of biology, squandering abusive metaphors drawn from anatomy and physiology, imagining the historical transformations of societies as similar to the development of a seed which, through a rigorously predetermined cycle of embryonic states, reaches maturity, old age, and finally death after having reproduced itself in a new seed which will follow the same course. No, to establish social science it is not necessary to conceive the evolution of societies in this manner, with a formula comparable to the type of itinerary planned in advance that the railroad companies propose to and do impose on tourists. Not that I reject analogies and comparisons (which actually I have used a great deal), but here it must be said that the terms of the comparison have been poorly chosen. The analogue of a living *being*, which reproduces itself according to a constant formula of evolution, is not a nation taken as a whole or even considered in one of its general aspects (language, government, religion, and so fourth). . . .

Furthermore, nothing obliges us to solve these problems; we know that a science is based on an order of facts when from among those facts we succeed in grasping the general facts allied to each other, that is, groups of similar facts which repeat themselves, groups which increase and decrease, whose increases and decreases are subject to measurement and calculation, and which present themselves as bound to one another in either direct or inverse relationship. Are these groups of similarities anything other than quantities? And quantity basically is only repetition and similarity, in other words, a general fact; and wherever there is quantity there is science. It seems, in truth, that the idea of quantity is found in its purest state only in the physical sciences, but perhaps this is only an illusion. In any case, here as elsewhere, quantity is always resolved into grouped repetitions. The weight of a given chemical substance, of a volume of oxygen or nitrogen, is no more than the more or less numerous group of similar molecules of which it is composed; the heat of a body consists of the more or less numerous group of more or less voluminous and rapid calorific vibrations with which it is agitated. The vitality of animal or vegetable tissue, of muscular or mucous tissues, is also a quantity which consists of a multiplication of entirely similar cells. Finally, when social statistics, as it always ought to have, has a bearing on similar human acts or human products and does not, as it too often does, group together heterogeneous things, its curves reveal numerical highs and lows which are comparable to the preceding ones. The parallelism or the inversion of these various curves have a significance analogous to that of the quantitative correlations expressed by the physicists' formulas or the naturalists' remarks. Thus before all else every science presupposes quantities and repetitions, but its own characteristic quantities and repetitions, which add themselves, as elements of its formulas, to the quantities and repetitions of those sciences inferior to it. This implies first of all that there is a mode of repetition particular to physical phenomena and another particular to biological phenomena and yet another particular to social phenomena. The autonomy of social science will thus be assured if it is shown that it has its own characteristic mode of repetition. . . .

VI

Now, just what is the characteristic social repetition? As we have already said, it is imitation, the mental impression from a distance by which one brain reflects to another its ideas, its wishes, even its ways of feeling. Once it can be shown that, despite exceptions or simply ostensible objections, it is imitation which is the elementary and universal social fact, I presume no one will deny the autonomy of social science. For, without any doubt whatsoever, imitation can be reduced neither to generation nor to undulation. This does not keep these last two modes of repetition, the so-called biological and physical factors, race and climate, from exercising a large influence on the direction of the currents of imitation, and thus from having considerable, though auxiliary and subordinate, importance for sociology.

It will be easy to prove that imitation is implied in all social relations whatsoever, that it is the common bond of these relationships. But let us say first that these social relationships can be classified in a certain number of categories: linguistic, religious, scientific, political, legal, moral, economic, aesthetic.

While we are still on the threshold of sociology, it is necessary to indicate a very remarkable characteristic which, in the field of individual consciousness—supposedly the domain of the sui generis, the unique, the incomparable, and pure quality—enables us to distinguish two homogeneous realities, identical not only from one state to another in the same mind but also from one mind to another. It is in this way, and this way only, that psychology can become exteriorized and be transformed into sociology. If the various "I's" (*les divers "moi"*) were as heterogeneous as is sometimes supposed, if they had nothing in common with one another, how could they transmit or communicate anything to each other? And with no communication, with nothing in common, how could they associate and form an "ourself," a "*we*" (*un "nous"*)? And even if we admit, against all possibility, that the juxtaposition of these heterogeneous individual selves or "I's" does give rise to what appears to be a social group, how could we derive any kind of a science by observing and comparing such diverse associations that cannot be compared with each other, are composed of dissimilar facts and have no link between them? Collective psychology, *inter-mental* psychology, that is, sociology, is thus possible only because individual psychology, *intra-mental* psychology, includes elements which can be transmitted and communicated from one consciousness to others, elements which, despite the irreducible hiatus between individuals, are capable of uniting and joining together in order to form true social forces and quantities, currents of opinion or popular impulses, traditions or national customs.

There is, I have said, in every elementary social relationship a transmission of, or the attempt to transmit, a belief or a desire. To be sure of this, it suffices to glance at the series of relationships enumerated above. All speech expresses a judgment or a plan, an idea or a desire, and tends to persuade or advise, to instruct or command. So is it for all the religious, scientific, political or legal types of speech, of clerical or lay instruction, and also of prayer, a ministerial decree, or a legal text. Every book, every newspaper, is essentially persuasive or impulsive, dogmatic or imperious. . . .

From the very beginning it is important to recognize this double, common basis of all minds, this double internal environment into which they plunge and which ceaselessly penetrates them during their continual exchanges. For here is the fundamental psychological and sociological duality. But if it is through the transfusion of these two energies that all communications from one mind to another resemble each other, in their form they differ strangely, because combined with those inner qualities is a marked and specific *sensate* element. A belief rendered as a specific idea, a precise judgment, a specific desire, a definite act or need: this is what imitation spreads from one consciousness to the next.

Looking at this phenomenon once again, what is imitation? A special type of action exercised from a distance by one mind on another, a mental imprint given or received, which is propagated in this way by a type of contagion completely different both from the transmission of periodic movements produced by two chemical substances in the process of combination and from the transmission of regulated life stages which occurs when an impregnated ovum grows and produces a living being. This mental imprint has two characteristics: first it is an imprint, an exact reproduction of the verbal articulation, the religious rite, the action ordered, the idea taught, the industrial or artistic process acquired, the virtue or vice inculcated—a reproduction of whatever model it copied, a print of the negative which has in turn become a negative. In the second place, the imprint is mental, spiritual, essentially psychological: hence the impossibility of expelling psychology from social science, as was attempted in defiance of all evidence; hence also the uselessness of seeking any other basis for sociology.

Imitation, I said, is the elementary and characteristic social fact. It is now time to explain the significance of this proposition. The members of a society do not have only social relationships: the relationships of the infant to its mother or those between the sexes are biological; the relationships between individuals who in a crowd press together, crush and fall upon one another without wishing to are mechanical and physical. But their social relationships proper are all imitative or formed by imitation, and wherever there is imitation, whether among men belonging to different societies, between man and the animals he has domesticated, or even among members of the so-called sociable species of animals, there is a society or the beginning of a society. . . .

Whenever there exists a relationship of mutual or unilateral assistance between beings, even between men, who do not also have between them similarities born of imitation, this relationship does not suffice to make them social associates (*sociétaires*). If, as classes of men become more necessary to one another and serve each other more, they also become more dissimilar to one another —because of the heterogeneity of their models, their language, culture, behavior and customs, work, and tastes—these classes, despite their increasing reciprocal utility but because of their decreasing imitative similarity, tend to form more and more distinct societies. The force and extent of the social bonds between members of a society (*sociétaires*) are a function of the number and importance of the types, the negatives, and the models they have in common, for example, the inventions, the old or new individual initiatives from which through imitative propagation they derive their manners of talking—even when they contradict each other—their ways of praying or sacrificing to their gods—even when they curse each other—their modes of work—even when they compete—and their ways of understanding duty—even when they quite dutifully kill each other.

Certainly in an established society, even the narrowest one, those who talk to each other do not always succeed in convincing each other. And there are many persons who, instead of attempting to imitate certain others, copying their style of dress, gestures, habits, expressions, and ideas, undertake to resist this contagion or do not even feel its pressure. Is this an objection to what was said above, an exception to the rule? Not at all. To the extent that these people rebel against imitation and against the reproduction of their states of mind, they tend to dissociate themselves; and if, despite this, they remain associated, it is because, while refusing to be marked by one another, they nevertheless bear the imprint of the same ancestors or contemporaries who through custom or mode transmitted to them the elements of their language, their thoughts, or their action. In this case imitation is their indirect rather than direct social bond, and it is by far the most important one. As biological kinship consists in having common ancestors, so does social kinship consist in having common models.

But why should two men, two Europeans, two Frenchmen, who moreover have an extensive set of common models reproduced in innumerable copies in their memories and their habits, seek—so often with success—not to copy one another? Sometimes the cause is a natural physical or physiological repugnance, which is the source of many inexplicable antipathies; but these cases do not concern us. Putting them aside we shall see that the most frequent cause, and only truly social cause, that explains these cases of obstinate non-imitation is the attraction of a model contrary to the one proposed, the influence of which is thereby neutralized. The truth of this explanation is obvious when at times of moral revolution people separate themselves from their traditions and begin to repudiate former customs, refusing to wear the traditional dress of their forefathers and ceasing to pattern themselves on the nobility or court which until then had been their model. This was a phenomenon of ever greater importance in France from 1761 to 1789. What happened was that, superimposed on and gradually replacing the exemplary prestige of the king in the kingdom as a whole, the prestige of the seigneur in each village, and that of the father in each family was the no less exemplary prestige of the new educators, philosophers, and writers, and through them the prestige of foreign models, notably the anglomania which raged during this period with unparalleled intensity. Every time a custom thus ceases to spread, it is due to the invasion of a style. The sources of imitation have changed—one has dried up, another has sprung forth—but the stream has continued to flow.

Here one can already see the error of those critics who believe that this theory of imitation leads to consideration of the social being as an automaton, to an effacement of his individuality. When he is born, the infant, it is true, is almost an automaton and resists imitative suggestion no more than the savage. But far from rooting himself in his automatism by the exercise of imitation, because he imitates more each day, especially in school, and because he copies more numerous and more diverse models, the child-automaton little by little becomes autonomous. These accumulated copies nourish his originality, and through the ever less forced and ever more spontaneous choice of his models he discovers for himself his own distinctive nature, displays it, and accentuates it. Free inquiry and free discussion arise through reading, *application,* study, intellectual discipline. All nonconformists began and had to begin as conformists, all leaders of a new school as disciples.

And if voluntary non-imitation, no matter how persistent or hateful, between two social compatriots, two men belonging to the same civilization, does not keep them from being bound to each other imitatively by a mass of indirect ties and by traditional and habitual models that they have in common, there are even fewer grounds on which to raise the objection of relationships of counter-imitation such as often occur between co-citizens. Some men think to distinguish themselves favorably from their peers by taking the opposite course from the current examples, the ruling ideas and habits; but their efforts only succeed in demonstrating the force of the imitative contagion which they are combating. Their paradoxes are only clichés in reverse, their originality nothing but an inverted banality. A negative image is still an image.

VII

Another observation and a very important one: when, after the discovery of an island or a continent or the crossing of a desert or a mountain considered impassable, two peoples, complete strangers until then, are brought in contact for the first time, they are often surprised at the coincidence which, despite profound dissimilarities, appears in some of their institutions. This indicates that under the external stimulation of the same bad climate to combat, the same flora and fauna to be used for the same human needs, certain inventions, certain fairly similar initiatives appeared spontaneously in the two countries, and that by the laws of imitation they were propagated and generalized in each society. Will the objection be raised that these similarities, imitative in a certain sense but recorded in two countries which, we hypothesize, did not borrow anything from one another nor imitated one another, nonetheless establish a social bond between them, and that this goes contrary to the basic principle of my argument? All that I can concede is that these encounters of institutions and of ideas, which moreover are always rather imprecise and are exaggerated by travelers, can predispose the peoples who become aware of such resemblances to enter into social relationships, unite with and cling to one another. But until this social relationship has begun, until this social action exercised by one and received by the other has materialized—through commerce, missionary activity, an interested or devoted apostolate, which always leads to importing examples—no truly social relationship can unite them. One has only to recall the treatment inflicted by the Spanish on the Aztecs and the Incas despite the similarities between these two American semi-civilizations and certain aspects of our own. China and Japan resembled us industrially, legally, even politically in many ways; yet we did not begin to regard the Chinese and the Japanese as possible allies, capable of forming an international society with us, until after we had begun to exchange our products and, with our products, our examples.

These non-imitative similarities between independent nations offer a very curious and vast subject matter which I shall not attempt to explore here, having treated it elsewhere with some of its implications, but I cannot by-pass it entirely. These similarities have served as pretexts for the social evolution formulas that naturalistic sociologists have attempted, which, according to them, are the whole of sociology. This is their favorite topic; hence the manifest tendency of these scholars on the one hand to increase the proportion of the spontaneous similarities as much as possible by including many imported or borrowed ones and, on the other hand, to reduce the importance of these borrowed similarities as much as possible, to the point of saying that they are of no interest for the historical philosopher and that spontaneous similarities alone should absorb his attention. They were led to this grave error by failing to perceive the universal presence of imitation in all social action and its extraordinary capacity for propagation. . . .

And yet I have been speaking of a simple invention,* of an idea so simple that it seems it must have been born of itself among even the most backward people. But in fact it must have had multiple centers of invention, each independent of the others. If it were a question of more complex ideas, more difficult to conceive or to execute, this multiplicity would be less probable and in certain cases even improbable. Here the accident of genius becomes necessary in order that the idea be conceived and executed. But this is exactly what certain sociologists—those who consider the progression of societies as a circular voyage more or less similar for all societies—do not want. Imbued with the error of thinking that social science is not possible without this condition, they need to explain everything by impersonal factors which eradicate the disturbing action of great men. This action visibly bothers them because their obvious preoccupation is doing away with genius. We could ignore the situation if genius alone were at stake in this serious problem; but it is not only genius but our individual originality, the individual quality of genius in each of us, whose efficacity and very existence are called into question; for in some way we all, whether obscure or famous, invent, perfect, and vary at the same time that we imitate, and there is not one of us who does not leave his mark, deep or imperceptible, on his language, his religion, his science, his trade, his art. If it had been proved that the great inventors, the great creators of poetry, myths, dogmas, arts, and sciences, were simple products of their times, illusory personifications of impersonal forces which acted through them and would have acted just as well without them—if this were true, it would be still more true to say that as great actions are a great illusion, the small action of each one of us is a small illusion, that none of us has served for anything, that human personality is a decoy. This is what we must necessarily concede if the true and

*   Tarde has been discussing pottery.—Ed.

sole actors in history are not men but the *factors* that we are told about. We can avoid this consequence and restore to individuality its true value and true raison d'être only by explaining history as a sequence of initiatives and repetitions, of inventions and imitations, and by showing that through the imitative if not the inventive side of their actions, human individuals are subject to laws that lend themselves to formulas very different from those of religious, political, moral, and industrial evolution, where, in order to reveal only the similarities of various societies, so much effort is expended to conceal their differences, their essential and characteristic aspects. The theory of imitation, which implies a theory of invention, does not require such a sacrifice of socially picturesque elements to social science. Rather it lets us include within the same point of view both statistics, which measure series or groups of similar acts and clearly determine the sphere of influence of different imitations, and archaeological exhumations, which disclose the successive order of inventions and trace the irregular ramifications of their geneological tree.

We can only point out in passing this important subject of non-imitative similarities. Let us add that precisely the most essential aspects of social life are those in which these non-imitative acts are remarkably rare and conjectural. Between any two idioms the vaguest and most hypothetical similarities will be grammatical or lexical, that is, those similarities which have not been caused by imitation, by transmission of the same mother tongue from father to son or from victor to vanquished, or by borrowings and imports according to the fancy of the day. Non-imitative similarities are no less problematical between two arts which have remained unknown to one another, and the more two arts develop the more they diverge. Finally, it would be superfluous to seek any similarities between our European sciences and other independent sciences, and with reason: there is only one scientific evolution worthy of the name and that is our own. Consequently we are forbidden to formulate the laws to which it would be subject. To have the right to legislate, one must be able to generalize, and a fact is generalizable only if there are at least two examples, not just one. It remains an established fact that our modern scientific evolution—the most eminent characteristic of superior societies—is a unique phenomenon and as such essentially eludes all evolutionary formulas.

VIII

To summarize the above, we have dismissed the objections to the construction of a social science. We have shown under what conditions and on what basis it is possible. We have seen that each of the great superimposed stages of reality is characterized by its own particular type of variation and repetition, and that it is the special role of science to consider these phenomena from their repetitive side. Physics studies facts reproduced by periodic movements, undulations, and gravitations; biology studies physico-chemical events reproduced by internal or external generation; sociology must study psychological events reproduced by imitation, and as soon as it has thus found its own area of repetition, numeration, and measurement, its autonomy is assured without the necessity to think up tyrannical and fantastic formulas of evolution. We added that not only in form but also in content the repetitions studied by social science differ profoundly from those studied by the natural sciences; that like the latter they include quantities but very different quantities—beliefs and desires—capable, however, like the exterior quantities, of ascending and descending an enormous scale of degrees, and of presenting the opposition, so fruitful in mathematics, of positive and negative.

As its basic subject every science has repetitions but also variations, and is characterized by the latter as well as the former. I am speaking of viable and fruitful variations, those which are the take-off point for a new series of repetitions. Biology in particular is eager to discover how these individual innovations are produced, these *adaptations* through which it attempts to explain the genesis of species. They can be compared to the inventions of genius from which new sciences or new industries arise. We have seen that in all types of facts the general arises from the individual, even though the individual does not always, nor even most often, succeed in becoming generalized. A science is therefore not permitted to neglect the variations which constitute the source of repetitions.

And as for those variations which die sterile, but which often have not lost their value or charm, they are the sought-after prey of the artist who, in both landscapes and faces, loves everything with a marked, or even and especially a transient, character. Hence the artist-historian passionately attaches himself to historical scenes, to singular encounters of actions and actors which were seen only once, for only an instant. The scholar-historian can be concerned only with the novelties and the innovators which introduced frequently imitated models into the social world. It is the lot of the philosopher-historian alone to consider and to reconcile the ideas of the artist and the notions of the scholar.

But this is a question of science, not of social philosophy. Sociology, as just defined, must attack two major problems: (1) What is the cause of inventions, of successful initiatives, of the social *adaptations* analogous to and no less obscure in their origin than biological adaptations? (2) Why were these initiatives imitated, and not others? Why was the preference accorded to such and such a model, among so many others which did not find any imitators? In other words, what are the laws of imitation?

Of these two problems, the first can only be dealt with and resolved after the second; and the lack of success of the sociological systems which have been devised up to now is a result of having reversed this order. Biology gives us an instructive example on this point: would it ever have thought of stirring up the question of the genesis of species without having thoroughly probed the laws of both hereditary and nutritive generation? Similarly, though of course the laws of imitation are not the whole of social science, they constitute its first chapter.

An investigation of the laws of imitation has been carried out elsewhere, and we need not formulate them here. Suffice it to say that, from different points of view, they present real and precise analogies to the laws of undulation and those of heredity in that the chosen models, like unsuppressed physical waves and victorious biological varieties or species, *tend* to propagate themselves by multiplying according to a geometric progression, a fact attested to by many regularly increasing statistical curves. But this analogy is not among those which attack the autonomy of social phenomena, the originality of individuals, or the eminent dignity of the human world in the midst of nature. To men, to peoples, it leaves free play of their own movements and is marvelously in accord with the exuberant diversity of their always unexpected, always new evolution, which forms the passionate interest of history. Even if we clearly understood the open hostility of racial historians to sociology when it is presented as a simple annex to biology, we would not explain their mistrust of a superior and transfigured psychology, an inter-psychic psychology completed by a social logic which is both a logic of ideas and of actions, founded on the elementary principles which we have just briefly indicated.

2

ECONOMICS AND SOCIOLOGY

1895

I said above that for the moment I did not propose to show the application of my ideas to politics and to moral ethics, but by applying them to political economy—fairly freely by the way and without binding myself to a methodical order—I am beginning partially to fill in this gap. Even though this science has for its proper subject that fraction of human activity engaged in industrial work, it long ago extended and increased its domain to include any form of activity. Precursors of the sociologists, the economists strove to expand over the whole field of the sociologists, who did not feel the insufficiency of their mutilated sociology until the socialists protested; these socialists were themselves forerunners of the sociologists, and no less defective than the economists. The error of the economists, let us say right away, was to construct only individual teleology, to present it falsely as a social teleology, as the whole of social teleology, and to think themselves able to create the latter without any considerations drawn from logic.

The successive encroachments of political economy are manifest. Think of its principal divisions—production, division, consumption of wealth—and examine them separately. It will be seen that basically all three are usurpations: the first from political science, the second from legal science, the third from ethics. As far as production is concerned, I am well aware that the liberal school of economists advocates the non-intervention of the state but advising the state to withdraw when its presence is indiscreet and harmful to its own ends is nonetheless speaking as a statesman

From *La logique sociale* (Paris: Alcan, 1895), pp. 339–45.

and positing rules for an intelligent policy. If politics, that superior art, claimed to become a science in its turn—imitating pedagogy, that modest art which suddenly presumed to inflate itself into a sublime science—it would be engaged in formulating the causes of the national strength as well as its constituent elements. But at a time when strength seems to be included in wealth, as the species in the genus, it seems that the best way to attain maximum power is to seek the maximum of general wealth. Moreover, individualism and liberalism seem to have been less a constitutional character-istic than a passing accident or a childhood illness, as it were, of the nascent political economy, misled by the Leibnitzian optimism of the harmonist Bastiat* and by blind faith in providence, which would make foresight useless. As it grows, political economy dis-closes its socialist goals and plays politics with everything. And in fact, what is a minister or a great king or leader of people for, if not to direct the productive forces of the nation in the direction most favorable to public enrichment? . . .

Thus the economist begins as a statesman and ends up as a jurist and moralist. This means that above and beyond economic science, itself somewhat limited, there is an economic point of view applicable to all branches of human behavior. What is the distinc-tive characteristic of this point of view? How should it be recti-fied? What are its gaps and its necessary complement? It is these questions that we shall now try to answer.

The economic point of view is a way of conceiving social teleol-ogy, a conception applicable to everything—military operations and administrative functions, artistic compositions and works of charity—and one that tends to prevail more and more in our age of imitation-fashion even if at some later time, when the spirit of tra-dition is reborn, it pales once again before a sufficiently increased legal and moral conception. Shall we say that the jurists and the moralists are primarily occupied with coordinating man's various goals, while the economist prefers to study *means*, which he terms values? This is a fairly well founded distinction, but here again

*   Frédéric Bastiat (1801–50), French economist, author of *Eco-nomic Harmonies* in which he postulated the existence of pre-established economic laws.—Ed.

is it not just a difference in the degree of attention? The economist himself is not loath to prescribe a particular duty, or to blame some other motive. What characterizes his manner, it seems to me, is the consideration of human activity from its *quantitative* and measurable side and not, like the jurist and the moralist, from its *qualified* and unmeasurable side. The jurist and the moralist think of their subjects as heterogeneous, often incommensurable and governed separately; thus they see the rights that they proclaim as innately singular privileges, the duties that they formulate as the consecration of particular instincts and of historical circumstances, the joys and the advantages that they sanction as original modes of feeling. For them the affective, sui generis side of impressions, volitions, passions, pleasures, and pains masks the common basis of this multicolored undulation—whence the predilection of ages of custom, and especially ages of primitive, or heterogeneously fragmented custom, for the juridical way of seeing things. But the economist implicitly affirms the fundamental identity hidden beneath this luxuriant diversity. He summarizes everything in the idea of wealth, which he regards as a homogeneous entity capable of indefinite increase and mathematical summation. If this view is legitimate, both its popularity and its scientific superiority are understandable. But is it legitimate? That is the first question to be asked, and political economy was wrong to pass by without taking notice of it.

It is thus a matter of proving what the economist affirms. We can do so by showing that wealth is the incarnation of a combination of desire and belief (in which desire plays the main role) and by recalling the following consideration: that all our passions, all our pains and our pleasures are simple or complex movements of positive or negative desires just as all our sensations and our ideas are extracts of judgments, of acts of faith; that either from one state to another within the same individual or from one individual to another, belief and desire do not change nature but include innumerable symmetrically opposable degrees of intensity, and consequently can legitimately be subtracted or added. Unfortunately, until now political economy has not been aware of its true support.

All the prescriptions of this science are based on judgments of greater or lesser general utility. All its formulas express or claim to express relationships between singular entities, simultaneously increasing or decreasing, which it treats as real quantities: work, credit, capital, value, and so forth. Now assuredly these are not at all real quantities, but no less certainly there is something quantitative about them, and I should say the same for everything that in popular parlance is considered capable of increasing and decreasing, of being superior or inferior to something else. Every time, then, that an economist uses, as he is forced to do, the usual terms of tightening or loosening of credit, of progress, of well-being and activity, and so forth, either he is talking and saying nothing or he is implicitly affirming that these diverse collections or accumulations of apparently so heterogeneous things (work, an accumulation of the most varied muscular or mental efforts; capital, a collection of all sorts of provisions; credit, a group of acts of faith, and so forth) are in fact summations of homogeneous and comparable things, which must be defined. And therein lies the difficulty—what are these things? Until now the answer has been the degrees of affliction or enjoyment which accompany the multiform states of mind grouped in this manner. Such is the defective analysis of the utilitarians. Completely misunderstanding the intellectual and *judicial* element, which nonetheless appears right on the surface in credit, and obstinately refusing to see anything more in security than an advantage reducible to pleasures or anything more in effort than a lively or not so lively pain of greater or lesser duration, they thought they could summarize in these two words, "pain" and "pleasure," the alpha and the omega, the cause and the goal of political economy. The ideal would be to procure for oneself the maximum of pleasure with a minimum of pain.

This is an enormous mutilation, which, far from clarifying anything, confuses everything. For in pleasures and pains, all sui generis, it is the qualitative, *nonmeasurable* character that predominates. But in examining these two ideas we see that it can be taken as self-evident that pleasure is simply the quality of a sensation *insofar as it is desired*, and pain simply the quality of a sensation *insofar as it is rejected*. If we push the analysis further we shall also see in physical or moral pain and in physical or moral pleasure simply on alternate, continual, unconscious *high* or a *low* of our *faith in ourselves*, in our value, our strength, our physical or moral, individual or social virtuality.

In a word, the question is whether faith and desire really have a quantitative nature. If so, economic science is possible; if not, it is rightly labeled bad literature. Political economy, once again, postulates necessarily but implicitly the propositions that I am putting forward, which this work develops.

As long as people persist in basing political economy on the equivocal idea of *services* and *satisfactions*, which, I repeat, presents desire and faith combined with dissimilar sensate elements and is of an especially salient heterogeneity, this science will be rendered radically inappropriate for any philosophical development whatsoever. The ambiguity of this idea of service encourages the continuing conflict between the theoretical, deductive, generalizing, unitary school of economists such as Ricardo, John Stuart Mill and the majority of the French, and the historical, inductive, particularist school, which, sometimes stronger, sometimes weaker, never succeeds in crushing its rival nor ceases to resist it. Why this battle? Because, without knowing it or perceiving it clearly, some lean on the fact that the most diverse pleasures and sufferings of sight, of hearing, of no matter what sense, be it physical or moral, have in the final analysis *something* comparable, something truly identical, measurable, or evaluable by an internal tribunal— whence they gain the right to *group* these things together; whereas others, protesting apparently not without reason, base their objection on the radical diversity of joy and pains considered as sensations. This second group, for example, analyzes the word *wealth*, which in political economy is what force is in mechanics, the fundamental thing whose production, direction, and expenditure must be studied. And what is wealth? The flocks of a pastoral people, the plowed land of the peasant, the casket of the miser, the wardrobe of a woman—just so many objects, so many special pleasures with no relation to one another, without any common measure, so to speak. . . .[1]

If they speak the truth, political economy rests on a mere name

[1]   See especially Mr. de Laveleye's article, *Revue des Deux-Mondes* April 1881.

flatus vocis, or on ground alien to science, for there is no science of the qualitative as such. And in this case we must agree with Cournot that the *common denominator* of values, money—whether metallic or paper—is a pure fiction and a matter of convention. But if in accordance with our way of seeing things we give each of these two schools its due, we see why, despite the erudition, the wit, the sharp good sense of the historical school, the theoretical school is unassailable. It would, however, be stronger yet if it were conscious of its true raison d'être, namely the theoretical possibility of measuring faith and desire. I say theoretical, and that is sufficient for it to take place in a science of economics. But what will always prevent this science from becoming fixed, from formulating itself in exact and verifiable laws is the impossibility of measuring belief and desire practically and conveniently other than as a single entity with inadequate approximations.

When, by accident, the economists struck on the idea of desire rather than service, they made fairly poor use of it. For example, as the source of production they gave desire for wealth. Desire for wealth is in political economy what desire for happiness is in ethics: a pure tautology. We might as well speak of *desire for the desired*, since the fact of being individually desired raises any state of being to the rank of happiness, and the very fact of being desired generally raises any object or service to the rank of wealth. Again it is necessary to distinguish between desire to produce wealth, which we call work, and desire to acquire or retain in in order to transform it into personal satisfaction, which we call consumption.

3

SOCIOLOGY,
SOCIAL PSYCHOLOGY,
AND SOCIOLOGISM

1894

IT IS NATURAL that a developing science lean on those already established, as for example sociology on biology. It is also natural that a growing science seek to fly on its own wings and to establish its own separate domain. Sociology has arrived at this point: it seeks to be established *by itself* and *for itself*. This is a sort of egotism or scientific individualism—useful to some degree, like all animal or human egotism, but beyond a certain point harmful to the individual himself. Biology and psychology have also experienced this separatist tendency, which, when exaggerated, has led them to the old principles of vitalism and a poorly conceived spitiualism.

Everyone is aware of the sterility of these pretensions, which refuse to recognize the solidarity of the various sciences, hence the profound unity of universal reality. The same vain aspirations are to be feared in sociology, and here and there I believe I can perceive symptoms of a similar error which could be disastrous. Let us try to prevent such an aberration, searching out, with all desirable precision but without pretending that it has absolute auton

Address given at the First International Congress of Sociology in October 1894, *Annales de l'Institut International de Sociologie* I:895, reprinted in "Les deux éléments de la sociologie," *Etudes de psychologie sociale* (Paris: Giard & Brière, 1898), pp. 63–94.

omy, the limits of the field that the science dear to us is called upon to cultivate.

Like all scientific research, this investigation is twofold: the study of phenomena of beings, and in order to pursue this, for each type of investigation the specification of the elementary phenomenon of being whose repetition and combination enable us to formulate laws.

We ask, therefore: (1) What is or rather what are the elementary social facts, the elementary social acts, and what is their distinctive character? (2) What is or what are social beings, that is—since *being* here means *group*—elementary social groups?

I

The first question, which will be our first concern, has already been treated by me at such length that I dislike returning to it, but the answer I gave has been misunderstood so often that I should be allowed to say a word about it. What is the elementary fact of mechanics? Is it movement? No, no more than the elementary social fact is consciousness. Consciousness is the postulate of sociology just as movement is the postulate of mechanics. The elementary mechanical fact is the communication or modification of a specific movement by the action of one molecule or mass on another; in particular, the elementary fact of astronomy is the attraction exercised by a sphere and also the effect of such repeated attractions—the elliptical movement of celestial bodies, which is itself repeated. Likewise the elementary social fact is the communication or modification of a state of consciousness by the action of one conscious being on another.

But what is the nature of this action? To be more precise, not everything done by members of society is sociological. Many of their acts, I was going to say most of them, are purely physiological or even purely psychological. Breathing, digesting, blinking one's eyelids, mechanically moving one's legs about, absent-mindedly looking at a landscape, or giving an inarticulate cry—there are all acts which are in no way social except when they result from a habit acquired in dealings with other men and born of a wish or

belief that those men communicated to us. But speaking to someone, praying to an idol, weaving a garment, cutting down a tree,
knifing an enemy, or sculpting a stone—these are social acts, for
only man in society acts in this manner and he would not do so
without the example of other men whom he has voluntarily or
involuntarily copied from infancy. The common characteristic of
social acts is that they are imitative. They alone have this characteristic, and when, exceptionally, a purely biological or mental
act becomes a social one, it is to the extent that imitation has
bestowed its special mark. Walking in step in a regiment, breathing as does a trained singer, eating with a fork are truly, and for
the reason indicated, social acts. Only a man in society walks,
breathes, eats in this way. As for those acts which consist of a new
initiative, a discovery, an important invention or an insignificant
one, they quit the individual sphere to enter the social world only
as they are propagated by example and little by little fall into public domain.

This, then, is a very clear and, more important, a very objective characteristic, for I take no account of the motivation for imitation. It can proceed from sympathy or even animosity, from envy
or admiration, from servile docility or a free and intelligent calculation; it makes no difference, for, once this subjective element is
set aside, the objective fact remains the same. Perhaps I shall be
allowed to say that the psychological source as well remains basically the same, namely a certain hidden attraction mixed with
admiration, envy, and even hate, which irresistibly pushes men
to reflect each other even while hating each other. Be that as it may,
I limit myself to establishing that everywhere and at all times the
distinctive characteristic of a thought, a wish, a social action, is to
be created in the image and in the likeness of the thoughts, wishes,
and actions of others. And I am astonished to find myself reproached for paying particular attention here to a fact which can
be grasped externally with no regard for its internal source, and
that this reproach was addressed to me by no other than the distinguished professor at Bordeaux, Mr. Durkheim—the very man
who expounds the necessity of basing sociology on purely objective
considerations and of exorcising this science, so to speak, by

driving away psychology, which, contrary to the ideas of all its founders from Auguste Comte to Spencer, is not the soul of sociology but rather its evil genius.

We shall soon examine what this idea is worth. For the moment let us consider the import of this author's criticisms. "A thought," he says, "found in all individual consciousnesses, a movement repeated by all individuals, is not for that reason a social fact. Repetition (read *imitation*) has so little to do with social facts *that they exist outside of the particular cases in which they are realized.* Each social fact consists either of a belief, or a tendency, or a practice which is that of the *group taken collectively and which is something quite different from the forms under which it is refracted in individuals.*" But how could it be refracted before it exists, and, to speak intelligibly, how could it exist *outside* of *all* individuals? The truth is that any social thing, a word in a language, a religious rite, a trade secret, an artistic process, a legal provision, a moral maxim, is transmitted and passed not from *the social group taken collectively* to the individual, but from one individual—parent, teacher, friend, neighbor, comrade—to another individual, and in this passage from one mind to another it is refracted. The totality of these refractions, starting from an initial impulsion due to some anonymous or illustrious inventor, discoverer, innovator or modifier, is all the reality of a social thing at any given moment. Like all reality, this reality changes by imperceptible nuances, but this does not preclude that from the individual variants there emerges a collective result which is almost constant, and which first strikes our attention and gives rise to Mr. Durkheim's ontological illusion. For there is no doubt that it is a veritable scholastic ontology that the learned writer is undertaking to inject into sociology in place of the psychology he opposes.

Nevertheless, the importance of repetition—continue to read imitation—cannot help making itself felt in his work, however much he is against it, even without his knowledge. In order to prove the radical separation, the absolute duality that he claims to establish between the collective fact and the individual facts which I say make it up but which he says refract it from the outside in some unknown manner, he writes: "Certain ways of acting or thinking acquire, through *repetition*, a sort of consistency which precipitates them, so to speak, and isolates them from the particular events in which they are incarnated. They thus take on a body, a perceptible form of their own which constitutes a reality sui generis very distinct from the individual events which manifest it." And what demonstrates this—listen to this carefully—is that the *collective habit*, some custom, "is expressed once and for all in a formula *repeated from mouth to mouth, transmitted by education*, and fixed in writing. Such is the origin of judicial rules, morals, aphorisms, and popular sayings." If he were not blinded by his preoccupation, our author would see what is perfectly obvious: that he has just involuntarily furnished new testimony to the eminently social, or rather *socializing* nature of imitative repetition. Indeed, is it not clear that in the case he describes there is simply a double action of imitation, namely: (1) the frequent repetition of the act resulting in a current of collective habit, the collective habit in turn giving someone the idea of articulating it verbally; (2) the repetition of this verbal formula by all those who learn it and who communicate it to each other?

Now in this case, where does the singularly accentuated character of the distinction between the collective fact and the individual facts come from? From the fact that, even though one admits that the first of these two kinds of imitation may have ceased to function, that some custom, law or rule has fallen into disuse, such a custom will still conserve a sort of diminished reality, a mouthed existence so to speak, as long as, even though not practiced, it continues to be articulated—and this is what happens so often for many moral maxims. But suppose that the second of these two repetitions is in turn extinguished like the first: what sort of life or reality would be left, I ask you, in a custom, a law, a rule that no one either practices or articulates, or even thinks of, and which may be written down or printed somewhere but is read by no one? Before Champollion there were many Egyptian laws and maxims which had not been known or practiced for thousands of years but which were engraved in hieroglyphics at the bottom of tombs guarded by the sphinxes. I should like to know if that was sufficient to give them a real existence and to raise them to the ranks of those transcendent social facts which Mr. Durkheim raises to the level of the resurrected Ideas of Plato. And when Champollion or his disciples had deciphered the norms of ancient Egypt, did that decoding bring them back to life? No, it only revived knowledge of them, thanks to the propagation of those discoveries and their repetition from Egyptologist to Egyptologist, resulting each time in a new and truly social link between these scholars. As proof, therefore, of the distinct and autonomous reality of the collective fact considered *in abstracto* let no one propose the verbal expression it assumes; one could say as much for all things named in human language.

Mr. Durkheim seems to gravitate toward some theory of emanation. For him, I repeat, the individual facts which we call social are not the elements of the social fact but only its manifestation. As for the social fact itself, it is the superior model, the Platonic Idea, *the* model—so true is it that in social matters the new idea of imitation imposes itself on its greatest adversaries. But let us move on. From this it follows, according to Mr. Durkheim, that the individual acts through which the social fact manifests itself—as, for example, the words of a speaker as a manifestation of *language*, or the kneeling of a worshiper as a manifestation of *religion*—may not be called social. No, since each of these acts depends not only on the nature of the social fact but also on the mental and biological constitution of the agent and on the physical environment, these are types of hybrid acts, *socio-psychical* or *socio-physical* facts with which we should no longer sully the scientific purity of the new sociology.

By joining our point of view, however, the learned logician creates an objection. This must be read, and especially the reply. "But, someone will say, a phenomenon can be collective only if it is common to all members of a society or at least to the majority of them, consequently, only if it is general. Doubtless—but *if it is general, it is because it is collective, that is, more or less obligatory, and it is far from being collective because it is general. . . .*" At first glance we do not understand, but once we are acquainted with the author's doctrine, its significance becomes clear: it is not the greater or lesser degree of generalization or imitative propagation of a fact which constitutes its more or less social character, but rather its greater or lesser degree of *coerciveness*, and indeed, according to him (for so far we have revealed but half his thought), the definition of the social fact is a double one. One of its characteristics, as we already know, is "a manner of thinking or acting which is general within the extent of the group but exists *independently* of its individual expressions." But another and no less essential characteristic is its coerciveness. Quoting once again, *"the social fact can be recognized by the coercive power it exerts or is capable of exerting on individuals."*

This last proposition is scarcely less surprising than the first. By this reasoning there would be nothing more social than the relationship established between victor and vanquished in the capture of a fortress or the reduction of a conquered nation to slavery, and nothing less social than the spontaneous conversion of an entire people to a new religion or a new political faith preached by enthusiastic apostles. To me the error here seems so palpable that we must wonder how it could arise and take root in a mind of such intelligence. The author himself tells us how: it seemed to him that the first of his two definitions entailed the second. Considering that the social fact is essentially exterior to the individual, "it can enter the individual only by imposition." I do not clearly see the rigor of this deduction. Food as well is exterior to us before being absorbed. Is this to say that agglutination and assimilation are constraints exercised by food on the cell that ingests it? That is not even true of the fowl that we fatten up in our farmyards, which certainly prefer being stuffed to dying of hunger. This is the same kind of example as the child who undergoes the harsh and restrictive form of education, which Mr. Durkheim has wrongly generalized and which has helped give him the idea about obligatory social constraint. The child, tossed into a social milieu, is nourished there by *intussusception*, like a cell in the blood, a seed in humid soil. It is true that at school and at home he is often chastised. But, first of all, the education that students receive from their teachers and parents is not the only one they have; considerable account must be taken of another education, involuntary, spontaneous and all the more effective because the students give in to one another and because, later on, there will continue to be free interchange among them for the rest of their lives. Then, too, school education itself is not always coercive; and finally, even when it is, when the child is put on bread and water, locked up and beaten in order to constrain him to act according to the rules or habits of society, is it certain, even in this case, that his initiation into social life is imposed on him by force? No, because at heart this rebellious child who is being punished remains attached, despite himself, to his family, sometimes to his teachers, to the society in which he was born, and he would be terrified at the very idea of living outside of it. He is similar to the enlisted man who, though he joined voluntarily, still behaves sometimes so as to bring himself before the police. The basis of it all is human sociability, innate in the most insubordinate child. When by chance it is missing in a child, it is useless to correct him, his education is impossible. The phenomena of being swept away in a crowd are *social facts*, the author concedes; consequently he hastens to say that these great currents of enthusiasm, of anger or hatred, which push a multitude to heroism or to murder, "have *no* particular consciousness as their place of origin," that they are facts exterior to all members of a crowd, and facts which constrain them all. Is it not evident here, however, that some are leaders and others followers, and that if, despite their eagerness to anticipate suggestions, we can speak of constraint with respect to followers, it is a contradiction in term to apply this expression to leaders?

But enough of the alleged coercive character of social facts. One more word about their supposed character of being exterior and alien to individuals. This whole system rests on a misinterpretation. To the extent that my language, my law, my work, my religion existed before me and exist outside me—in at least a certain metaphorical sense of *outside*—and to the extent that the same can be said for each member of a society taken individually, does it follow that a language, a religion, a law, an industry, and so forth can be considered to exist independently of *all* the people who speak this language, practice this religion, conform to this law, practice this industry? If it can be said that these social things are independent of every one of the members in the sense that if one member disappears the social things do not, is it not simply because without him their reality is their presence *within* the consciousness or the memory of all the other members? I say *within* because they are interior and not exterior to these members, and if they begin by being exterior to each new arrival who is not yet a member of the association, as he becomes incorporated into the association, they actually enter into him and finally become that which is most intimate and most dear to him, most his own. *Social things*, which maintain and perpetuate themselves by the individual consciousnesses through which they evolve, are like an ocean wave, which crosses innumerable molecules and seems to animate them even while living from their force. One can say just as well (or not so well) of the wave that it is exterior to the waters of the sea and that it imposes itself on them. But where is the physicist who does not know what to think of such metaphors?

I am afraid that I shall be reproached for breaking down an open door by refuting a profound but isolated thinker who tranquilly writes sentences such as this: "Individuals aside, only society remains." What can society be when *all* individuals are disregarded? For, no doubt about it, this is precisely what the author means.

Still, far from excusing myself for the time devoted to this refutation, I must say that there are few sociological truths as useful to examine as Mr. Durkheim's errors, however evident they may be. And he must be thanked for having expressed them so boldly and so clearly. They were in the air and asked to be incarnated in a logical and vigorous mind; it was fortunate that it was his mind they encountered. He pushed to the extreme all the scattered tendencies of an emancipated sociology, freed not only from biology, as was necessary, but also from psychology, which is impossible, and esconced in its invisible and imaginary domain in the clouds.

The source of this illusion merits examination, for it is very widespread among cultivated minds—nothing more banal than the idea that a combination differs or can differ entirely from its elements and that from the simple meeting of these elements can emerge an entirely new reality which has in no way existed previously in another form. Chemistry and biology gave credence to this prejudice. One can see the contrast between the properties of composite bodies and those of the simple bodies of which they are composed. One can see a living being composed exclusively of chemical substances which, before being assembled in an organism, had nothing biological about them. And most of all, out of living cells that we assume to be unconscious, we see the self arise and we call it a miracle. After this we ought not to judge it surprising a priori that the social meeting of different *selves* should bring forth an *us*, which is supposedly something supra-psychological, or essentially nonpsychological, and which exists independently of all individual consciousnesses.

But even if, *all else granted*, this does not suffer from difficulties a priori, observation unfortunately is absolutely contrary to this hypothesis. We are singularly privileged in sociology to have intimate knowledge of its element—our individual consciousness— as well as of the composite—the assembly of consciousnesses —and here one cannot make us take words for things. Now in this case, we clearly establish that without the individual element the social element is nothing, and that there is nothing, absolutely nothing, in society which does not exist piecemeal in a state of continual repetition in living individuals and which did not exist in the ancestors of the present individuals.

I say that this is a singular privilege because everywhere else we are completely ignorant of what there is in the depths of the element. For what is there in the innermost depths of a chemical molecule or a living cell? We do not know. How then can we affirm, when these mysterious beings meet in a certain manner, itself unknown, and cause the appearance of new phenomena, an organism, a mind, a conscience, that there has been a sudden apparition at each degree of this mysterious scale, a creation ex nihilo of something that was not there before, not even in germinal form? Is it not probable that if we had an intimate knowledge of those cells, those molecules, those atoms, those *unknowns* that are so often taken as *givens*, we should find that the exteriorization of phenomena seemingly created by their rapprochement—phenomena which at present make us marvel—are in reality very simple? Note the enormous postulate implied by these current notions, on which Mr. Durkheim deliberately leans in order to justify his chimerical conception: that the simple relationship of several beings can itself become a new being, and one often superior to the others. It is odd to see these men, who pride themselves above all on being positive and methodical, everywhere pursuing the very shadow of mysticism, clinging to such a fantastic notion.

Thus, in the only case in which the elements are known to us, we observe that they contain within themselves the complete explanation and the complete existence of their composite. What should we conclude from this? Precisely this: by a reasoning which is just the reverse of that of our learned adversary we must infer that in all other cases it is the same. And if I, too, dared to push this idea to its extreme, if I ventured to indicate the possible remodeling of universal science under the inspiration of sociology, perhaps I should be led in turn into deep mysteries such as the Leibnitzian region of monads, onto which, from many different avenues, the inquiring thought of our day seems to converge. Perhaps then I should be led to say that one must choose between the ontological phantasmagoria of Mr. Durkheim and our own neo-monadological hypothesis and that once the latter is rejected the former must be accepted. But I do not care to venture on such metaphysical flights, preferring to stay on the shores of fact.

Thus, like Auguste Comte and John Stuart Mill, like Herbert Spencer, let us solicit the secret of sociology from collective psychology and from that accumulated psychology of the dead called history, and from logic as well. We are told, however, that "between psychology and sociology exists the same solution of continuity as between biology and the physicochemical sciences. *Consequently every time a social phenomenon is directly explained by a psychical phenomena, we may rest assured that the explanation is false.*" This is like saying that in social matters any clear explanation is necessarily an erroneous one. Further, "a purely psychological explanation of social facts cannot help but overlook what is unique to them, that is, what is social." I reply yes, if one wishes to account for a collective fact only through the psychology and the logic of individuals and of real individuals, but not if one also considers the psychology and the logic of the masses and of the dead.

Then we are told that "if in fact social evolution had its true origin in man's psychical constitution, it is impossible to see how this evolution could have occurred." It seems to me that one can see even less clearly without this psychical constitution how it could have arisen and developed. With it, on the contrary, social progress is most simply explained, always on condition, however, that it be a question of the mental nature and of states of mind not of *man* but of *men*, of men dissimilar and unequal to a certain degree, gifted with diverse capabilities and aptitudes, sometimes touching on genius. It is certain that if one supposes in the beginning a gathering of men (which may or may not be divided into equal segments), men all identical, all similarly inert and stupid or situated at the same mediocre level of intelligence, with no man superior to those around him, then human progress, social evolution, remains inexplicable psychologically just as it does from any other point of view. Ideas of genius, conceived in one brain and then propagated in many others, which presupposes, on the one hand, the rather rare good fortune, either fortuitous or planted, of genius or ingenuity, and, on the other hand, the imitative docility of mediocrity; and that, if I am not mistaken, is what the historical mystery amounts to.

Furthermore, our century has seen whole new societies established in the many American, African, and Oceanic colonies that it has spawned. It is not clear that we are dealing here with entirely psychological causes—causes which were doubtless mutually stimulated, overexcited, transfigured, and, moreover, directed by the example of surrounding or distant societies but still via psychological causes? In these spontaneous generations of new states, it is not also evident that responsible for their birth is a basis of natural attraction, a tendency toward association (and this despite the unleashing of egoistic passions) and not an external constraint exercised on all (we are not told by whom)?

But Mr. Durkheim does not see it this way. He formulates and emphasizes the following rule, which to him seems of capital importance: "The determining cause of a social fact must be sought among antecedent social facts and not among individual states of consciousness." Applying this we find that the determining cause of our railroad system should be sought neither in the states of consciousness of Papin, Watts, Stephenson, or others, nor in the logical series of ideas and discoveries which dawned on these great minds, but rather in the preexisting network of roads and the parcel post service.

There is a fetish, a deus ex machina that the new sociologists utilize like an "open Sesame" each time they are perplexed, and it is time to indicate this abuse, which is becoming really disquieting. This explanatory talisman is *environment*. Once this word is uttered, everything has been said. *Environment* is the all-purpose formula whose illusory profundity serves to cover the emptiness of the idea.[1] Hence it has been pointed out without fail, for example, that the origin of all social evolution must be sought exclusively in the properties of "the internal social environment." Now what can this be, the properties of the internal or external social environment, if not everything contained in the minds brought together in society, their notions and memories, their aptitudes and habits? Certainly I know that the idea of social environment has a real significance whenever men act en masse and not ut singuli, as in the case of an impulsive crowd, or a charging regiment, and also wherever the ideas of a group of men, considered as a group instead of individually, impress someone as a whole. But this must be understood to mean that each person acted upon and impressed by the environment is a part of that environment which acts upon and impresses his peers. As to this phantom-environment, which we revive at will, to which we attribute all sorts of marvelous virtues in order to dispense with recognizing the real geniuses who really do good, by whom we live, in whom we move, without whom we would be nothing, let us expulse this phantom from our science as fast as possible. Environment is the constellation which, when looked at more closely, changes into distinct stars of very unequal size. I observe many individuals, some of whom exercise reciprocal influ-

[1]   Needless to say, this expression, "the emptiness of the idea," does not apply to Mr. Durkheim who, despite his bias, remains withal one of the most serious sociologists we know.

ence on each other, and some of whom model themselves on others; nowhere do I see them swim together in this sort of subtle and imaginary atmosphere which, with much less reason than the ether in physics, is the supposed *factotum* of sociology.

II

After this admittedly incomplete investigation of the nature of the elementary social fact we should ask what is the nature of the elementary social group, which is not at all the same thing. It is true that every social act—speaking, professing a belief, working, obeying, dancing, singing—implies an imitative relationship between men, some being models, the others copiers, or all copying an ancient common model. In this sense there is a social bond between all those who speak the same language, practice the same profession or religion, or do business together. But the group formed by each of these bonds considered separately has only an incomplete and abstract reality. The concrete and living group presupposes a superposition of several of these groups, a bundle of several of these bonds, just as a rope is composed of many twisted and intertwined strings. And that is not all. In addition, at least in the beginning, in order for the group to be alive and fruitful it is necessary to add something else to these various sorts of imitation, and that something is the action of heredity, the real or fictional bond of blood, which serves to tie all the rest together. Thus, just as we had to define the social fact in essentially psychological terms, we are now forced to define the social group in terms that are both psychological and physiological, and which expose its roots deep in the soul and in life.

Shall I say then that the elementary social group is the family? This would be most audacious: there is nothing so outmoded, so highly despised by today's sociologists as this simple solution. A few years ago it was still used everywhere and looked upon as an obvious truth. When one of the most industrious and devoted pioneers of documentary sociology, a man of the highest moral character, possessing both love for and rare intelligence about inferior, savage, or half-civilized societies, when Le Play dedicated his life to a detailed study of what I shall call social histology, or the cellular tissue of peoples—the idea that if one cell were known, all the others would be as well—did he hesitate one second in choosing the group which would be the subject of his investigation? No, it did not occur to him to trace anything other than monographs of families. At present even his disciples have some doubts on this count, and several of them are in the process of substituting for rather than adding to the studies of the master with monographes *of professions* conceived on an entirely different plan.

As for Mr. Durkheim, he completely rejects any mixing of a biological idea in the subtle sociology he traces. For him, the elementary social group is not the family at all but the horde, brought together any which way and staying together no one know why or how—the horde, and then the repetition of hordes, the clan. To a lesser degree, the same prejudice against the family is found almost everywhere, even among scholars who are generally to be commended for their insight and moderation. According to Starke, cohabitation has played a far greater role in the formation of the social bond than consanguinity. Along with the community formed by tatooing, the totem, or a name, cohabitation supposedly provides the true origin of the clan and even furnishes the origin of matriarchy, whose explanation had been sought to no avail by hypothesizing universal promiscuity in the beginning of mankind. For Starke the clan is thus a sort of hereditary corporation into which one enters less by consanguinity than by religious consecretion. The child is given—I was going to say at baptism—the name of an animal or plant which from then on becomes his protector, his miraculous and invisible doctor. "Mr. Morgan recounts," says Starke, "that according to a fairly widespread custom the mother enters her son into the clan she prefers by giving him a certain name; and indeed each clan does possess a series of names which are its particular property; to receive such a name therefore is to enter into the clan." To understand this it must be recalled that, both among the primitives and ourselves, the name given to a child is held to have a very real effect on his future. Something of this ancient belief subsists in the Christian's cult toward his patron saint.

Bees of the same hive, ants of the same anthill are all sisters. This is enough to say that it is impossible to look to animal societies for an argument to support the thesis of a supposed *antagonism between the family and the society*. In the same way the members in the majority of lower human tribes consider themselves brothers. To be sure this is often a fiction, but this fictitious fraternity, an artificial and ingenious extension of real fraternity, necessarily assumes the preexistence of the latter, which serves as its model.

The truth is that social evolution utilizes two different processes to develop the family in society and that, since one occurs at the expense of the other, these two processes can be considered antagonistic. Both, however, issue from the primitive domestic group. Whatever the nature of this group, monogamous or polygamous, it can spread either through simple growth and internal complications (leading to the tribe and the clan) or from exterior colonization and a tight or loose federation between its offshoots separated and scattered across a certain area. This distinction is reminiscent of the one between monocellular organisms, where the single cell grows and differentiates itself internally as much as possible, and polycellular organisms. In sociology, moreover, as in biology, only the second mode of development is capable of a great rise up the scale of progress.

It must be agreed, nonetheless, that in itself the family group is something very vague and very indeterminate if no foreign element enters into the picture to circumscribe it and make it more precise. Unfortunately, by making it more precise we also make it more complicated, and it is from this complication that arise the multiple forms of the family brought to light by numerous illustrious ethnographers, which at first seemed to have only a nominal link between them. However, if one looks at the matter closely, one cannot help but notice the common basis which serves as a theme for these variations. One of the most original forms of kinship is surely that of the Iroquois and of many other peoples who practice what is called *syndiasmian marriage*, the collective marriage of a series of brothers with a series of sisters. Here uncles as well as the real father are called father, both nephews and sons are called sons,

cousins and brothers alike are called brother. This is what is called
the *classificatory* kinship system as opposed to our European descriptive system. As strange as this American notion of the family
may appear to us, it seems to me that Mr. Gaston Richard somewhere gives an account of it which is both very plausible and very
appropriate for relating the origins of this form to those of our own
system. This perspicacious writer explains the question by the
almost permanent state of war in which the tribes with this strange
system live. The more the social group is menaced, the more it
feels the need to grow by collecting more members, to extend and
also strengthen the special bond which unites its members. Consequently if this bond is principally that of kinship—for this is the
necessary hypothesis—an effort would be made to enlarge the kinship circle as much as possible and by the boldest means. This occurs for the same reason that we civilized peoples tend to reduce
this circle as our customs become refined and more pacific. Now
this circle is limited to father, mother, and child, whereas during
the Middle Ages, the era of insecurity, everyone was a cousin. The
desire for a numerous and strong kinship group caused this assimilation of nephew to son, of cousin to brother, which surprises us
now but would have surprised a *magnate* of fifteenth-century Florence much less.

In the groups united by a special bond other than that of kinship the same need for common defense produces analogous effects.
When the professional group is or thinks it is threatened, one sees
similar workers in various provinces or countries form unions and
international congresses, where they treat each other as brothers
and where foreigners are assimilated to the national group. When
the religious group is threatened, quarrels over details are forgotten, and the dissidents treat each other as co-religionists.

We should note that matriarchy is easily explained as the almost inevitable successor of syndiasmian marriage or, more generally, of polyandry. When a child does not actually know who
among the men whom he calls by that name is his father, the authority of each of these is partially neutralized by that of the others,
while the authority of the mother makes itself felt without rivalry.
This situation is singularly apt to increase the power of the mother

even without the nomadic habits of the fathers and their weak attachment to a child held jointly with others. "Perhaps everything would become clear," says Mr. Richard, "if we were reconciled to seeing in this famous matriarchy another name for the father's abandonment of the mother, an abandonment which must have been frequent at a time when man's propensities to wander had not been repressed by the habits stemming from civilization." It should be noted that matriarchies are the rule in the deserts or prairies crossed by commercial caravans, from the Caucasas to the Sahara, among the ancient Amazons and the present-day Touaregs, everywhere that women, left alone at home for months on end, were forced to arm themselves and become more masculine in order to defend themselves against surrounding enemies. In conditions so unfavorable for conjugal fidelity, the uncertainty of kinship makes it advisable to call the child by its mother's name alone.

In short, we see everywhere that the vital bond of generation serves to link, to pull the bundle of social bonds vigorously together into a concrete, real, and active group. Not that non-family groupings of individuals do not play a role in our societies as in animal societies. Among the savages and among the animals the young who are separated from their families join together in bands, much like conscripts in our army regiments; these bands and regiments are certainly well defined, lively, and active aggregates, which, next to and outside the family, have their place in the sun. But do not forget that this place is due to the family. Without families and without a certain social organization of the family, which alone enabled the children to learn a trade and free themselves, no band, horde, or regiment would be possible. The band, horde, or regiment is the element, not of society itself, but of the militant, plundering and murdering society of the army. It is not the repetition, the multiplication, the grouping of bands or hordes that produces a nation, but the repetition, multiplication, and grouping of families.

Perhaps instead of families we should say *households*. And in fact instead of monographs on families as he himself thought, it is monographs on households that Le Play has given us. In every age and on all continents, in the Old as well as the New World, we always perceive a given population divided into houses or, amount-

ing to the same thing in a big city like Paris, into distinct and separate apartments. Each of these households consists of a family
group clearly and arbitrarily divided according to the dominant
custom; it may be either pure or, as is most frequent, mixed
through a more or less intimate alliance of adopted members,
slaves, apprentices, servants. You say that before houses were invented there could of course be no households? True, but there
were analogous groups in the age of the Troglodites, called *caveholds*, if I may use a neologism. Among nomadic shepherds there
were caravans, a sort of ambulant household, which I would classify as such even though there was no sort of tent or hut, no hearth
or site—a situation which must have been the same for many a
forgotten people.

Here it is certainly not to the relationship of cohabitation that
we attribute the origin of the social group. But is it not at least the
relationship of *coperegrination* that establishes such a close bond
between the nomads of each caravan, similar to the bond between
migratory birds of each flock wandering in the sky? To walk or fly
together, to wander together and encounter the same dangers—this
must certainly have been one of the first and most intimate of
social bonds. But this bond also presupposes the bond of kinship,
which it so obviously followed and modeled itself on. Indeed, where
did animals, or humans, learn to walk or fly together, to follow one
another, to mass together and unite if not when they were very
small by following their mother step by step or by taking shelter
with their brothers close to their father? Thus arose the instinct for
grouping, the tendency to march in step, to imitate. The family is
thus the cradle of imitation because the first and always the principal motivation of imitation is the confident and credulous attraction which would not exist were it not for filial piety, maternal devotion, and domestic tenderness. It would be a grave error to think
that, with the progress of civilization and the extension of artificial
groups arising from industry and politics, the social value of these
deep attachments diminishes or that the importance of natural
groupings lessens. Far from it: to become civilized is to find more
affinities with others each day; the increased social field requires
a better human heart, greater and more tender, just as a larger

garden requires more abundant water. Where can this be found if not by delving ever deeper into the only inexhaustible source, or rather by multiplying those sources which are smaller but more pure? Hence it is clear that civilization multiplies households equally with population, and by simplifying them, by dividing up the family, civilization purifies it and strengthens its most tender and essential aspects. If the population of Paris were lodged in *long houses* like those of the Iroquois, which were a sort of phalanstery or barracks, there would be ten to twenty times fewer homes than in the present division into apartments and tiny dwellings.

At the Trocadéro Museum can be seen the principal types of *households* in different countries and the various provinces of France. But within each province and each canton there is great diversity and inequality between the hovel and the château, as between the little tents and the big tents of the nomads. To think of primitive societies, then, as a juxtaposition of equal and similar segments is to carry the spirit of methodical simplification a little far. These primitive social groups, caveholds, caravans, and bands, products of proliferation and splitting of one or several initial families, are very dissimilar, precisely because they are self-contained and alien to one another. Each one of these groups has its own language or dialect, its own customs, gods, and trade secrets, and its own government. From this dissimilarity we arrive little by little at the relative resemblance produced by mutual or unilateral imitation from clan to clan or tribe to tribe.

It should not be said that this division into families, or at least into groups of an essentially family nature united by real or supposed kinship, was later replaced by a division according to job or class, religion or state, and that the consanguinal element is increasingly repressed or eliminated from our societies by their specifically social forces. The power attached to ties of blood has neither disappeared nor even diminished, but has instead increased like these so-called new forces which in reality are contemporary to that power and do not develop inversely but rather parallel to it. If the professional group has grown constantly from its embryonic state within the primitive family to our present-day unions, which extend throughout a nation or a federation of states, has not the family group undergone the same increases? The city of antiquity did not really exist until the time when the two or three more or less heterogeneous tribes, whose original alliance founded it, fused physiologically via repeated intermarriages. And despite its faculty (used, however, relatively infrequently) of growing through naturalization, what is a modern nation but a vast family, an enormous genealogical tree? The proof lies in the fact that when, like Austria, a state is composed of an amalgamation of several races, the feeling of a single strong nationality does not arise until several centuries have enabled these races to cross and combine, at least at their borders, into a new race or races. Inversely, a people such as the Poles have been divided among several states to no avail, because the original community maintains the feeling of common nationality indefinitely. In a word, the physiological bond, which was the principal basis of the small domestic societies of the past, then of the tribes, then of the cities of antiquity, is still the essential basis of the great national societies of today. In this way it has manifestly acquired ever more power and importance, since before the formation of cities and nations the innumerable families or tribes spread across a territory such as Gaul or the Teutonic empire were related to each other, as they are now in modern states such as France and Germany. But this kinship did not yet have the power to establish a social bond between them or the feeling of such a bond; they were and felt themselves to be foreign to one another, whereas at present they feel themselves intimately and fraternally united. Civilization has thus singularly increased the family in a national or *interfamily* sense of the word as much as it has decreased the family in the narrow and specific sense of the word.

This gradual development of the *genetic* social circle was accomplished at the same time as the increase in the professional circle. At first, occupational identity closely linked only a small number of men, slaves, or women in each house or cave who were assigned to the same military, pastoral, agricultural, or industrial task. Later, and precisely because the family tie was extended, the working community came to be felt as a new source of affinities and social solidarity among people belonging to different families, tribes, or cities. There is not, therefore, an inverse relationship between the progress of the consanguinal bond and the progress of the social bond which is attached to labor, that is, to the imitative reproduction of the same types of wealth and services.

And what I have said of the working community I could say just as well about cohabitation on the same land and the communion of beliefs and desires. All these various causes of social aggregation exist in germinal form from the beginning and develop harmoniously. However, those which have an entirely social nature develop much more quickly and go much farther, so that there comes a time when, under the influence of a respected authority, a common faith or aspiration in the same civilization, peoples of the most diverse races aggregate or tend to aggregate into a sort of vast supranational nation such as the Roman world, medieval Christendom, or the European federation of tomorrow. But here we are not concerned with this glorious final stage, toward which these social developments march with unequal though parallel strides, but with their first stage. From the beginning, the inhabiting of the same cave or the same lake shelter, later the same tent, and the covering of the same region as regular nomads with unvarying periodical wanderings was added to—and not substituted for, as Sumner-Maine erroneously believes—consanguinity as the constitutive element of the group thought of as the *fatherland* (*patria tellus*). From the beginning, similarly, those who undertook the same tasks (weaving, sewing, milking, hunting, fishing, and so forth) felt themselves drawn together. From family to family, the fishermen with the fishermen, the hunters with the hunters, the weavers with the weavers, each was drawn to form a *class*, while their families tended to form a *nation*. This was the first step toward *internationalism* as well as toward nationhood. Another cause of the tendencies toward internationalism—and one that existed from the very beginning—was the community of superstitions, which tended to unite in the same *church* the dispersed worshippers of the same god. As for the communities of desire, of plans, of collective interest, without them no human aggregate would ever have been possible; for they are the necessary soul of every political society, of every *state*.

Thus, from the outset, the idea of *nation, fatherland, class, Church,* and *state* coexist and become more precise and spread, though, I repeat, at different rates. Such is the concrete and living reality, the subject of our studies to which not only historians, philosophers, jurists, moralists, and humanists ought to contribute but also naturalists, anthropologists, and doctors. All the sciences meet in sociology even though it assuredly has its own special domain—but not in the clouds or in the fog of ontology.

Sociology can be and has been thought of in turn as (1) social physics (the economists, Auguste Comte), (2) social biology (Spencer), (3) social psychology. Each of these conceptions has a plausible side, although only the third, in my opinion, is as comprehensive as it is insightful. But the worst idea one can have of our science is, I think, as (4) a social ideology.

Now that we have defined the social group and the social fact, it remains for me to speak of their relationship, the social state, and of the logic which regulates the composition of social states and their evolution or rather evolutions. This would also be the moment to ask wherein lies the distinction between healthy and morbid states of society, and whether Mr. Durkheim, whom we encounter here once again, is correct in saying that a high rate of criminality is not a pathological social state but on the contrary "an integral part" of the health of the national body—a peculiar view to which, he says, he is led logically by the application of his method. I should also say a word about method. But besides the fact that this would take us much too far and it is already time to finish, I believe that the best method for each of us is one which develops by itself from study, just as primitive peoples create their original customs and legislation through action. One learns to swim by jumping into the water.

If I were to formulate a maxim on this subject, it would treat the essential moral, and not just intellectual, conditions required for the discovery of truth. A little modesty and simplicity suit both an adolescent science and a young man embarking on life; the science, for one, should avoid a doctrinaire tone and academic jargon. One must bring to it a familiar and well-intentioned bent of mind and above all a love of the subject matter. The first condition for a naturalist is to love life, to fraternize with all the living, to sense the good hidden in the worst of things. For even the tiger is good, the boa constrictor is good, and I am told that the rattle-snake only agitates his rattle to warn the passerby of the danger, rather like our cyclists. Similarly, the first condition for a sociologist is to love social life, to sympathize with men of all races and all nations united around one hearth, to seek with curiosity and discover with joy the affectionate devotion that lies hidden in the hut of the reputedly most ferocious savage or in the retreat of the miscreant, and, finally, never to believe easily in the stupidity or the absolute wickedness of man in the past, nor in his present perversity, and never to give up hope for his future.

4

A DEBATE WITH
EMILE DURKHEIM

1904

Lecture by Mr. Durkheim

Must sociology continue to be a philosophical speculation which encompasses social life in a formula? Or, on the contrary, must it become fragmented into different sciences, and if it
is to specialize, how is this specialization to occur? Purely philosophical sociology is based entirely on the idea that social phenomena are controlled by necessary laws. Social facts are linked by
bonds that human volition cannot arbitrarily break. This truth
assumed an advanced mentality and could only be the fruit of
philosophical speculations. Sociology is the daughter of philosophical thought; it arose in the heart of Comtean philosophy and is its
logical crown.

But for Comte sociology does not consist in the plurality of
definite problems that scholars study separately, but is embodied
in a single problem, and in order to perceive the law that dominates
it as a whole, sociology must embrace within an indivisible instant
the course of historical development. Detailed studies are dangerous, Comte said, because they distract the attention of the sociologist from the fundamental problem which is the entirety of sociology. Social facts are solidaristic, and only by profoundly altering
their nature can one study them in isolation. All Comte's disciples

Resumés of lectures given by Durkheim and Tarde at the Ecole Pratique
des Hautes Etudes in December 1903, reprinted with the discussions that
followed in the *Revue Internationale de Sociologie*, 1904, pp. 83–87. The
resumés, unsigned, were presumably penned by René Worms, editor of the
Revue.

have done is to reproduce the thought of their master, and the same formulas have been repeated without any advances in sociology.

But why should sociology consist of a single problem? Social reality is essentially complex, not unintelligible but just uncongenial to simple forms. Sociology is not a unitary science, and, even while respecting the solidarity and interdependence of social facts, it must study each category separately. But the conception that reduces sociology to a single and unique problem is still, even among contemporary authors, the one most generally held. It is always a question of discovering the general law of sociality. Since they are social, all the facts studied by the separate social sciences supposedly have a common character, and the subject of sociology is the study of the social fact in abstraction. By comparing social facts we shall see the elements found in all types and shall distinguish the general characteristics of sociality. But where and how will this abstraction be achieved? The given facts are concrete and complex; even the most inferior civilizations are extremely complex. How can we extract the elementary fact, with its abstract characteristics, if we do not begin by studying the concrete phenomena in which it is realized?

If sociology wants to live, then, it will have to reject the philosophical character that it owes to its origin and approach the concrete realities via special research. It is desirable for the public to know that sociology is not purely philosophical and that it requires precision and objectivity. But this is not to say that in order to become truly sociological sciences the special disciplines need only remain what they are already. They have not yet been adequately penetrated by the ideas brought to light by social philosophy. They need to be transformed, to orient themselves in a more expressly sociological direction. At the present time one can only pose the problem.

Lecture by Tarde

Should we speak of social science or of the social sciences? Sociology must be the science and not the philosophy of social facts, for today that would be insufficient. The social sciences preceded social science and prepared its evolution. These sciences based on the comparative and evolutionary method need themselves to be compared. And this comparison of comparisons would be sociology. The specialists attacked the problem of social life, and each of them has observed the social facts that concern him. But institutions did not all arise identically in all countries. When one verifies imitative and spontaneous similarities between instituitions, it is always psychological and inter-psychological facts that we are dealing with; in one case there was imitation, the action of a model mind on a copying mind, and in the other case the work of a single human mind which, using the same logic on givens of a similar nature, of necessity arrived at fairly similar results. As the naturalists would say, these are functional analogies which moreover attach far greater price to homologies—the equivalent of imitative similarities.

The study of social facts can only concern acts relevant to inter-mental psychology. It is therefore to this inter-psychology that we must turn for the explanation of social facts.

The comparative method can verify a preconceived hypothesis, but if this view is false, the results are nil. This is the way the soothsayers of antiquity, who used the comparative method so abundantly, completely wasted their time. Great thinkers did not always achieve the results that they were hoping for—witness Herbert Spencer with the organicist hypothesis and Le Play with the study of family monographs. The family is a poorly defined unit, and one must descend as far as the individual in order to find the social element. Mr. Durkheim believes that scientific progress requires increasing division of social work and that the social sciences must divide. But there are two sorts of division of labor: one anterior to unification, the other posterior to convergence. Scientific progress for the first consists of moving towards unity; and progress for the second consists of an ever-growing differentiation There are therefore two movements: (1) separate investigations the different sciences converging toward one point, and (2) the synthesis of these different sciences. Inter-mental psychology must be to the social sciences what the study of the cell is to the biological sciences. These special sciences must use the comparative method, but to unite them, define them, increase them, the aid of inter-mental psychology is indispensable.

In the social sciences one discovers elementary agents and acts common to all sciences; these are incorporeal or inter-mental acts, but the first cannot exist without the second. This inter-mental psychology is indispensable to the study of social facts, because psychology, which studies only the individual confronting nature, is incapable of studying phenomena such as the intimidation produced by a man meeting his peers.

As each of us enters social life, we feel the influence of certain great persons; these individual examples fuse with many other influences of the same type and form a collective product that acts on us who have formed it with an air of personal or external command and can only have a false air of exteriority. This collective appearance is the result of a psychological synthesis.

It does not suffice for sociologists to observe the direction of evolution of the various sciences. All the sciences that took off from an objective point of view have become psychological (as for example the psychological nature of modern economic study).

There are two categories of social things to study: (1) groups of people acting inter-mentally (families, classes, nations); (2) groups of actions (languages, customs, institutions). And it would be desirable for the social sciences to keep this distinction in mind instead of frequently nourishing themselves with vain entities.

Inter-mental psychology is an elementary, that is, general, sociology, and thanks to it sociology can be a central science and not just a common name given to the collection of social sciences.

The third session, presided over by Mr. Croiset, dean of the Faculty of Letters, was devoted to the discussion of the first two lectures summarized above. Mr. Durkheim and Mr. Tarde maintained their respective theses with enthusiasm.

Mr. Tarde granted the importance of general laws extracted by the comparative method, but asked that another method be followed at the same time and that one use the social microscope of inter-mental psychology.

Mr. Durkheim replied that the general sociology exterior to

the social sciences can only be the synthesis of the results from the particular sciences and that one cannot say what these results will be nor whether they can be achieved by inter-mental psychology as long as the special sciences are so little advanced. "Mr. Tarde claims that sociology will arrive at such and such results; but in the present state of our knowledge we cannot say what the elementary social fact is. There are too many things that we do not know, and under these conditions the construction of the elementary social fact can only be arbitrary. Whatever this inter-mental psychology is worth, it is inadmissible for it to exercise a sort of directive action on the special disciplines of which it must be the product."

Mr. Tarde replied that to formulate laws it is not necessary that the sciences be definitely established. A directive idea is necessary in research. Social sciences do not owe their progress to rules of objective method but to their development in the direction of psychology. Once again in social life there are only acts from one individual to another. Does Mr. Durkheim think that social reality is anything other than individuals and individual acts or facts? "If you believe that," said Mr. Tarde, "I understand your method, which is pure ontology. Between us is the debate between nominalism and scholastic realism. I am a nominalist. There can only be individual actions and interactions. The rest is only a metaphysical entity, mysticism."

Mr. Durkheim thought that Mr. Tarde was confusing two different questions, and declined to say anything about a problem that he had not touched upon and, he maintained, had nothing to do with the discussion.

II. General Principles of Sociology

5

BASIC PRINCIPLES

1902

LET US briefly examine the general relationships of adaptation and repetition, which in the biological, physical, and social worlds are the two fundamental processes. Everywhere there are harmonies which repeat themselves: a wave is actually a harmonious succession of movements, equilibrium in motion, falling back on itself like a musical phrase. It is the same, though more complex, with a living being, which we may see as a very complicated wave that is born, grows, and declines like a wave of liquid or sound, and whose adult state corresponds to what the physicists call the antinode of the wave. Similarly, any sort of imitative act—a word or phrase spoken, a religious ritual performed, a job executed, or a legal procedure enacted—each of these is a *whole* having a beginning, middle, and end and comprising a series of integrated and unified changes collecting around a center of gravity—the accented syllable of the word, the accented word of the phrase, the essential act in the religious ritual, the central point of the job or procedure.

How were these harmonies formed? It is extremely important not to confuse this problem with that of how they repeat themselves—a confusion we find hidden in the heart of the Darwinian idea. It was pointed out to Darwin that the struggle for existence presupposes the association for life, that is, an *organization*, which the multiplying repetitions of organisms and ensuing battles do not explain but imply. It is as if one wished to explain the formation of undulating chemical molecules by the impact of undulations or

From *Psychologie économique* (Paris: Alcan, 1902), 1:32–36, 37–41.

to explain the genesis of imitative inventions by competition in imitation.

Not that these battles, impacts, competitions and *oppositions* need not be considered. *Opposition* is a general fact, though less general than adaptation and repetition, which must take its place between and below them, as a frequently necessary but still simple auxiliary or intermediary. Because of their multiplying repetitions, repeating harmonies can occasionally harmonize directly with one another simply by meeting and can thus form higher adaptations. But more often they are in some way opposed, and through clashes and mutual corrections they prepare the way for higher harmonizations, which these conflicts and clashes condition and provoke rather than cause. Everywhere in the social and biological worlds and even the physical world we see harmonious things which, by multiplying, come into conflict with one another; we see adaptations which oppose each other, microbes against cells, organism against organism, corporation against corporation, nation against nation, molecule against molecule—a conflagration preceding chemical combination, which appears to be an innumerable multitude of impacts, and so forth. And everywhere, because of this crisis, we see oppositions which adapt: phenomena of commensalism and acclimatization, fecundations, treaties of alliance, chemical combinations. The passage from militarism to industrialism can be cited as a noteworthy example of this same transformation.

Since we have identified three major concentric circles of reality, the physical circle, the biological circle, and the social circle (the latter two being more closely linked to each other than to the first)—circles which could easily be subdivided or synthesized —we shall have no difficulty distinguishing in each a form of adaptation, a form of repetition, and a form of opposition which characterizes and dominates in it.[1] A typical physical adaptation is

---

[1] One can begin the series of three terms enumerated with whichever term is preferred. Here I prefer to begin with *adaptation* followed by repetition and opposition. This is more logical since repetition and opposition presuppose something which can repeat and oppose itself, and this something can only be an aggregate, an *adaptat* (I apologize for this neologism). Elsewhere, for didactic reasons, I have chosen to begin with repetition. Actually the order of terms forms an endless chain, whose beginning may elude us.

chemical combination, whose internal equilibrium of linked movements is perhaps only vastly amplified in the mobile equilibrium of the solar system (for the law of magnification seems applicable to exterior nature). Is not fecundation, the fruitful coupling which results in a new variety or a new viable race, the most perfect example of biological adaptation? And is not the typical elementary example of psycho-social adaptation found in invention, by which I mean viable, imitable invention, which begins by linking ideas and ends by linking men? For at the origin of every association between men there is an association between ideas which made it possible; and everything now effected through collaboration owes its origins to conception and an individual process. This fact tends to be forgotten when the marvels created by individual genius are attributed to collective work, the so-called spontaneous division and association of work. If hundreds of workers collaborate in the same workshop, it is because the work they do together (weaving, metallurgy, ceramics) was first conceived in its entirety by an illustrious or obscure inventor and then developed by an entrepreneur. And if hundreds of shops collaborate without any overall direction, but with an apparent spontaneity, to make the same products, such as a locomotive or silk materials, it is because the locomotive or the silk materials were invented by some particular person.

The marked difference between the three forms of universal harmony just compared is that the first two remain very mysterious while the nature of the third is fairly clear. Every invention signifies either that facts, previously unrelated or apparently so (the movement of the moon and an apple falling, an electric spark and thunder), were perceived as consequences of the same principle, confirmation of the same proposition, diverse affirmations of the same basic thing—or that procedures and tools which were previously useless to each other (rails, wheels, and steam engines; sewing needles and a pedal; electric current and writing) were placed in a relation to one another such that they served reciprocally as means to the same end, that is, they responded to a desire for one particular thing. It clearly appears here that social concord, or social harmony, basically consists of a set of judgments which affirms the same idea or of actions which imply the pursuit of the same goal. But what is the harmonious accord of two invisible movements produced by chemical combination? Is it certain that this is common gravitation around the same center, and is it only this? Do we know any more about the harmony of organic functions born of the fertilized ovum? Is it convergence to one end or toward multiple associated goals? Or is it perhaps a concordance of another sort that we would be wrong to confuse with finality, differing from the latter as a theory differs from a machine? Nothing could be more of a conjecture.

There are also three forms of universal repetition which I identified long ago. The physical form is the most widespread: undulation, whose spherical and interlaced radiations fill the immense ether, while its more restricted and polarized radiation or linear series penetrates bodies to their innermost depths. The biological form is generation, by which competing and growing populations of plants and animals cover the earth, the air, and the seas. . . .

Finally there are forms of opposition specific to each sphere of reality. The clearest form of physical opposition is an impact, the encounter of two diametrically opposed movements on the same straight line. The sharpest form of biological opposition is *murder* in the most general sense of the term, which includes the suffocation of one plant by another or the destruction of a plant by an animal as well as a fatal duel between two animals. The most violent form of social opposition is *war*, which appears to be no more than the magnification of an animal duel but which basically differs greatly from the latter by the nature and precise awareness of its internal cause: the *contradiction* of the judgments or the *contrariness* of the schemes involved.

General considerations can be formulated—call them laws if you will, a slight misuse of vocabulary but one with the convenience of a monosyllable—concerning the various forms of adaptation, repetition, and opposition. We have seen that the general law of the three forms of repetition is their common tendency, which is most often hindered, to indefinite multiplication. The same law of progressive enlargement necessarily applies to the three forms of adaptation and of opposition, since the oppositions and adaptations multiply along with the repetitions with which they interfere either through battle or alliance. Opposition has led to another very simple generalization, one which has had a great success, greater, I believe, than its explanatory ability merits: all forms of biological, social, and even physical battle terminate in victory for the stronger, called in biology survival of the fittest. This is as true for the competition of physical forces or chemical affinities as it is for the competition of species or nations—whence there follows a selection, alternately physical, biological, or social, whose main property is elimination or purification but not creation.

Does adaptation also have its general laws? Despite frequent substitutions and destruction, is not a tendency toward increasing *accumulation* common to the three forms of adaptation: to chemical combination, which increases in complexity from so-called simple bodies to organic substances; to the fertile coupling, which is a treasury ceaselessly enlarged by hereditary legacies from monera to man, from the mushroom to the highest mammal; and to invention, which grafts a new idea to the previous inventions of which it is composed and is destined, in turn, to support new grafts, and so on from prehistoric inventions of the lever and the wheel to today's most highly perfected machines? Every invention adds something to previous ones, which it synthesizes rather than replaces, in the same way that each new species or race, created by a succession of small but vital innovations through auspicious marriages, is a synthesis of previous species or races. Similarly, new chemical bodies are complications of previous chemical bodies.

No less than this principle of accumulation, the principle of *irreversibility* which derives from it appears applicable to all forms of adaptation. We observe no law that predetermines the appearance of all or almost all inventions at a particular time and place. There is nothing to prevent us from imagining that the compass was discovered two or three centuries earlier or later, likewise America, the printing press, or electricity. But of a given invention we can say that it could not occur before some other invention which preceded and stimulated it, and to a large extent we know beyond doubt that there is a logical chain of discoveries and inventions, that is, an irreversible order in their appearance. The paleontological series of flora and fauna, no less than ideas and human progress, are conceived as essentially irreversible[2] as are astronomical or geological series of chemical formulations. According to thermodynamics, even transformations of physical forces are, owing to their final conversion into heat, thrown against a hill impossible to reascend. Thus all three of these aspects make life in the universe appear to us to *have a meaning* and a raison d'être.

This principle of irreversibility has such great significance that one might be tempted to exaggerate its importance. It is advisable to circumscribe it in order to understand it well because, clearly understood, it leaves a large share in social destinies to individual irregularities, personal initiative, and genius. Irreversibility is far from a rule without exceptions. There are series of discoveries which can always be conceived of as having followed one another in exactly inverse order—geographical discoveries for instance. However, they also retain the particular quality that they necessarily are deduced one from another, that one is inevitably led from one of them to not *one* other but *others* in the immediate vicinity. Thus, a sociologist thought of seeking a formula for the evolution of geographical discoveries, he would certainly be wasting his time. On the other hand, it is certain that by *no matter which* evolution of sufficiently extensive geographical discoveries, one ought inevitably to arrive at a world map which in its basic features would be more or less the same as the map studied by the students of today. Whatever the starting point in America, the series of explorations pushed to their conclusion would have led the navigators of whatever nation and whatever race to the map of America as we now know it. All routes, each essentially reversible, would have led inevitably to this result. And what I say here can be said as well concerning discoveries of *anatomy*, or *crystalography*, or in general of all purely *descriptive* sciences whose entirety is clearly circumscribed and whose form alone is important.

[2]   Without this, how can we comprehend that the series of embryonic stages repeats to some degree the order of succession of previous species? One can only explain the mystery of this repetition, even abbreviated, by supposing that the paleontological succession of species in which that of the individual originates is above all a *logical* succession, a sort of biological deduction which, in shorter form, must be recommended *ab ovo* with each new generation.

6

INVENTION

1902

I

HOWEVER DANGEROUS it may be to generalize here, let us try to formulate a few general considerations concerning the psychological or exterior conditions for invention, its different classes, social consequences, and finally the direction it appears to follow in its infinite meanderings.

About the physiological conditions of invention we know little for certain except that this cerebral creative effort more or less congests the brain. "Low, short pulse, cold pale skin, feverish head, glistening, bloodshot, wandering eyes: such is the classic description" of this state given by Ribot. Furthermore, it seems that some connection exists between the generative function and creative imagination. If one admits, as I am tempted to do, that generation is a sort of vital invention, this correlation is not surprising. In the case of certain inventors, it is certain that the height of their inventiveness corresponded to their period of greatest sexual force. Between the ages of twenty-five and thirty-five arose those concepts that they spent the rest of their lives developing, correcting, and illuminating.[1] But this rule (which is never without exception) is

---

From *Psychologie économique* (Paris: Alcan, 1902), 2:234–53.

[1] An inventor who corresponded with Ribot wrote: "My imagination was most intense at about age twenty-five to thirty-five (I am now forty-three). After this period it seems that the rest of existence only serves to produce less important ideas and thus forms the natural follow-up of the principal ideas born during youth."

most applicable to aesthetic inventions, least applicable to industrial ones: the precocity of industrial innovation is as remarkable as the extension of their productivity into old age. From adolescence, even from childhood, their special aptitudes are revealed in the construction of small machines of often striking ingenuity. There is no schoolyard without its fledgling mechanic, its born engineer, an instinctive builder like the beaver.

The psychology of the man of imagination in every realm of ideas has been traced by Ribot[2] and less extensively by Paulhan, who emphasizes the logic and teleology typical of the inventor. This is in basic agreement with Ribot's idea that the imaginative person is not only a dreamer but an impassioned man whose *idée fixe* is nourished by a fixed sentiment. According to him there is no invention which does not imply an emotional element or a desire, and there is no emotion, be it fear or anger, sorrow or joy, hate or love, which cannot be a ferment to invention. Such a tenacious preoccupation explains the profound distraction of genius, its "internal finality" (to use Souriau's terminology), which becomes fruitful if it happens to encounter a favorable "exterior chance." That is why, contrary to the normal state of affairs, images in the inventor's hallucinatory reverie tend to become *strong states* while sensations become *weak states*. This unnatural tendency may be realized to a greater or lesser extent: its extreme degree is insanity, which here appears not the condition of genius nor even its usual accompaniment but rather a fortuitous malady, the decline of genius into the excesses which destroy it. Nor should the inventor's faith in his mission, which he needs to support him in his battles and in his concentration on his ideas, be confused with the megalomania of a lunatic.

When the self is absorbed in a goal for a long time, it is rare that the *sub-self*, incorrectly called the unconscious, does not participate in this obsession, conspiring with our consciousness and collaborating in our mental effort. This conspiracy, this collaboration whose service is faithful yet hidden, is *inspiration*, which re-

2   *Essai sur l'imagination créatrice* (1900) ; Paulhan, *Psychologie de l'invention* (1901) ; see also Séailles, *Essai sur le génie dans l'art*; Souriau, *Théorie de l'invention.*

mains no less mysterious even when we remove the myths concerning it. Without the continual activity of this internal hive, of this mass of small auxiliary consciences (perhaps) serving our own, not one single phenomena of even the most ordinary intellectual life, not one association of ideas recalled at the opportune moment, remembered just in time as if by some invisible and infinitely diligent librarian, could be explained. But there are times when the help given to the self by the sub-self surprises us by its abundance, by the importance of its results, or by the sudden solution it brings to problems whose solutions have been sought in vain for days and months. Poets in such cases say they are *inspired*; scholars and engineers would have just as much right to say so—and that is one of the reasons why the inventor's work cannot be confused with work as such, with the tasks of a worker, in which there is no noticeable collaboration of the unconscious.

In his enumeration and examination of the various forms or courses of imagination—poetic, artistic, mythological, scientific, moral, political, economic—Mr. Ribot correctly subdivides economic imagination into two branches, industrial and commercial. We shall return to this. I reproach him only for omitting from his otherwise substantial list one important item, that of *linguistic imagination*, the source of verbal invention. Was not this probably the first great manifestation of human genius? Like mythical imagination it arose from the logic of analogy. The need for personification came to light in language by the *sentence*, in which every subject is thought of as a self, and in thought by *animism*. In literature metaphors or "felicitous expressions" originate in this same logic and must be counted among the most successful (being both aesthetic and practical) and the most imitated of all inventions. What a prodigious outlay of verbal invention is implied in the creation of a language or even just a dialect! And if one considers the diversity and multiplicity of original idioms which have since been reduced in number, there is no doubt that the spoken word was the first imaginative exercise of prehistoric man, a response to his most urgent need, that of inter-mental action. Although they always have coexisted, the various linguistic, mythological, poetic, scientific, industrial types of imagination to some extent seem to have reached their zeniths one after another in a series which, in some respects, is irreversible. This is also true in the life of an individual when, as frequently happens, his attitudes change as he grows older. As an extraordinary exception Ribot gives the following example: "I can cite the case of a well-known scholar who began with a taste for the arts (especially the plastic arts), went rapidly through literature, dedicated his life to biological sciences, in which he acquired a merited reputation, and then, becoming completely disgusted with scientific research, returned to literature and finally to the arts, which at present occupy him fully."

The social conditions of invention are much easier to specify than its industrial conditions, and I have in fact often discussed them. It is from this point of view that many of the inequalities of class and the injustices of fate are partially justified. For there are certain classes, as there are certain nations, which are more inventive than others, and whose superiority may be explained thus. Invention being the daughter of leisure and study, it is the leisure classes, the liberal professions, which generally bring forth the ideas destined to revolutionize manual labor and raise the level of the lower classes. It is incorrect to attribute to the workers a large share in the invention of machines or at least in their original conception. Our Académie des Sciences contributed greatly both to the conception of inventions and their popularization. During the eighteenth century it was consulted about every invention, and its greatest scholars, like Réaumur, were inventors. Réaumur advanced the state of metallurgy and ceramics; Vaucanson, another academician, is known only for his mechanical duck, yet he invented extremely useful machines which advanced the weaving of silk goods. Differences of inventiveness among nations are no less than among classes and may also be explained by social rather than biological considerations, by the influence of education rather than race. The most inventive nations are not always those which profit the most from their own good ideas, as is shown by World Fairs, where the industrial inventions of nations are compared instead of their industrial prosperity, that is, the imitative propagation of inventions. The classification of nations in these international competitions is therefore quite different from that which would be established by glancing through industrial and commercial statistics.

The influence of the social environment has often been improperly understood and exaggerated to mean that the man of genius is a simple product of the masses, a being simply representative of his surroundings. Ribot remarks that if this were true, such a man would first of all not arouse so much antagonism in his environment. But his environment furnishes all the elements of which his invention constitutes but an original hybrid. Any machine is merely a composite of previous, simpler ones, springs and forces which were known about individually. The new conception arises from these prior inventions, which are propogated through example and meet in one particular mind. Every invention, be it theoretical or practical, is only a combination of imitations, but the nature of this combination remains to be explained. First, this synthesis presupposes a preliminary analysis or abstraction which has dissociated the elements of former inventions and perceived therein the possibility of new associations. This dissociation, like the association, occurs through an intense need for either finality or logic (depending on whether it is a practical or a theoretical invention). In a new type of architecture—Gothic architecture for example—we only find forms which were already popular; but bringing them together for the first time was not just a simple meeting of ideas in someone's mind, for the meeting raised the further idea of their common adaptation to a goal which, in this manner, was realized for the first time: such a goal, which generally preexists (and often has done so for a long time), is in the case of Gothic style the forceful expression of certain exaltations or impulses of the Christian soul, certain characteristic hopes and fears. Everything in Gothic architecture concurs in this goal and at the same time constitutes a response to the need of bringing greater crowds around the pulpit or the alter. Likewise, the invention of the windmill contained only those elements in use for centuries: grindstones, the motor force of the wind, a tower, a mobile roof. The ingenuity consisted in bringing these things together in order to realize an ancient wish: grinding wheat with the least possible effort. Seen from this point of view, brought together in this manner, these things, which once appeared foreign to one another, appear as collaborators. Similarly, when Huyghens conceived the theory of light waves, he perceived the phenomena of luminous radiation and propagation of sound waves or waves formed by the wind on the surface of a lake as consequences of the same principle, applications of the same formula, whereas until then they had not seemed to have any relation to one another.

Thus we see that the inventive idea can be utilitarian or disinterested, that is, its subject may be a relation of means to end or of consequence to principle (of species to genus). But this does not prevent the inventive idea from being in both cases a purely intellectual fact, a deductive analysis, provoked to be sure by a ferment of passion, a special desire, which this conception satisfies but which has nothing in common with those completely different desires that the conception is destined to satisfy when it is utilitarian in nature. The conception of industrial invention is one thing, the wish to see it materialize quite another. On this point I note the comparison, made by both Mr. Ribot and Mr. Paulhan, between *invention* and *volition*. "Imagination," according to Mr. Ribot, "is to the intellectual order what will is to the order of movements." Creative imagination has its miscarriages comparable to the weaknesses of will. Reveries are equivalent to loss of will power. The unexpected is a characteristic common to invention and voluntary decision, as is unpredictability. Perhaps these striking analogies will acquire a different significance if we note that in every act of will there is an invention, be it large or small, a plan, more or less new (for without this there would be only habit and automatism) of which the act of volition is only the executor. Every act of volition is preceded by a teleological syllogism which concludes in favor of a *necessity for action*. Now, does not a syllogism or some such analysis always imply an invention, and does not an invention imply a syllogism whether implicit or clearly formulated? From two premises—two affirmative or negative propositions— I deduce a third proposition which expresses a new *necessity for affirmation*, the logical, scholastic, ordinary syllogism. From those two premises, of which one expresses a volition or a goal, and the other a means to this goal, I deduce a *necessity for action* which consists of putting this means into action: and this is the syllogism of finality.

I know that traditionally the syllogism is not considered a process of discovery but only a method of verification, whereas the famous canons of induction are supposedly the only true paths to invention. But precisely the opposite seems true to me.[3] Before any experimental research there must be a hypothesis based on an association of judgments from which a hypothetical conclusion has been deduced as a simple, more or less probable possibility. Empirical methods are then useful in order either to raise the conjecture up the scale of probability to certainty or to strip it of all semblance of truth. Empirical methods serve to verify the conjecture. By constructing a syllogism (and usually without realizing it), a Pasteur, a Helmholtz, a Lavoisier, who begins by "suspecting" the existence of oxygen before demonstrating it experimentally, is doing an inventive thing. Through experimentation they establish *facts* which prove the real or imaginary character of the invented hypothesis.

II

The essential deductive character of invention explains the sequence of theorems or laws successively formulated by a science, and the successive technical developments of an industry. But however deduced, these innovations were nonetheless unex-

3   Mr. Paulhan clearly saw that relations exist between invention and reasoning, but he fails to specify them and thinks perhaps that they are more superficial than they really are. With respect to Sardou's* and Zola's methods of composition, he says that "the development of invention here reminds us of the linking of terms in a syllogism. Thus we see reasoning given by Mr. Sardou as the method of invention and deduction invoked for the same purpose by Mr. Zola." And he adds that, according to Binet, for Sardou "the process of work always retains the same psychological nature, that of reasoning. Sardou employs reasoning in the construction of his plays from beginning to end." All the more reason, or apparent reason, for us to say that every industrial or mechanical invention is syllogistic.

   * [Victorien Sardou (1831–1901), playwright, known for his well (i.e., logically) constructed plays.—Ed.]

pected and unforeseen and occurred partially by chance. When one looks back over the types of locomotion from the litter to the most recent locomotives, or when one sees in a museum the paleontological series of vertebrates from the first rudiments of walking, swimming, or flight to their higher order perfection, one is struck by a double impression of logic and peculiarity; here is the mystery of living individuality—always original, though always inferred from its two parent premises.

Even in the arguments of an irreproachable logician, each new argument appears as a felicitous, but surprising, discovery. This surprise is due to the spontaneous placing of one memory on another so that even an argument which stays centered on its basic theme never develops in a straight line but follows a picturesque trail. Very rarely, however, is there only a single logic operating in a mind and even more rarely in a society, which is essentially a collective and enormously inclusive mind. These most diverse and mutually contradictory deductions advance by zigzags, crossing each other, swerving, mingling sometimes, then separating once again. Hypnotists have noted that between deep hypnosis and total awakening some of their subjects go through a *somnambulist awakening*[4] during which they remain open to suggestion and indiscriminately subscribe to contradictory suggestions superimposed on and accumulated in their minds. The same may well hold true for the reason and freedom of people plunged into an intense social environment in which they strongly and unwittingly influence one another, like the hypnotized subjects mentioned above. Even in the thirteenth century, when Catholicism had attained its relative perfection and purity, it is surprising to note the number of not just non-Christian but antichristian elements in the customs, laws and institutions. The facility with which an unorthodox idea slipped into those minds is quite remarkable. Emperor Frederick II, who was after all the right arm of the Church, was host to both bishops and emirs (and at the same time), and churchmen often did likewise. In his *Introduction to Social Science* Spencer brought to light the contradiction between the "religion of hate" and the

[4]   This is Delboeuf's term. On this subject see the *Revue Philosophique*, February 1887.

"religion of love" which have coexisted in all Christian countries since the beginning of Christianity. When social logic is itself so complex and spreads its time fighting itself with different inventions, the fray of inventors is naturally full of the most surprising ups and downs.

As an example of the highest degree of both capricious and logical deduction, one can cite the series of female fashions, generally considered the realm of pure fantasy. How are the new styles invented that are made fashionable each year by an elite and are subsequently propagated from Paris to the large cities, then to the small towns and rural areas, to all strata of society from the richest to the poorest, according to the general law of examples? Mr. du Maroussem will tell us how.[5] This author denies that the sketches in magazines constitute "scenes of inspiration" for a style (or rather a new variation of a style already popular). Because, pursuing this goal, we must satisfy the "apparently contradictory double requirement of the elegant woman: to be dressed like no one else and yet like everyone else." This is not really a contradiction but only a difficulty which consists in "discovering an original idea within the general tone of the style already prevailing." Given this goal, it is clear that the problem could have several solutions, which must be formulated or deduced and from which a choice must be made. First, the important dressmakers, tailors, and designers call in the artists. "Designers from the professional classes submit their delicate watercolors: they have taken from their frames doges' wives of the fifteenth century, legionnaires' wives of the sixteenth century, marquises and eccentrics* of the eighteenth century, in order to give an expert lesson in flirting to these women's great-granddaughters. Then the workshop heads had to create the technical work." In other words inventions do not come from the tailors and dressmakers who profit from them but from the artists who combined styles of the past with those cur-

5   *Le Vêtement à Paris*, vol. 2.
*   "*Les Merveilleuses*," which we have translated as "eccentrics," was the name bestowed upon certain women after 1794 who adopted an elegant but extravagant style of dress inspired by the costumes of ancient Greece and Rome.—Ed.

rently accepted. "Moreover, the creations multiply by imitating neighboring creations. Plagiarism between rival studios is a common custom." There is competition among projected models as they fight for the heart of the woman of fashion. This public competition takes place at certain gatherings, such as an important marriage or the Grand-Prix at Longchamps. The jury, a tribunal of the most frivolous of people, decides what it likes, and its decision is docilely accepted by the entire world.

The important role of chance in inventions has been misunderstood so often—it being incorrectly assumed that chance negates the logic of inventions[6]—that it is important to stress the point here. Chance in invention is demonstrated first of all by the lack of similar industries among the Oceanic islanders, that is, among savages having the fewest reciprocal relations and living mostly on indigenous inventions—whence the sometimes extraordinary gaps in their inventions. The Tahitians visited by Wallis in 1767 had certain industries and simple arts like sculpture and music; they knew how to make fire[7] and had recipes that the English captain deemed exquisite. But they did not know what pottery was and only had plates of bark and cups made from coconuts. Further, these people who made fire so well had no idea of hot water and were stupefied at the sight of a pot full of boiling water. They had only shells for knives, not even flints.

No matter how ingenious, any tribe left alone in isolation dis-

---

[6]   In a passage from Bacon (in which he exaggerates the fortuitous nature of inventions) we find the confusion of ideas noted above. "You would not assert that Prometheus owed the knowledge of how to light fire to his own meditations, and that when he struck a flint for the first time he expected fire to burst forth. You will certainly admit that he owed this invention to chance . . . and that we owe the discovery of plasters to the wild goat, musical modulations to the nightingale, enemas to the stork, and gunpowder to the pot cover which flies into the air; *in brief for all these discoveries we are obliged to chance and to something very different from dialectic reasoning.*"

[7]   Certain peoples, on continents and hence with more means of communicating with others, still did not have fire in the eighteenth century. Such, according to a letter written in 1730 (*Lettres Edifiantes*), were the "long eared" Indians of Guiana. These savages were still in the age of polished stones or rather the age of pebbles sharpened against one another.

covers very little (and that by chance) and does not develop very far the apparently logical consequences of its good ideas. What is discovered by one people is seldom what has been found by another on a neighboring island.[8] If, instead of being agglomerated in several large continents, the land which emerged from the sea had broken up into a myriad of small islands, separated by dangerous seas, it is highly probable that (1) civilization would not have developed anywhere in such a worldwide Micronesia, and (2) these innumerable embryos of human culture would be an incoherent motley lot. Reciprocal stimulation, reciprocal exchange of spontaneous discoveries alone enabled some of these peoples to become civilized and allowed all of them to harmonize and fuse together.

The role of impulse and chance in the direction of inventive genius will cease to amaze us if we recall that such genius almost always begins in the service of a game or is dependent on a religious idea or a superstition. Many economic institutions have a religious origin. Grant Allen[9] is not alone in thinking that the explanation of the first agricultural practices is to be found in totemism. Wherever economic evolution has just begun, we find "markets [mingled] with church celebrations, pilgrimages with merchants' trips, missions with colonization, treasures of temples with the functions of a bank, among pagans and Moslems as well as among Christians." Going back still further, the link between these two phenomena is even closer. Consequently the nature of collected inventions depends on the nature of mythological ideas, and these vary enormously from one people to another. Inventions also depend on the way people amuse themselves. Galton explains the domestication of animals as a consequence of playing with them. And as further support for the proposition, one may note with Roscher that the Indians who, according to him, did not bother to

---

[8]   The same remark is applicable to more civilized peoples which, although in fairly close proximity, do not communicate with each other. We are surprised to learn for example that the Incas had scales while the Aztecs did not.

[9]   See *Rivista di sociologia*, September-October 1899, Salvioli's article on "Gli asordi dell'agricultura."

domesticate the useful buffalo or reindeer were expert at taming parrots and monkeys, both of which were as numerous as the men in many of their huts. Galton's observation can be generalized to a large degree. Social evolution begins and ends with games and celebrations. It was in play that little by little man learned most of his types of work; development of even the most difficult and least profitable industries tends to make life happier, filling the longer leisure hours with more varied pleasures. Work is a stage to cross between the carefree idleness of primitive peoples and the lively gaiety of future civilized peoples.

If savages disliked innovation as much as is believed, they would not give each other the technical secrets discovered in each of their tribes, and observers would be struck by the dissimilarity of these secrets, the peculiarity of their juxtaposition. But fortunately the abhorence of novelty ascribed to primitive peoples is quite apocryphal. Their masses, even more than ours, easily become infatuated with things exotic and yet routine, but the elite often escapes the yoke of custom. There is always an innovator among the islanders themselves, usually a chief or an aristocrat, or else a queen like the forty-five-year-old Tahitian princess who took a fancy to Wallis. "One of her principal followers seemed to us more disposed than the rest of the Tahitians to imitate our manners," recounts the great navigator. "He soon became a friend of our servants, who named him Jonathan and dressed him in an English outfit which looked very well on him. He wanted to use a knife and fork, but when he had taken a bite, habit led his hand to his mouth and the fork went toward his ear." All the more reason for savages to imitate each other. And it is this imitation which leads to the relative similarity of their social status, a similarity that misleads travelers and some sociologists about the role of *instinct* and *necessity* in their development.

Even if it were true—which it is not—that any relatively simple invention can lead to only one other relatively complex invention, in other words, that inventions follow one another like the links of a single chain, it would still be true that these links follow one another at highly variable intervals, sometimes of a few days or months, sometimes of several centuries. This difference, due to chance, has incalculable consequences. It was certainly easier to discover that a magnet attracts iron, as was already known in antiquity, than to note that the magnet is directed toward the pole; hence it is easy to understand that the first of these discoveries came before the second, but it was not at all necessary that they be separated by more than a thousand years. Imagine what it would have been like if this interval had been much longer or shorter, and just think of the changes in the course of history. If the Romans or the Carthaginians had had a compass, they probably would have discovered America. Imagine the effect produced by that miraculous transatlantic voyage carried out under Hadrian or Severus; what an awakening for a sleeping world, what a whip lash to the sluggish activity of those times, to the spirit of conquest and enterprise, to the spread of Christianity! And since the invention in question is the greatest discovery of modern times, let us use this example to show the lasting, continually magnified effects that may originate in the unforeseen consequences of events. Could one have guessed that Ferdinand's and Isabella's capture of Grenada would have a direct and decisive influence on the discovery of the New World? Yet nothing is more obvious. In fact, just before the capture of the Moorish town Christopher Columbus had received a second humiliating refusal from the two sovereigns and was deeply discouraged. Rebuffed by his fellow Genoans, then by the king of Portugal, the king of England, and twice in succession by the Spanish monarchs, he could do nothing but resign himself to his fate. But once Grenada had been taken, there was a change in the attitudes of Ferdinand and especially Isabella. This conquest gave them an appetite for greater expansion, made them more confident and enterprising. They received the new overtures of Columbus' supporters, and a few months later his ships landed in America.

Moreover, all things being equal, once an invention becomes a possibility, it is more likely to materialize if the problem of which it is one possible solution preoccupies more people and, particularly, more enlightened people. But at least to a certain degree need is stimulated by whatever satisfies it; inventive genius is more likely to turn towards a particular area of research if, under pressure from a more general or more intense need, successful inventions have already been made in that area. If previous inventions were partially due to chance, in subsequent discoveries the part attributed to chance can only increase. In the fourteenth and fifteenth centuries we see the avidity for geographical discoveries and colonial empires arise, grow, and spread, seconded by the strengthened and popularized passion for religious proselytism, which either served the royal ambition or opposed it. This avidity was born the moment the invention of the compass (1302) made it possible for it to be satisfied. It was first revealed among princes desirous of distinguishing themselves, beginning with the kings of Portugal. John I had the west coast of Africa explored, somewhat timidly, as far as the Boyador Cape; then a shift in wind led a Portuguese vessel to discover the Island of Madeira. However small the island, it was an encouragement of the spirit of adventure, whereupon the exploration of the African coast was pushed farther and the islands of Cape Verde and the Azores were discovered. With each discovery the thirst for travel redoubled and spread, and under John II it became an obsession. Under his reign and on his orders, Bartholomew Diaz reached the Cape of Good Hope. Following the example of the Portuguese princes, the Spanish, English, and French sovereigns in turn encouraged long sea voyages. This series of successful explorations is so methodical that chance seems to play almost no role in it. But if one remembers that without the discovery of the compass, which was entirely fortuitous, the series would not have evolved, since the goal of this evolution was never prescribed, one is forced to agree that chance has the right to claim a large part in engendering this marvelous geographical progress.

And then, what one finds is so rarely what one was looking for! There is so little resemblance and proportion between the clear objective result of a given period of labor and the inner motives of its actors. So many human souls, linked end to end and exchanging their desires and hopes, their characteristic but later incomprehensible passions, are needed to bring about a great human event. From its results, who would have guessed the incomparable spirit of the great sixteenth-century Spanish colonizers? In the first place, accustomed to discovering miraculous things, strange plants and animals, unheard-of lands, these Spaniards had developed a credulity which can be measured by the following story.[10] When they heard among the islanders of Puerto-Rico that on the island of Bimini there was a Fountain of Youth which made the old young again, they were convinced of its existence, and their faith in this legend led them to conquer the whole group of islands (the Bahamas) and to comb them minutely and with great difficulty, all in search of the fabled fountain. Did not Columbus himself think he had discovered terrestrial paradise? It is absurd, but the imaginations of nearly all the Spaniards were so excited by this that Spanish audacity could be fully exploited and could conquer the world.

The exultation which took hold of this great people became one of the great forces of history. This immense torrent, now run dry, was an exultation of united passions, unique in history, whose meeting and combination will not be seen again. Present-day British imperialism—the frenzy to colonize the world in order to make everyone into good Anglicans but above all to inundate it with British merchandise—has nothing in common with the Spanish ambition, which was complex and noble in quite a different way and which was intermingled with large proportions of proselytism, thirst for adventure, greed for gold, imaginative credulity, passionate curiosity, and untempered heroism. A confluence of circumstances, a historical accident is at the origin of this transient grandeur, just as another confluence of fortunate accidents led to the more lasting grandeur of Britain.

For there are accidents which have indefinite, even eternal consequences. How can we suppose that whatever is accidental excludes the rational when at the origin of every habit is a caprice, and at the base of every natural law, in the words of John Stuart Mill, an "arbitrary classification of causes"? The air, like the sea,

10   In different terms, has not the same cause produced an analogous effect in our own time? From the prodigious inventiveness of the nineteenth century have not our own contemporaries, under the guise of skepticism, developed an equally extraordinary credulity? Witness not only the progress of spiritualism and the renaissance of mysticism, but more generally the avid collection by the enlightened classes, and even the masses, of any sort of novelty, whether remedy, legislative reform, or experiment in social dissection based on some utopian ideal.

is furrowed with invisible routes followed by birds and boats in their periodic migrations. Because they are so unvarying despite their meanderings, many of these paths have a semblance of necessity, of law based on nature. When they cross continents, migratory birds follow big river valleys such as the Rhine or the Rhone instead of going straight. Human migrations also passed through valleys, followed by the first roads, the royal routes, finally the train lines. Thus the geologic accidents which once traced the water routes and so capriciously and even, in large part, arbitrarily sketched their dividing lines, imposed as law on the voyages of animals and men the same eternal arbitrariness, the same fixed disorder. The sociologists of certain schools should think of this when they make their science into a seeking and formulating of supposed laws of evolution which subject the social transformations of all peoples, regardless of their reciprocal borrowings, to the same itinerary decided, to some extent, in advance. Even admitting that they may find some formula which is not too much in contradiction with the facts, would not the approximate regularity of these social changes be like the regularity of the voyages I was just discussing? Would such regularity not be due to simple accidents which had permanent consequences? And if this is the case, is there anything more to be seen than interesting documents to interpret and complex facts to explain by the application of true laws of the science of societies, laws which would better be sought elsewhere?

7

OPPOSITION

1898

LET US, first of all, come to a clear understanding with
regard to the different meanings of the word *opposition*. In my
work on *Universal Opposition* I proposed a definition and a classification to which I may be permitted to refer. Let us sum the matter up briefly from our present point of view. Opposition is erroneously conceived by the average thinker as the maximum degree of
difference. In reality, it is a very special kind of repetition, namely,
of two similar things that are mutually destructive by virtue of their
very similarity. In other words, opposites or contraries always constitute a couple or duality; they are not opposed to each other as
beings or groups of beings, for these are always dissimilar and, in
some respect, sui generis; nor yet as *states* of a single being or of
different beings, but rather as tendencies or *forces*. For, if we
regard certain forms or certain states, such as concave and convex,
pleasure and pain, heat and cold, as opposites, it is by reason of
the real or assumed contrariety of the forces which produce these
states. Thus we see that it is necessary to eliminate from the start,
as so many pseudo-oppositions, all the antitheses of mythology and
the philosophy of history which are based on assumed *natural* contrarieties; for example, the contrarieties between two nations, two
races, or two forms of government (such as republic and monarchy, to cite certain Hegelians in this matter); or between occident and orient, two religions (such as Christianity and Moham-
medanism), or two families of languages (such as the Semitic and

Reprinted from *Social Laws*, translated by Howard C. Warren (New York:
The Macmillan Co., 1899), pp. 85–133, with elisions.

Indo-European). These contrasts chance to be partially true, if we take into consideration the manner in which the things in question deny or affirm the same notion, and desire or reject the same end, under certain more or less ephemeral circumstances. But if the antipathy of these things for each other be regarded as essential, absolute, and innate, as many ancient philosophers seemed to believe, they are wholly chimerical.

Thus, every real opposition implies a relation between two forces, tendencies, or *directions*. But the phenomena by means of which these two forces become actualities are of two kinds— qualitative and quantitative—that is, they may be composed of either heterogeneous or homogeneous parts. A series made up of heterogeneous factors is a species of evolution that can always be *conceived of* (whether rightly or wrongly) as reversible, or capable of going back by following the same road in precisely the opposite direction. For example, if a chemist, taking a piece of wood and going through a series of operations, ends by extracting brandy from it, this does not of course imply that it would be possible to reconstruct the piece of wood by a series of inverse operations; yet if this is not a possibility, it is at least conceivable. And this was the dream of the ancient philosophers with respect to the transformations of humanity. A series made up of homogeneous factors is an evolution of a special sort, known as increase or decrease, wax or wane, rise or fall. Without entering too minutely into the facts, we must notice how, as social science develops with the advance of civilization, instances of exact and measurable oppositions of this sort continue to appear and multiply, giving us fluctuations of the stock market and statistical diagrams on which are registered in wave-like curves the rise and fall of some particular security, of some particular species of crime, of suicide, the birth-rate, marriage, or thrift as measured by the returns of the savings banks, insurance companies, etc.

The distinction just made is between oppositions of series (evolution and counter-evolution) and oppositions of degree (increase and diminution). A still more important category to be considered consists of oppositions of *sign*, or, if we prefer, *diametrical* oppositions. Although these last are often confused with the preceding in the language of mathematics, in which plus and minus symbolize increase and diminution as well as positive and negative directions, it is nevertheless true that the alternate increase and decrease of a force acting always in the same direction constitutes a very different sort of opposition from that of two forces, one of which acts from A toward B, and the other from B toward A, both along the same straight line. Similarly, the contrast between the increase and decrease of a credit balance must not be confused with the contrast between such a credit and an equal debt; and the growth or diminution of the tendency to theft or crime, in a given society, is quite a different thing from the antithesis between this tendency and the tendency to charity and philanthropy. In order to give at once a psychological explanation of these and many other social contrasts, we may observe that an increase followed by a diminution of our *affirmative* belief in a notion, whether religious or scientific, legal or political, is quite a different matter from our affirmation followed by our *rejection* of this same idea, and that an increase followed by a diminution of our desire for something, for instance our love for a woman, is quite a different matter from a desire followed by a repugnance to the same object, such as our love toward this woman and then our hatred of her. It is certainly interesting to note that each of these subjective quantities, belief and desire, possesses two opposite signs, the positive and negative, and that in this respect they admit of comparison with objective quantities, such as mechanical forces which act in opposite directions along the same straight line. Space is so constituted as to admit of an infinity of couples whose members are opposed to each other in direction, and our consciousness is so constituted as to admit of an infinity of affirmations opposed to negations, or an infinity of desires opposed to repugnances, each having precisely the same object. Except for these two unique instances, whose coincidence is remarkable, the universe would know neither war nor discord, and all the tragic side of life would be both impossible and inconceivable.

One observation is necessary, however. The oppositions of every sort—of series, degrees, or signs—may take place between terms that find expression either in one and the same being (whether molecule, organism, or *self*), or in two different beings (molecules, masses, organisms, or human consciousnesses). But we must distinguish carefully between these two cases. This is of primary importance for the sake of another distinction that is no less essential, namely, the distinction between the case where the terms are simultaneous and the case where they are successive. In the former there is a collision, strife, and then equilibrium; in the latter there is alternation and rhythm. In the former there is always destruction and loss of energy; in the latter there is neither. Now when any oppositions whatsoever, whether of series, degrees, or signs, occur in two different beings, they may be either simultaneous or successive—either strife or rhythm. But when both of their terms belong to one and the same being, body, or self, they can only be both simultaneous and successive if they are oppositions of signs. As for the oppositions of series and degrees under this hypothesis, they admit only of a succession or alternation of terms. For instance, it is impossible for the velocity of a body moving in a given direction to increase and diminish at the same time; it can only do so successively. But it may well happen that it is impelled at the same time by two distinct forces to move in two opposite directions; this is the case of equilibrium, which is often characterized by a symmetry of opposite forms, notably in the case of crystals. Similarly, it is impossible for the love of a man for a woman to increase and diminish at the same time: such a thing can only occur alternately; but it may easily occur for him to love and hate the same woman at the same time—an antinomy of the heart that finds illustration in many crimes of passion. Again, it is impossible for the religious faith of a man to increase and diminish at the same time: this can only occur successively; but it may easily happen that he has in his thoughts, at the same time, though often without being himself aware of it, a vigorous affirmation and a no less vigorous if implicit denial of certain dogmas; that he holds at once a certain Christian belief, and a certain worldly or political prejudice which is opposed to it. . . .

A discussion of each of the species of oppositions here pointed out would carry us beyond our limits. We must be satisfied with a few general reflections. First, then, if *external oppositions* exist (for so we may term the oppositions of tendencies between different beings or men), they are rendered possible by the fact that *internal oppositions* (between different tendencies within the same being or man) exist or may exist. This applies to oppositions of series and degrees as well as to oppositions of sign, but more particularly to the latter. If certain men or groups of men are developing in one direction, while other men or groups of men are developing in the contrary direction, it is because each individual man can either develop or counterdevelop in this way; as, for example, in the transition from naturalism to idealism, or from idealism to naturalism, in art, and from an aristocracy to a democracy, or *vice versa*, in government, etc. If religious faith is on the increase among certain races or classes, while among others it is on the decline, it is because the consciousness of each individual man admits of either an increase or a diminution in the intensity of religious faith. Finally, if there exist political parties and religious sects which affirm and desire what other parties and sects deny and reject, it is because the mind and heart of each individual man is capable of containing both the *yes* and the *no*, the *pro* and the *con*, with respect to any given concept or aim.

Nevertheless, I am far from wishing to identify *external* with *internal* contests. In one sense they are incompatible; for it is only when the internal struggle is ended, when the individual, after having been pulled hither and thither by contrary influences, has made his choice, and adopted a certain opinion or resolution rather than some other—it is only when he has made peace with himself—that war between himself and those who have made the opposite choice becomes possible. Nor is this of itself sufficient to bring about such a war. The individual must *know*, in addition, that the others have chosen the opposite of what he has himself chosen. Without this, any external opposition of contraries, whether simultaneous or successive, would be practically non-existent, for it would present none of those characteristics that render an external struggle really effective. To bring about religious war or strife, it is essential for every adherent of one faith to know that the adherents of some other faith deny exactly what he affirms; and this negation must be placed side by side in his consciousness with his own affirmation, not as though adopted imitatively, but rather as being definitely rejected by him, and hence redoubling the intensity of his own belief. To bring about industrial competition, as, for instance, among the bidders at the sale of a house, each one must know that his desire to possess the building is opposed by his competitors, who wish him not to get it; and he will desire all the more to get possession of it if he knows that the rest do not wish him to do so. Without this, mere competition would be fruitless, and political economists have erred here in not clearly distinguishing the special case where there exists, in the minds of the competitors, no knowledge at all of the competition, from the varying measure of that knowledge, as shown in the infinite number of degrees that separate complete understanding from complete ignorance of the fact.

This was my ground for saying, as I did further back, that the fundamental social opposition must be sought, not, as one might be tempted to think, at first sight, in the relation of two contrary or contradictory individuals, but rather in those logical and teleological duals, those curious combats between thesis and antithesis, between willing and *nilling*, whose stage is the consciousness of the social individual. Of course the question may be asked: If this be true, how does this social opposition differ from any purely psychological opposition? To this I reply: It differs in cause, and still more in effect.

First, as to its cause. When a solitary individual receives from his senses two apparently contradictory impressions, he hesitates between two sense judgments, one of which says that that spot down there is a lake, while the other denies it. Here is an internal opposition of purely psychological origin, a thing which occurs but seldom, however. Indeed, we may assert without fear of error that every doubt or hesitation experienced by even the most isolated man belonging to the most savage of tribes is due to an encounter within himself, either of two rays of instances which come together and interfere in his brain, or else of a single ray of instances which runs athwart of some sense perception. In writing, I often hesitate between two synonymous phrases, each of which appears preferable to the other under the given circumstances; here it is two rays of imitation that interfere within me—I refer to the two human series which, beginning with the first inventor of each of these phrases, have reached on down to myself. For, each of these phrases I learned from some individual, who learned it from some other, and so on up to the first one who uttered it. (This, let me say again, is what I mean by a *ray of imitation*, or imitative ray; and the sum total of rays of this kind derived from any single inventor, originator, or innovator, whose pattern is reproduced, is what I call an *imitative radiation*. Our social life includes a thick network of radiations of this sort, with countless mutual interferences.) ...

But let us face the question in a still more general way. When an individual becomes aware of a contradiction existing between one of his conclusions, aims, notions, or habits—such as a dogma, turn of phraseology, commercial procedure, species of arm or tool, etc.—and the conclusion, aim, notion, or habit of some other man or men, one of three things happens. On the one hand, he may allow himself to be completely influenced by the other, and abruptly abandon his own mode of thinking or acting; in this case there is no internal strife, the victory occurs without a struggle, and presents one of the many instances of imitation which make up the social life. On the other hand, our individual may only half submit to the other's influence; this is the case we were considering above, and the shock is here followed by a diminution of its force, so that it becomes more or less weakened and paralyzed. Or, finally, he may actively oppose the strange action or habit—the belief or volition with which he has come in contact—and assert or desire all the more strenuously what he asserted and desired before. Yet, even in this last case, where he rouses all the strength of his conviction or passion to repel another's example, he experiences a certain unrest, an internal strife—though of another sort, it is true, and as inspiring as the former was enervating. This unrest, also, for the very reason that it results from an over-excitement and not a paralysis of one's individual force, is likely to spread contagiously; and this is what causes the splitting up of a society into parties. A new party always consists of a group of persons who, one after another and copying one another, have adopted a notion or course contrary to that which had hitherto reigned in their midst, and with which they themselves had been imbued. On the other hand, this new dogmatism, becoming more intense and intolerant as it spreads, raises against itself a coalition of those who, remaining faithful to tradition, have made exactly the opposite choice, and thus two fanatical parties find themselves face to face.

So we see that, whether in a violent, dogmatic form, or in a weaker, sceptical one, the juxtaposition of two opposite terms is social in character, provided it spreads by imitation. . . .

One may ask himself in this connection, as I asked long ago, in one of my first articles, which is worse for a society: to be divided into parties and sects fighting over opposing programmes and dogmas, and into nations continually warring with one another, or to be composed of individuals at peace with one another, but each individually striving within himself, a prey to scepticism, irresolution, and discouragement? . . . Were it true that we must choose between these two solutions, it must be admitted that the social problem would be exceedingly difficult to settle. . . .

Fortunately, the truth is not so sad and discouraging as they make out. Observation proves that every condition of strife, whether external or internal, always aims at, and ends by passing into, a decisive victory or a treaty of peace. As far as internal strife is concerned, whether we call it doubt, irresolution, anguish, or despair, one thing, at least, is evident: this sort of struggle always appears as an exceptional and transient crisis, and no one should take it upon himself to consider it the normal state of affairs or to judge it preferable (with all its painful agitations) to the so-called effeminate peace involving regular work under the guidance of a decided will and a securely formed judgment. And as regards external strife, the struggle among men, can it be otherwise? If history be correctly interpreted, it shows that war is forever developing in one particular direction, and that this course, repeated hundreds of times and easy to disentangle among the thickets and undergrowth of history, seems to indicate its ultimate disappearance, after it has gradually become rarer. In fact, as a result of that imitative radiation, which labors constantly and, so to speak, clandestinely to enlarge the special field of social phenomena, all the latter are in process of enlargement, and war is participating in the movement. From a countless number of very small but exceedingly bitter wars between petty clans, we pass to a smaller number of somewhat larger and less rancorous wars: first between small cities, then between large cities, then between nations that are

continually growing greater, till finally we arrive at an era of very
infrequent but most impressive conflicts, quite devoid of hatred,
between colossal nations, whose very greatness makes them inclined to peace. . . .

. . . But this extension cannot go on indefinitely; this flitting
mirage cannot forever torment our view, since the globe has
limits and we have long since encircled it. What characterizes
especially our own epoch and differentiates it widely, in a sense,
from the entire past, although the laws of history apply to it no
less nor more than to its predecessors, is this: that now, for the first
time in history, the international polity of the great states of civilization embraces within its purview, not merely a single continent,
or two at most, but the whole globe, so that the last stage of the
evolution of war is at length discovering itself, in a vista so dazz-
ling that we can scarcely believe our eyes; the end of this vista is
certainly difficult to attain, but it is a real end, and no deception
this time, and it can no longer move away as we approach it. . . .

. . . There are other forms of strife besides war, notably competition. But what has just been said applies also to competition,
which is a social opposition of the economic instead of the political
type. Like war, competition proceeds from the small to the great,
and from very numerous instances of the very small to very infrequent instances of the very great. . . . It begins with countless
rivalries among petty merchants who contend over miniature markets, originally side by side, yet almost without communication.
But as the latter, breaking down their barriers, pass over into
greater but less numerous markets, the petty rival shops also con-
solidate, either voluntarily or perforce, into greater but less numerous factories, in which the work of production, hitherto a prey to
its own jealous opposition, is now harmoniously coordinated; and
the rivalry of these factories reproduces, on a larger scale, the
former rivalry of the shops, until, with the gradual expansion of
the markets, which tend to become a single market, we arrive at
a stage where there remain merely a few giants of industry and
commerce, which are still rivals, unless, indeed, they also have
come to some understanding. . . .

. . . Competition, then, tends either to monopoly (at least a
partial and relative one) or to the association of competitors, just

as war leads to a crushing of the vanquished, or to the conclusion of a fair treaty with him—in either case, to at least a partial and relative pacification. . . .

A third great form of social strife is *discussion*. This is doubtless implied in the preceding; but, if war and competition are discussions, one is a discussion in deeds of blood, the other a discussion in deeds of ruin. Let us say a word now with regard to verbal discussion, pure and simple. This, too, when it develops—for there are any number of little private discussions which, fortunately, do not develop, but die on the spot—develops in the way just described, though here the process is far less obvious. It is only after the mental discussion between contradictory ideas within the same mind has ended (this should not be forgotten), that any verbal discussion is possible between two men who have solved the question differently. Similarly, if verbal, written, or printed discussions between groups of men, and groups that are ever widening, takes the place of verbal discussion between two men, it is because the more limited discussion has been brought to an end by some relative and temporary agreement, or some sort of unanimity. These groups are first split up into an endless multitude of little coteries, clans, churches, forums, and schools, which combat one another; but at length, after many polemics, they are welded into a very small number of great parties, religions, parliamentary groups, schools of philosophy, and schools of art, which engage one another in mortal combat. . . .

To sum up. The strife of opposition in human society, in its three principal forms—war, competition, and discussion—proves obedient to one and the same law of development, through ever widening areas of temporary pacification, alternating with renewals of discord more centrally organized and on a larger scale, and leading up to a final, at least partial, agreement. It would appear from this—and we have many other reasons for the conclusion—that the strife of opposition fulfils the role of a middle term in the social, as it does in the organic and inorganic, worlds, and that it is destined gradually to fade away, exhaust itself, and disappear, as a result of its own growth, which is merely a progress toward its own destruction. . . .

III. The Laws of Imitation

8

LOGICAL LAWS OF IMITATION

1888

OUR PROBLEM is to learn why, given one hundred different innovations conceived of at the same time—innovations in the forms of words, in mythological ideas, in industrial processes, etc. —ten will spread abroad, while ninety will be forgotten. In order to solve this question systematically let us first divide those influences which have favored or hindered the diffusion of successful or non-successful innovations into physical and social causes. But in this book let us pass over the first order of causes, those, for example, which make the people of southern countries prefer new words composed of voiced to those composed of whispered vowels, and the people of northern countries, the opposite. In the same way there are in mythology, in artistic or industrial technique, or in government, many peculiarities which result from a racial conformation of ear or larynx, from cerebral predispositions, from meteoric conditions or from the nature of fauna and flora. Let us put all this to one side. I do not mean that it has no real importance in sociology. It is of interest, for example, to note the influence which may be exerted upon the entire course of a civilisation by the nature of a new and spontaneous production of its soil. Much depends upon the spot in which it springs; the conditions of labour, and, consequently, the family groups and political institutions of a fertile valley are different from those of a moor more or less rich in pasture-land. We must thank those scholars who devote themselves to researches of this character, researches which are as useful

Reprinted from *The Laws of Imitation*, translated by Elsie C. Parsons (New York: Henry Holt, 1903), pp. 140–85, with elisions.

178   THE LAWS OF IMITATION

in sociology as studies upon the modification of species by the action of climate or general environment are in biology. It would be erroneous to think, however, that because we had shown the adaptation of living or social types to external phenomena we had thereby explained them. The explanation must be sought for in the laws which express the internal relations of cells or of minds in association. This is the reason why, in this discussion of pure and abstract, not of concrete and applied, sociology, I must set aside all considerations of the above nature. . . .

Invention and imitation are, as we know, the elementary social acts. But what is the social substance or force through which this act is accomplished and of which it is merely the form? In other words, what is invented or imitated? The *thing* which is invented, the *thing* which is imitated, is always an idea or a volition, a judgment or a purpose, which embodies a certain amount of *belief* and *desire*. And here we have, in fact, the very soul of words, of religious prayers, of state administration, of the articles of a code, of moral duties, of industrial achievements or of artistic processes. Desire and belief: they are the substance and the force, they are the two psychological quantities which are found at the bottom of all the *sensational* qualities with which they combine; and when invention and then imitation takes possession of them in order to organise and use them, they also are the real social quantities. Societies are organised according to the agreement or opposition of beliefs which reinforce or limit one another. Social institutions depend entirely upon these conditions. Societies function according to the competition or co-operation of their desires or wants. Beliefs, principally religious and moral beliefs, but juristic and political beliefs as well, and even linguistic beliefs (for how many acts of faith are implied in the lightest talk and what an irresistible although unconscious power of persuasion our mother tongue, a true mother indeed, exerts over us), are the plastic forces of societies. Economic or aesthetic wants are their functional forces. . . .

Now, how is progress effected? When an individual reflects upon a given subject first one idea comes to him and then another until from idea to idea, from elimination to elimination, he finally seizes upon the guiding thread to the solution of the problem and then, from that moment, passes quickly out from the twilight into the light. Does not the same thing happen in history? When a society elaborates some great conception, which the curious public pushes forward before science can correct and develop it, the mechanical explanation of the world, for example, or when it dreams in its ambition of some great achievement like the use of steam in manufacture or locomotion or navigation before it can turn its activity to exploiting it, what happens? The problem that is raised in this way at once prompts people to make and entertain all kinds of contradictory inventions and vagaries which appear first here and then there, only to disappear, until the advent of some clear formula or some suitable mechanism which throws all the others into the background and which serves thenceforward as the fixed basis for future improvements and developments. *Progress*, then, is a kind of collective thinking, which lacks a brain of its own, but which is made possible, thanks to imitation, by the solidarity of the brains of numerous scholars and inventors who interchange their successive discoveries. (The fixation of discoveries through writing, which makes possible their transmission over long stretches of time and space, is equivalent to the fixation of images which takes place in the individual brain and which constitutes the cellular stereotype-plate of memory.)

It follows that social like individual progress is effected in two ways, through substitution and through accumulation. Certain discoveries and inventions can only be used as substitutes, others can be accumulated. Hence we have logical *combats* and logical *alliances*. This is the general classification which we will adopt, and in it we shall have no difficulty in placing all historical events.

Moreover, in different societies discord between fresh desires and old, between a new scientific idea and existing religious dogmas, is not always immediately perceived nor perceived within the same period of time. Besides, when the discord is perceived, the desire to put an end to it is not always equally strong. The nature and intensity of the desire vary with time and place. In fact, *Reason* exists in societies as well as in individuals; and *Reason* in all cases is merely a desire like any other, a specific desire which like others is more or less developed by its own satisfactions as well as created by the very inventions or discoveries which have satisfied it; that is to say that systems, programmes, catechisms, and constitutions, in undertaking to render ideas and volitions coherent create and stimulate the very desire for their coherence. . . .

Everything, *even the desire to invent*, has the same origin. In fact, this desire completes and is part of the logical need for unification, if it is true, as I might prove, that logic is both a problem of a maximum and a problem of equilibrium. The more a people invent and discover, the more inventive and the more eager for new discoveries they grow. It is also through imitation that this noble kind of craving takes possession of those minds that are worthy of it. Now, discoveries are gains in certitude, inventions, in confidence and security. The desire to discover and invent is, consequently, the twofold form which the tendency toward achieving a maximum of public faith takes on. This creative tendency which is peculiar to synthesising and assimilating minds often alternates, is sometimes concomitant, but in all cases always agrees with the critical tendency towards an equilibrium of beliefs through the elimination of those inventions or discoveries which are contrary to the majority of their number. The desire for unanimity of faith and the desire for purification of faith is each in turn more fully satisfied, but in general their ebullitions either coincide with, or follow closely upon each other. For just because imitation is their common source, both of them, the desire for stable as well as that for absolute faith, have a degree of intensity proportionate, other things being equal, to the degree of animation in the social life, that is, to the multiplicity of relations between individuals. Any fine combination of ideas must first shine out in the mind of the individual before it can illumine the mind of a nation; and its chance of being produced in the individual mind depends upon the frequency of the intellectual exchanges between minds. A contradiction between two institutions or two principles will not harass a society until it has been noted by some exceptionally sagacious person, some systematic thinker, who, having been checked in his conscious efforts to unify his own group of ideas, points out the aforesaid difficulty.—This explains the social importance of philosophers.—And the greater the amount of mutual intellectual stimulation and, consequently, the greater the circulation of ideas within a nation, the more readily will such a difficulty be perceived.

In the course of the nineteenth century, for example, the relations of man to man having been multiplied beyond all expectation as a result of inventions in locomotion, and the action of imitation having become very powerful, very rapid, and very far-reaching, we should not be surprised to see that the passion for social reforms, for systematic and rational social reorganisations has taken on its present proportions, just as, by virtue of its previous conquests, the passion for social, especially industrial, conquests over nature has known no bounds. Therefore it is safe to predict that a century of adjustment will follow upon the past century of discovery. (Does not the nineteenth century deserve this name?) Civilisation requires that an afflux of discovery and an effort to harmonise discoveries shall coincide with or follow one another.

On the other hand, when societies are in their uninventive phases they are also uncritical, and *vice versa*. They embrace the most contradictory beliefs of surrounding fashions or inherited traditions; and no one notes the contradictions. And yet, at the same time, they carry within themselves, as a result of the contributions of fashion and tradition, much scattered thought and knowledge which would reveal from a certain angle a fruitful although unsuspected self-consistency. In the same way they borrow out of curiosity from their different neighbours, or cherish out of piety as a heritage from their different forefathers, the most dissimilar arts and industries, which develop in them ill-assorted needs and opposing currents of activity. Nor are these *practical antinomies*, any more than the aforesaid theoretical contradictions, felt or formulated by anybody, although everybody suffers from the unrest which they provoke. But at the same time neither do such primitive peoples perceive that certain of their artistic processes and mechanical tools are fitted to be of the greatest mutual service and to work powerfully together for the same end, the one serving as the efficient means of the other, just as certain perceptions serve as intermediaries in explaining certain hypotheses which they confirm. . . .

I have now pointed out how the social need for logic, through which alone a social logic is formed, arises and develops. It is at present necessary to see how it sets about to obtain satisfaction. We already know that its two tendencies are distinguishable, the one creative, the other critical, the one abounding in combinations of old *accumulable* inventions and discoveries, the other in struggles between *alternative* inventions or discoveries. We shall study each of these tendencies separately, beginning with the latter.

Suppose that a discovery, an invention, has appeared. There are straightway two facts for us to note about it: its gains in faith, as it spreads from one person to another, and the losses in faith to which it subjects the invention which had the same object or satisfied the same desire when it intervened. Such an encounter gives rise to a logical duel. . . .

Studied in detail, then, the history of societies, like psychological evolution, is a series or a simultaneous occurrence of logical duels (when it is not one of logical unions). What happened in the case of writing had already happened in that of language. Linguistic progress is effected first by imitation and then by rivalry between two languages or dialects which quarrel over the same country and one of which is crowded back by the other, or between two terms or idioms which correspond to the same idea. This struggle is a conflict between opposite theses implicit in every word or idiom which tends to substitute itself for another word or grammatical form. . . .

The conclusion of society's logical duel occurs in three different ways. (1) It quite often happens that one of the two adversaries is suppressed merely by the natural prolongation of the other's progress. For example, the Phœnician writing had only to continue to spread to annihilate the cuneiform. The petroleum lamp had only to be known to cause the brazier of nut oil, a slight modification of the Roman lamp, to fail into disuse in the shanties of Southern France. Sometimes, however, a moment arrives when the progress of even the favoured rival is checked by some increasing difficulty in dislodging the enemy beyond a certain point. Then, (2) if the need of settling the contradiction is felt strongly enough, arms are restored to, and victory results in the violent suppression of one of the two duellists. Here may be easily classed the case in which an authoritative, although non-military, force intervenes, as happened in the vote of the Council of Nicaea in favor of the Athanasian creed, or in the conversion of Constantine to Christianity, or as happens in any important decision following upon the deliberations of a dictator or assembly. In this case, the vote or decree, like the victory in the other case, is a new external condition which favors one of the two rival theses or volitions at the expense of the other and disturbs the natural play of spreading and competing imitations somewhat as a sudden climatic change resulting from a geological accident in a given locality disturbs the propagation of life by preventing the multiplication of some naturally fertile animal or vegetal species and by facilitating that of others which otherwise had been less prolific. Finally, (3) the antagonists are often seen to be reconciled, or one of them is seen to be wisely and voluntarily expelled through the intervention of some new discovery or invention. . . .

Now that we have discussed the inventions and discoveries which fight and replace each other, I have to deal with those which aid and add to each other. It must not be inferred from the order I have followed that progress through substitution originally preceded progress through accumulation. In reality, the latter necessarily preceded, just as it plainly follows, the former. The latter is both the alpha and the omega; the former is but a middle term. . . .

But we should not overlook the fact that the kind of accumulation which precedes substitution by means of logical duels is different from that which follows it. The first kind consists of a weak aggregation of elements whose principal bond lies *in not contradicting one another*; the second, in a vigorous group of elements which not only do not contradict one another, but, for the most part, *confirm one another*. And this should be so, because of the continually growing need of strong and comprehensive belief. From what has preceded we can already see the truth of this remark; it will presently become still more apparent. I will show that along all lines there are two distinct kinds of inventions or discoveries, those that are capable of indefinite accumulation (although they may also be replaced) and those that, after a certain degree of accumulation has been reached, must, if progress is to continue, be replaced. Now, the distribution of both kinds takes place quite naturally in the course of progress. The first both precede and follow the second, but in the latter instance, after the exhaustion of the second, they present a systematic character which they previously lacked. . . .

We have seen that social progress is accomplished through a series of substitutions and accumulations. It is certainly necessary to distinguish between these two processes; and yet evolutionists have made the mistake, here as elsewhere, of merging them together. Perhaps the term evolution is badly chosen. We may call it social evolution, however, when an invention quietly spreads through imitation—the elementary fact in society; or even when a new invention that has already been imitated grafts itself upon a prior one which it fosters and completes. And yet why should we not use, in this second instance, the more precise term of *insertion?* A philosophy of universal Insertion would be a happy contribution to the correction of the theory of universal Evolution. Finally, when a new invention, an invisible microbe at first, later on a fatal disease, brings with it a germ which will eventually destroy the old invention to which it attaches itself, how can the latter be said to evolve? Did the Roman Empire evolve when Christianity inoculated it with the virus of radical negations of its fundamental principles? No, this was counter-evolution, revolution perhaps, but certainly not evolution. At bottom, of course, in this case as in the preceding, there is nothing, elementarily, but evolution, because everything is imitation; but, since these evolutions and imitations struggle against each other, it is a great mistake to consider the sum formed by these conflicting elements as *a single* evolution. . . .

9

EXTRA-LOGICAL LAWS
OF IMITATION

1888

IMITATION, then, contrary to what we might infer from certain appearances, *proceeds from the inner to the outer man.* It seems at first sight as if a people or a class began to imitate another by copying its luxury and its fine arts before it became possessed of its tastes and literature, of its aims and ideas, in a word, of its spirit. Precisely the contrary, however, occurs. In the sixteenth century fashions in dress came into France from Spain. This was because Spanish literature had already been imposed upon us at the time of Spain's pre-eminence. In the seventeenth century, when the preponderance of France was established, French literature ruled over Europe, and subsequently French arts and French fashions made the tour of the world. When Italy, overcome and downtrodden as she was, invaded us in the fifteenth century, with her arts and fashions, but, first of all, with her marvelous poetry, it was because the prestige of her higher civilisation and of the Roman Empire that she had unearthed and transfigured had subjugated her conquerors. Besides, the consciences of Frenchmen were Italianised long before their houses or dress or furniture through their habit of submission to the transalpine Papacy.

Did these very Italians who fell to aping their own Greco-Roman restorations begin by reflecting the externals of the ancient world, its statues, its frescoes, its Ciceronian periods, in order to become gradually filled by its spirit? On the contrary, it was to

Reprinted from *The Laws of Imitation*, translated by Elsie C. Parsons (New York: Henry Holt, 1903), pp. 189–254, with elisions.

their hearts that their transplendent model made its first appeal. This neo-paganism was the conversion of a whole community, first its scholars and then its artists (this order is irreversible), to a dead religion; and whenever a new religion, it matters not whether it be living or dead, that is made fascinating by some compelling apostle, takes hold of a man, it is first believed in and then prac- tised. . . .

The invention of language wonderfully facilitated, but did not originate, the inoculation of ideas and desires of one mind by an- other and consequently the progress of imitation *ab interioribus ad exteriora.* For had not this progress already existed, the birth of language would be inconceivable. It is not difficult to under- stand how the first inventor of speech set to associating in his own mind a given thought and a given sound (perfected by gesture), but it is difficult to understand how he was able to *suggest* this relation to another by merely making him hear the given sound. If the listener merely repeated this sound like a parrot, without attaching to it the required meaning, it is impossible to see how this superficial and mechanical *re-echoing* could have led him to under- stand the meaning of the strange speaker or carried him over from the *sound* to the *word*. It must then be admitted that the sense was transmitted with the sound, that it reflected the sound. And whoever is acquainted with the feats of hypnotism with the miracles of suggestion, that have been popularised to so great an extent of late, should certainly not be reluctant to admit this postulate. . . .

This progress from *within* to *without*, if we try to express it more precisely, means two things: (1) That imitation of ideas precedes the imitation of their expression. (2) That imitation of ends precedes imitation of means. Ends or ideas are the *inner things*, means or expressions, the outer. Of course, we are led to copy from others everything which seems to us a new means for attaining our old ends, or satisfying our old wants, or a new expres- sion for our old ideas; and we do this *at the same time* that we begin to adopt innovations which awaken new ideas and new ends in us. Only these new ends, these needs for novel kinds of consump- tion, take hold of us and propagate themselves in us much more readily and rapidly than the aforesaid means or expressions.[1]

A nation which is becoming civilised and whose wants are multiplying consumes much more than it is able or than it desires to produce. That amounts to saying, in the language of æsthetics, that the diffusion of sentiments anticipates that of talents. Sentiments are habits of judgment and desire which have become very alert and almost unconscious through repetition. Talents are habits of activity which have also gained a mechanical facility by repetition. Both sentiments and talents, then, are habits; the only difference between them is that the former are subjective, and the latter, objective facts. Now, is it not true that æsthetic sentiments form and spread long before the talents which are fitted to satisfy them? And have we not a proof of this in the commonplace observation that the virtuosity of periods of decadence survives the exhaustion of their inspiration? . . .

In the second place, even when the action of logical laws does not intervene, it is not only the superior who causes himself to be copied by the inferior, the patrician by the plebeian, the nobleman by the commoner, the cleric by the layman, and, at a later period, the Parisian by the provincial, the townsman by the peasant, etc., it is also the inferior who, in a certain measure, much less, to be sure, is copied, or is likely to be copied, by the superior. When two men are together for a long time, whatever may be their difference in station, they end by imitating each other reciprocally, although, of the two, the one imitates much the more, the other much the less. The colder body imparts its heat to the warmer. The haughtiest country gentleman cannot keep his accent, his manners, and his point of view from being a little like those of his servants

[1]   I do not mean to deny that the outside of the model is sometimes imitated to the exclusion of the inside. But when we begin in this way, as women and children often do (less often, however, than one might think), with outward imitation, we stop short there; whereas, if we begin with inward imitation, we pass on from it to the other. Dostoevsky tells us that after some years of prison life he became like his fellow convicts superficially. "Their habits, their ideas, their dress, left their colour upon me and became mine on the surface, without penetrating at all into my inner nature."

and tenants. For the same reason many provincialisms and countri-
fied expressions creep into the language of cities, and even capitals,
and slang phrases penetrate at times into drawing rooms. This influence from the bottom to the top of a scale characterises all
classes of facts. Nevertheless, on the whole, it is the generous radiation of the warm body towards the cold, not the insignificant
radiation of the cold body towards the warm, that is the main fact
in physics and the one which explains the final tendency of the universe towards an everlasting equilibrium of temperature. Similarly,
in sociology, the radiation of examples from above to below is the
only fact worth consideration because of the general levelling which
it tends to produce in the human world.

10

PROCESSES OF IMITATION

1890

After having studied the principal laws of imitation we have still to make their general meaning clear, to complete them by certain observations, and to point out several important consequences which proceed from them.

The supreme law of imitation seems to be its tendency towards indefinite progression. This immanent and immense kind of ambition is the soul of the universe. It expresses itself, physically, in the conquest of space by light, vitally, in the claim of even the humblest species to cover the entire globe with its kind. It seems to impel every discovery or innovation, however futile, including the most insignificant individual innovations, to scatter itself through the whole of the indefinitely broadened social field. But unless this tendency be backed up by the coming together of inventions which are logically and teleologically auxiliary, or by the help of the prestige which belongs to alleged superiorities, it is checked by the different obstacles which it has successively to overcome or to turn aside. These obstacles are the logical and teleogical contradictions which are opposed to it by other inventions, or the barriers which have been raised up by a thousand causes, by racial pride and prejudice, for the most part, between different families and tribes and peoples and, within each people or tribe, between different classes. Consequently, if a good idea is introduced in one of these groups, it propagates itself without any difficulty until it finds itself stopped short by the group's frontiers. Fortunately, this arrest is only a

Reprinted from *The Laws of Imitation*, translated by Elsie C. Parsons (New York: Henry Holt, 1903), pp. 366–93, with elisions.

slowing up. It is true that, at first, in the case of class barriers, a happy innovation which has happened to originate and make its way in a lower class, does not, during periods of hereditary aristocracy and of physiological inequality, so to speak, spread further, unless the advantage of adopting it appear plain to the higher classes; but, on the other hand, innovations which have been made or accepted by the latter classes easily reach down, as I have shown already, to those lower levels which are accustomed to feel their prestige. And it happens that, as a result of this prolonged descent, the lower strata gradually mount up, step by step, to swell the highest ranks with their successive increments. Thus, through assimilating themselves with their models, the copies come to equal them, that is, they become capable of becoming models in their turn, while assuming a superiority which is no longer hereditary, which is no longer centred in the whole person, but which is individual and vicarious. The march of imitation from top to bottom still goes on, but the inequality which it implies has changed in character. Instead of an aristocratic, intrinsically organic inequality, we have a democratic inequality, of an entirely social origin, which we may call inequality if we wish, but which is really a reciprocity of invariably impersonal prestiges, alternating from individual to individual and from profession to profession. In this way, the field of imitation has been constantly growing and freeing itself from heredity. . . .

Here then we have the laws of the preceding chapters in focus from the same point of view. Through them, the tendency of imitation, set free from generation, towards geometric progression, expresses and fulfils itself more and more. Every act of imitation, therefore, results in the preparation of conditions that will make possible and that will facilitate new acts of imitation of an increasingly free and rational and, at the same time, precise and definite character. These conditions are the gradual suppression of caste, class, and nationality barriers and, I may add, the lessening of distances through more rapid means of locomotion, as well as through greater density of population. This last condition is realised in the degree that fruitful, that is to say, widely imitated, agricultural or industrial inventions, and the equally fruitful discovery of new lands promote the world-wide circulation of the most inventive and, at the same time, the most imitative races. Let us suppose that all these conditions are combined and that they are fulfilled in the highest degree. Then, wherever a happy initiative might show itself in the whole mass of humanity, its transmission by imitation would be almost instantaneous, like the propagation of a wave in a perfectly elastic medium. We are approaching this strange ideal. Already, in certain special phases, where the most essential of the conditions which I have indicated happen to be combined, social life reveals the reality of the aforesaid tendency. We see it, for example, in the world of scholars, who, although they are widely scattered, are in constant touch with one another through multiple international communications. We see it, too, in the perpetual and universal contact of merchants. Haeckel said in an address delivered in 1882 on the success of Darwin's theories: "The prodigious influence which the decisive victory of the revolutionary idea exercises over all the sciences, an influence which *grows in geometric progression* year by year, opens out to us the most consoling perspectives." In fact, the success of Darwin and Spencer has been amazingly swift.

IV. Personality and Attitude
Measurement

11

BELIEF AND DESIRE

1880

AMONG THE many continuous dimensions that the soul
seems to present us with—degrees of heat or cold, more or less
vivid bursts of color, increasingly or decreasingly vivid pains and
pleasures, and so forth—it would be scientifically desirable to isolate one or two real quantities which, while everywhere mixed with
the qualitative elements of sensations, would lend themselves in
theory or in practice to measurement.[1] Even if measurable only
theoretically but not in practice, the demonstration of their basic
albeit latent measurability would still be worthwhile. If these
quantities appeared, it would be natural to conjecture that they
are characteristic of the subject and there would be reason to in-

From *Essais et mélanges sociologiques* (Paris: Maloine, 1895), pp. 253–
40, 264–75.

[1]   This study, which appeared in August and September 1880 in Mr.
Ribot's *Revue*, was my first philosophical publication. If I bring it to light
after such a lapse of time, it is not because I am blind to its being old or
out of date here and there; but even this is instructive, as an indication of
the changes which have taken place in contemporary thinking. Furthermore,
the problems, social more than psychological, to which this essay is addressed have not lost any of their importance, and indeed the socialist
preoccupations of the present day render them even sharper, more disquieting, more arduous in nature. As for the solution that these problems receive
here, it still seems to me essentially correct, and the application which I
made of it in my later work to various aspects of social life seems to confirm it adequately. Is this an illusion? The reader may judge. I reprint
these pages without any textual change even though in several places I am
now inclined to put question marks where I formerly made resolute asser-
tions. [Tarde added this footnote in 1895.—Ed.]

quire whether they reveal through other characteristics their distinct, fundamental, and irreducible nature.

But do these psychological quantities exist? This question cannot be approached before something has been said about the forceful and profound, though not always successful, researchers who developed psychophysics. Despite their laudable intention of quantifying the soul, the psychophysicists seem to me to ignore precisely the only two internal dimensions whose continuous variations and homogeneous degrees naturally suggest the use of calculation even though they cannot be measured by physical instruments: namely, belief and desire, and their reciprocal combinations, judgment and will.

What these bold scholars claim to calculate are the degrees of sensation: the Fechner law is well known along with other equally ingenious formulas whose almost total inaccuracy has been demonstrated. When by chance these attempts at subjective measurement are reasonably successful and become generally accepted, it is in cases where they are applied either to sensations considered agreeable or painful—those which arouse more or less desire or aversion —or to sensations considered more or less intense—those which arouse more or less attention.

For the first case we have La Place's remark on the parallel and unequally rapid increases in the wealth of a man and the happiness it procures for him. For the second case we are told how great must be the difference in vibration of two notes for us to perceive the difference in the corresponding aural sensations. Or we are told that a sensitive dispatch is transmitted by our nerves' telegraphic system with a speed that varies according to whether the brain *does* or *does not expect* this transmission, or whether its attention is occupied by some other sensation. Summarizing the work of numerous experimenters Mr. Ribot says, "We come to the general conclusion that the reproduction of states of consciousness, like their immediate perception, depends on the level of attention."[2] When a bell is struck beside us, a certain time passes before we perceive the sound. If at the same time as the bell is struck an electric spark is given off, the two sensations reach us together,

[2]   See the *Revue Philosophique*, March 1876.

with a noticeable delay. It seems quite probable and almost certain that this delay is due to the disturbance of attention, which, essential to the very existence of sensations, has two tasks to fulfill. Other experiments leave no doubt on this point. Thus, without attention, no sensation; and everything in sensation which is susceptible of increase or decrease (such as length, intensity, and particularly the clarity of visual sensations) can and must be attributed to attention unless it is attributed to desire.

Just what is attention? One reply might be that it is an effort to specify an nascent sensation. But one must be aware that, once all accompanying muscular action is eliminated, the purely psychological aspect of effort is desire, and that which is commonly called a sensation is always, if not a simple cluster of instinctive judgments as Wundt tries to show, at least a mixture of a weak sensitive element and a tangle of extremely rapid judgments and even conclusions. The horse that we say we see in the distance and judge to exist, actually, we *infer* its reality even without looking at it, as painters know very well. Our "seeing" the horse is a result of our instinctively assigning to a retinal impression, the possibility, the conditional certainty of the tactile, olfactory, and aural sensations that we connect with the horse. It is a judgment of localizing, a judgment of simultaneous coexistence with other impressions, a classificatory judgment which enables us to anticipate vaguely what will follow or makes us reflect on what has just preceded our impression. As the sensation supposedly becomes clearer, these judgments multiply and become the object of a firmer belief.

If, then, attention is the desire to specify the incipient sensation, this amounts to saying that it is the desire for an increase of present belief. Consequently, by showing the important role of attention, psychophysics has proved the great interest attached to the study of the two distinct elements of this complex quantity as well as the necessity to break it down into them. Almost the same definition could be applied to the source of hypotheses, the question, because the attentive mind is essentially inquisitive. A similar analysis can explain this singular faculty of saying *if*, which, no less than the faculty of saying *yes* or *no*, contributes to the formation of all our ideas (since all scientific laws are only verified hypotheses encompassing basically the vast array of facts adjudged possible). Before hypothesizing, the child questions. Before thinking of saying to himself, "If this rock falls, it will crush me," the child begins by asking himself implicitly, "Will this rock fall?" Let us analyse the question. The image of a rock (or the sight of that rock) and the image of its falling motion occur together in the mind of the child; and by exception (since thesis and antithesis are ordinarily the rule), the child's mind does not establish any bond of positive or negative belief between these two ideas. Yet he desires, he needs to know, to affirm or to deny. This desire, whose object is a future belief, is interrogation.

One might ask in passing, just what is belief, what is desire? I admit my inability to define them. Others have failed at it. In his *Treatise on Human Nature*, after giving belief a definition which cannot be supported and which, like all the definitions put forth since, would be equally applicable to desire (belief as an active idea attached to or associated with a current impression), Hume recognizes in his appendix, and with his usual frankness, *that it is not possible for him to explain belief perfectly.* More important than making a definition of this type is to note that belief, no more than desire, is neither logically nor psychologically subsequent to sensation; that, far from arising out of an aggregation of sensations, belief is indispensable both to their formation and their arrangement; that no one knows what remains of sensation once judgment is removed; and that in the most elementary sound, in the most indivisible colored point, there is already a duration and a succession, a multiplicity of points and contiguous moments whose integration is an enigma. Through what power do successive aural moments combine themselves when one has already ended by the time the next has begun? What makes possible this productive coupling of the living and the dead? The image? But the image is memory—then explain memory, the *fait ultime* according to a discouraged John Stuart Mill. The alternatives: either explain belief (and desire as well) by the sensations everyone knows, that is, veritable clumps of preexisting propositions— thereby presupposing what you claim to explain—or else have recourse to conjectural, elementary, mathematically instantaneous sensations—and these sensitive elements turn out to be the zeros of sensation with which you must construct a quantity. . . .

It is not, unfortunately, the increases and decreases of belief such as they are which determine the calculations in question, but such as they would be if they adapted themselves exactly to the augmentations or diminutions of what might be called the mathematical reasons for believing (*les raisons mathématiques de croire*). One must avoid regarding these reasons for belief as intrinsic characteristics of things, thereby restoring objectivity to probability. These reasons are themselves subjective and consist in our knowledge, not of the *causes* of an expected and unknown events but of the limits of the field beyond which we are sure that these causes will not operate, and of the division of this field into two unequal portions, one called favorable odds, the other unfavorable odds, whose inequality can be calculated. I do not know by what combination of physical, physiological, and psychological causes the hand of a child draws one number and not another at a lottery; but I know (negative certainty) that the number which comes up will be between 1 and 100 and not above, since there are only 100 tickets, and further (positive certainty) I know that I have 10 tickets and that consequently there are 90 I do not have. Here the hypothesis consists of considering these two certainties as the partial equivalent of the knowledge of the causes, which I cannot have.

Once this hypothesis is accepted, everything follows easily, and it appears fairly natural to think that the degree of belief of a man invincibly ignorant of the real causes must be proportional to the mathematical value of the reasons as I have defined them. From this point of view, the calculation of *credibility*, that is, what may be affirmed and denied, would be the very kind of algebraic logic that modern logicians have dreamed of; the symmetrical counterpart of this science would be the utilitarian doctrine of Bentham, the ethics of *a* plus *b* which would be called the calculation of positive and negative *desirabilities*. But for the mathematician as for the utilitarian the difficulty is justifying the duty they impose on me to believe or desire more or less, or otherwise than I do in fact believe and desire. And as far as the mathematicians are concerned, why should I accept the debatable hypothesis which serves as the basis for their elaborate scaffolding of formulas? Now in reality these mathematical reasons for belief which I was discussing are to belief what, according to the psychophysicists, the degree of outside excitation, such as luminous intensity, is to the degree of the impression of light. Not that it is appropriate to extend to this new case the famous *logarithm of sensations*. But according to whether faith is influenced by desire or by repulsion it should be noted that the increases proceed more rapidly or more slowly than the parallel increases of mathematical probability. The inhabitants of a town of 10,000 are frightened when 10 cases of cholera break out. If the next day there are 20 cases, their alarm will more than double, whereas if there were 20 cases from the beginning, the initial alarm would not have been noticeably different. If I have 10 lottery tickets and take 10 more, will my hopes of winning double? Not at all, though certain personalities predisposed to fancy and inclined to hope rather than to fear may be exceptions on this point.

Then note that in the same man and concerning the same type of event, increases of faith (*foi*), after being more rapid than parallel increases of probability, can become slower, or vice versa. In general when belief has nearly attained its maximum state (which we call certitude), its rate of increase slows down appreciably. In the sciences one may note the singular resistance to the definitive establishment of a theory which was already recognized as almost proved at a time when it could explain only half as many facts. Each day new facts are found to support the transformist or atomistic hypotheses, but the faith of their proponents is not thereby increased nearly as much as it was at first by the discovery of much less convincing facts. With simple indications Newton *almost* acknowledged his conjecture as a law. Since then multiple astronomical observations have increased the proofs of his theory a hundred times over, but the scholars' faith in it could not become one hundred times greater. Even though certitude is not essentially different from the other degrees of belief and is simply one of the extremes of their series, the passage from belief to certainty we know to be a kind of change of state, like the solidification of liquids, and like all changes of state, it presents its own obstacles.

If we take these considerations into account, we see that having no objective base, the calculation of probabilities is applicable to an actual subjective quantity, which, however, it cannot measure. To me the major merit of calculation is to show clearly that the quantity is indeed measurable. If one must absolutely have an objective foundation, it can only be a greater or lesser *tendency* of future events to take place. But how can we conceive of this tendency if not as a type of desire? This calculation is thus necessarily based on the hypothesis that desire is measurable, if not belief.

At election time one sees candidates' hopes and fears rise and fall several times in the same day as a consequence of the slightest new information or the most insignificant gossip. The calculation of probabilities certainly plays no role here. But what is very clear is the markedly quantitative character of these hopes and fears. As time passes, and without any calculation of the probabilities, each of us senses in himself a fairly regular decline of confidence in our memories, and a word suffices to arouse or trouble us. When we see one of our friends in the distance and we are uncertain at first whether or not it is he, we feel, as he comes closer, a regular increase in our belief in the reality of his presence. Here again calculation of probabilities is neither possible nor imaginable. I believe, however, that these are quantitative variations just like the rise or fall of temperature. One cannot thus claim that measurability is a property that belief borrows from the language of calculation, since measurability persists after calculation is forced into silence.

Certainly the grossest method of measuring internal qualities (though the one which seems most rigorous) would be to express them by the quantity of action which exhausts a desire or realizes an idea every time that such an action is made of gestures, movements, expenditures of muscular force, all reducible to quantities of molecular movements. One would say that the thirst satisfied by one glass of water is equal to half of that which requires two glasses of water to be quenched, and so forth.

Though difficult to discover, an approximate measure of even individual beliefs and desires would eventually have been thought up if most men had felt its need as strongly as the need of a measure of opinion or general inclination. But unfortunately in practical life the degree of an individual opinion or inclination is not important, or rather is of no interest; consequently no one observes that an opinion has degrees. For the same reason, according to the law formulated by Helmholtz in his *Optics*, visual phenomena that, although visible, are useless with respect to practical knowledge of objects (flies in flight, accidental images) are simply not seen except perhaps by the sick or by occulists. Similarly it is only psychologists who pay attention to their nascent ideas or sentiments, to slight disturbances, and to the slow decay of their religious and political faiths, to their affections and their loves. The practical man is not aware of such breakdowns until the completed ruin returns his freedom of action to him. A desire, like an opinion, can be used to manage public or private business, by vote or notarized act, only if it is considered absolute and not relative. The man of action appears to give himself completely to everything he undertakes and, indeed, he believes he does so—a situation having many drawbacks. A court doctor is not asked, "Are you entirely, almost, three-quarters, one-half convinced that there was poisoning? Do you believe this as strongly as you believe in the existence of Theseus, or of Romulus, or in the existence of Tarquin the Proud, or that of Louis XIV, or that of your father?"; he is asked instead, "Was there or was there not poisoning?" And most of the time when the court doctor replies to this question, he implicitly makes a certainty of something about which he is still to some degree doubtful.

An all too infrequent mark of philosophical honesty is the attempt to render exactly not only the precise nuance of one's thought but the *level* of confidence (*le "taux" de confiance*) one has in it. The examples of Cournot, Renan, and Sainte-Beuve on this point have not caught on. It is surprising that even among logicians, demi-assertions do not count. I do not know why, particularly with syllogisms, we always reason as if we were affirming or denying the premises with equal energy and without any doubt whatsoever. Let us try to take into account, in major and minor premises, the various degrees of intensity of affirmation and negation.

As a hypothesis I affirm, with an intensity equal to 5, that all bodies have weight, and, with an intensity equal to 10, that air is a body. Is it not clear that the conclusion—air has weight—should be affirmed with an intensity equal to 5 and not 10? I forcefully assert that no animal is insensitive. I timidly add that *I am inclined to believe* the sponge insensitive. The conclusion must be that *I am inclined to believe* that the sponge is not an animal. Experiments can be made on all sorts of syllogisms, and it will always be found that the lesser of the two degrees of affirmation or negation contained in the premises is the only one which subsists in the resulting proposition.

This simple observation enables us to explain the necessity of the often observed deep and incurable skepticism into which logicians are led by the abuse of deduction. All the force of our belief and our desire, which flows—albeit with leakage—into our behavior and thoughts, is produced or rather provoked by the continual experiences of our senses. It is the nature of this double power to transmit itself in order to be preserved, but to be preserved only through dispersal. As we have just seen, logical transformation requires an expenditure of faith tantamount to sheer loss, like the expenditure of useless force required by a machine to function. If, then, without checking these conclusions in order to augment or cancel out the proportion of belief accruing to them, we use them just as they are for new deductions, the newly engendered conclusions will be less affirmative than their predecessors, and, from one extension to the next (the first ideas ordinarily being forgotten rather than simply becoming enlarged by the new ones), we shall end up ineluctably with no belief at all. Up against this inability to believe anything, the logician has left to him only one resource: to conjecture that nothing is believable. Analogously, the moralist, too proud of having eradicated all his passions, becomes inert and calls himself a quietist.*

Attention given in logic to the quantitative character of belief would introduce many changes that I cannot go into here, but I cite the above remark as an example.

Having demonstrated the measurability of individual belief and desire, we must now ask if the beliefs and desires of different

* Quietism is a form of mysticism stressing passivity and abandonment of effort, reason, emotion in order to achieve union with God.—Ed.

individuals taken together can be legitimately considered as a totality. They can if one considers that the act of desiring or rejecting, of affirming or denying, abstracted from the objects or the sensations and memories to which it applies, is constantly the same not only from one moment to another in a given individual but also from one individual to another. It is not the immediate perception that proves this, as above, but an unavoidable induction. That attests to it. We have reason to believe that the ways of experiencing odors and tastes, of seeing blue, of hearing the sound of a violin, of experiencing the sixth sense impressions differ from Peter to Paul, from John to James. The outstanding example of colorblindness, of people who have a bad ear or a head cold, proves this point. We can comprehend that Peter lacks a sensation and that Paul has one of a special kind; in fact the daily enthusiastic practice of an art or doctrine by a fervent religious sect that has long prevailed without opposition has led to the formation here and there if not of sensations, at least of accessory quasi-sensations on the way to becoming true sensations. There was a *Hegelian* spirit in Germany, a *Christian* spirit in the Middle Ages; and there is still a *poetic spirit*, a *legal spirit* of things. It may be said in passing that with regard to these slow acquisitions of our senses we take the transformation of reiterated judgments into ideas and of ideas into sensations at face value, an evolution which is the inverse of the one usually observed—and this suggests perhaps some probable hypothesis about the origin of our elementary sensations in our distant ancestors. Be that as it may, there is nothing incomprehensible in all this. But can we conceive of someone who cannot distinguish between yes and no in the way some cannot distinguish between red and green, or of another person who manifests signs of what we call desiring something and then expresses contentment when it is denied to him? Can we concede that there are two ways of *listening* or of *looking* just as there are two ways of hearing and of affecting the retina? If, in addition to sensations, belief and desire differed from one man to another, tradition would be but an empty word, and nothing human could be transmitted unchanged from one generation to the next. When someone proves to me that he does not smell the way I do, I feel alien and indifferent; but if he contradicts me, I immediately feel jarred by a force contrary, hence similar to my own. If someone tried to placate me by saying that perhaps the person in question does not deny just the way that I do, I would take it as a bad joke. Solely through belief and desire do we both collaborate and compete; only through them, therefore, are we alike. And no better reason can be given. Moreover, is it not clear that at the bottom of all human battles there is a *yes* or a *no*, a *velle* or a *nolle?** It is true that in religious, political or social debates, the storm is most often aroused by two propositions which are not only contradictory but distinct, two schemes not only contrary but heterogeneous. But it arises solely because, in asserting itself, each thesis denies the other and because each volition opposes the other. History is but the recital of such conflicts. On the contrary, it is our ways of feeling, either natural or acquired, that isolate us in the struggle. Subtle or strong, delicate or coarse, they are, for each of us, the inoffensive but inviolable presence which renders the surrounding world of discord and hate, charlatans and fanatics alien to us.

If this is true, it is legitimate to aggregate the quantities of belief or desire of separate individuals. It has in fact been tried with complete success and adequate approximation. Variations in the monetary value of things, statistical numbers, and also, as we shall see, the military triumphs or defeats of nations, are, in diverse ways, valid processes for this type of measurement.

I shall not dwell on the first. Except where government bonds are the sole outlet for available capital, stock market fluctuations are reasonably acceptable indicators of the vicissitudes of credit, of natural confidence in the financial success of the state, or of some industrial enterprise. One bets more or less heavily at the races according to the degree of confidence one has in the speed of a horse. Taking into account the depreciation of precious metals and the variations in national wealth, the elevation or decline of religious faith or of the certainty attached to threats of hell or promises of heaven is evidenced at all times and in all places by the comparative number of monetary sacrifices made at the alter

*   "Wish—not wish."—Ed.

and by bequests or donations to the clergy. It would be a delicate but not insoluable problem to determine, with the help of these numbers (the comparative size of the population and the total public fortune at two different periods, and several other numerical givens), the exact fraction which would express the relation of the two total quantities of religious faith manifested in the same country during these two periods. If, from one year to the next, shares were sold at 1,500 francs after having been sold for 500 (without any variation in a company's shareholder dividends or in general conditions of credit), would it not be well founded to say that public confidence in the duration or future increase of profits had tripled?

When properly handled, statistics can also furnish odd measures of general desire. According to Mr. Bertillon, for example, in the Netherlands, out of 1,000 boys between 25 and 30, 112 marry each year, and out of 1,000 widowers 355 remarry.* What we may conclude from this is that the desire for marriage is about three times greater among the widowers than among the unmarried men of the same age. For widows as compared with unmarried girls, it is only twice as great. Through the figures for births in different months of the year we learn by what numerical proportion physical love is more intense in spring than in winter. When we see than 1,000 married women aged 15 to 50 have, in an average year, 248 children in England, 273 in Prussia, and 173 in France, and since we know from the remarkable fecundity of the French in Canada that no physiological factor plays a dominant role in this result, we are authorized to think that if the desire among us is equal to 1, it is equal to 1.59 in Prussia and 1.43 in England. Criminal and civil statistics can serve to evaluate the increase or decrease of litigious instincts and violent passions.

*   Bertillon was a leading statistical sociologist at the turn of the century who completed important research on the causes of depopulation. See Terry N. Clark, "Jacques Bertillon," *International Encyclopedia of the Social Sciences* (New York: Macmillan-Free Press, 1968) and "Discontinuities in Social Research: The Case of the *Cours Elémentaire de Statistique Administrative*," *Journal of the History of the Behavioral Sciences*, vol. 3, no. 1 (January 1967), pp. 3–16.—Ed.

V. Methodology, Methods, and Quantification

12

EMPIRICAL BASES OF
SOCIOLOGICAL THEORY

1883

THANKS TO the archaeologists we learn where and when a
new discovery first appeared, how far and how long it has spread,
and by what roads it has travelled from the place of its origin to its
adopted country. Although they may not take us back to the first
furnace which turned out bronze or iron, they do take us back to
the first country and century in which the pointed arch, printing,
and oil-painting, and, still much more anciently, the orders of
Greek architecture, the Phoenician alphabet, etc., displayed themselves to a justly marvelling world. They devote all their curiosity[1]
and activity to following up a given invention through its manifold
disguises and modifications, to recognising the atrium in the
cloister, the praetorium of the Roman magistrate in the Roman
church, the Etruscan bench in the curule-chair, or to tracing out
the boundaries of the region to which an invention has spread
through gradual self-propagation and beyond which, for yet to be
discovered reasons (in my opinion they are always the competition
of rival inventions), it has been unable to pass, or to studying the
results of the intersection of different inventions which have spread

---

Reprinted from *The Laws of Imitation*, translated by Elsie C. Parsons
(New York: Henry Holt, 1903), pp. 366–93, with elisions.

[1]   I know that the curiosity of the antiquarian is often vain and puer-
ile. Even the greatest among them, men like Schliemann, seem more bent
upon discovering something relating to a celebrated individual, to a Hector
or Priam or Agamemnon, than upon following out the course of the principal inventions of the past. But the personal aim and motive of the workers is
one thing, the net gain and specific fruit of their work, another.

so widely that they have finally come together in one imaginative brain.

In short, these scholars are forced, perhaps unconsciously, into surveying the social life of the past from a point of view which is continually approximating that which I claim should be adopted knowingly and willingly by the sociologist. I refer here to the pure sociologist, who, through a necessary although artificial abstraction, is distinguished from the naturalist. In distinction to historians who see nothing else in history than the conflicts and competitions of individuals, that is, of the arms and legs as well as of the minds of individuals, and who, in regard to the latter, do not differentiate between ideas and desires of the most diverse origins, confusing those few that are new and personal with a mass of those that are merely copies; in distinction to those poor carvers-up of reality who have been unable to perceive the true dividing line between vital and social facts, the point where they separate without tearing, archaeologists stand out as makers of pure sociology, because, as the personality of those they unearth is impenetrable, and only the work of the dead, the vestiges of their archaic wants and ideas, are open to their scrutiny, they hear, in a certain way, like the Wagnerian ideal, the music without seeing the orchestra of the past. In their own eyes, I know, this is a cruel deprivation; but time, in destroying the corpses and blotting out the memories of the painters and writers and modellers whose inscriptions and palimpsests they decipher and whose frescoes and torsos and potsherds they so laboriously interpret, has, nevertheless, rendered them the service of setting free everything that is properly social in human events by eliminating everything that is vital* and by casting aside as an impurity the carnal and fragile contents of the glorious form which is truly worthy of resurrection.

To archaeologists, then, history becomes both simplified and transfigured. In their eyes it consists merely of the advent and development, of the competitions and conflicts, of original wants and ideas, or, to use a single term, of inventions. Inventions thus become great historic figures and the real agents of human progress.

---

* Biological or physical.—Ed.

The proof that this idealistic point of view is the just one lies in its fruitfulness. Through its [fortunate], although, I repeat, involuntary, adoption, do not philologist and mythologist, the modern archaeologist, under different names, cut all the Gordian knots and shed light upon all the obscurities of history and, without taking away any of its grace and picturesqueness, bestow upon it the charm of theory? If history is on the way to become a science, is it not due to this point of view?

Something is likewise due to the statistician. The statistician, like the archaeologist, considers human affairs from an entirely abstract and impersonal standpoint. He pays no attention to individuals, to Peter or Paul; he concerns himself only with their works, or, rather, with those acts of theirs which reveal their wants and ideas, with the act of buying or selling, of manufacturing, of voting, of committing or repressing crime, of suing for judicial separation, and even with the acts of being born, of marrying, of procreating, and of dying. All these individual acts are related on some of their sides to social life, in as much as the spread of certain examples or prejudices seems to aid in raising or lowering the rates of birth and marriage, and to affect the prolificness of marriages and the mortality of infants.

If archaeology is the collection and classification of similar products where the highest possible degree of similarity is the most important thing, Statistics is an enumeration of acts which are as much alike as possible. Here the art is in the choice of units; the more alike and equal they are, the better they are. What is the subject of Statistics unless, like that of archaeology, it is inventions and the *imitative editions* of inventions? . . .

To be sure, the methods of these two sciences are precisely opposite to each other, but this is because of the difference in the external conditions of their investigations. Archaeology studies the scattered examples of the same art a long time before it is able to hazard a conjecture about the origin or date of the primary process from which it has developed. For example, all the Indo-European languages must be known before they can be related to a perhaps imaginary mother tongue, to Aryac, or to their elder sister, Sanskrit. Archaeology laboriously travels back from imitations to their source. The science of statistics, on the other hand, almost always knows the source of the expansions which it is measuring; it goes from causes to effects, from discoveries to their more or less successful development according to given years and countries. By means of its successive records, it will tell you that, from the time that the invention of steam engines began to gradually spread and strengthen the need for coal throughout France, the output of French coal increased at a perfectly regular rate and that from 1759 to 1869 it multiplied sixty-two and one-half times. In the same way you may also learn that after the discovery of beet sugar, or, rather, after the utility of the discovery was no longer doubted, the manufacture of this commodity was increased at an equally regular rate from seven millions of kilograms in 1828 (until then it was almost stationary for the reason implied above) to one hundred and fifty millions of kilograms thirty years later (Maurice Block).

I have taken the less interesting examples, but do we not witness by means of even these dry figures the birth and gradual establishment and progress of a new want or fashion in the community? In general, there is nothing more instructive than the chronological tables of statisticians, in which they show us the increasing rise or fall, year by year, of some special kind of consumption or production, of some particular political opinion as it is expressed in the returns of the ballot box, or of some specific desire for security that is embodied in fire-insurance premiums, in savings-bank accounts, etc. These are all, at bottom, representations in the life of some desire or belief that has been imported and copied. Every one of these tables, or, rather, every one of the graphical curves which represent them, is, in a way, an historical monograph. Taken together they form the best historical narrative that it is possible to have. Synchronous tables giving comparisons between provinces or between countries are generally much less interesting. Let us contrast, as data for philosophic reflection, a table of criminality in the departments of France with a curve showing the increase of recidivists during the last fifty years; or, let us compare the proportion of the urban to the rural population with that of the urban population year by year. We shall see in the latter case, for example, that the proportion increased from 1851 to 1882 at a regular and uninterrupted rate from twenty-five to thirty-three per cent, *i.e.*, from a fourth to a third. This fact evidences the action of some definite social cause, whereas a comparison of the proportions between two neighbouring departments, between twenty-eight per cent, for example, in the one, and twenty-six per cent in the other, is not at all instructive. Similarly, a table giving the civil burials which had occurred in Paris or in the provinces for the last ten years would be significant; just as a comparison of the number of civil burials in France, England, and Germany at any given time would be relatively valueless. I do not mean that it would be useless to state that in 1870 the number of private telegraphic despatches amounted in France to fourteen millions, in Germany to eleven millions, and in England to twenty-four millions. But it is much more instructive to know that in France, especially, there had been an increase from nine thousand despatches in 1851 to four millions in 1859, to ten millions in 1869, and, finally, to fourteen millions in 1879. We cannot follow this varying rate of increase without being reminded of the growth of living things. Why is there this difference between curves and tables? Because, as a rule, although there are many exceptions, curves alone deal with the spread of imitation.

Statistics evidently follows a much more natural course than archaeology and, although it supplies the same kind of information, it is much more accurate. Its method is pre-eminently the sociological method, and it is only because we cannot apply it to extinct societies that we substitute the method of archaeology. How many trivial medals and mosaics, how many cinerary urns and funeral inscriptions, we should be willing to exchange for the industrial, the commerical, or even the criminal statistics of the Roman Empire! But in order that Statistics may render all the services which we expect of it and may triumph against the ironical criticism to which it is exposed, it must, like archaeology, be conscious both of its true usefulness and of its actual limitations; it must know where it is going and where it should go, nor must it underrate the dangers of the road which will take it to its goal. In itself it is merely a substitute. Psychological statistics which would take note of the individual gains and losses of special beliefs and desires called forth originally by some innovator, would alone, if the thing were practically possible, give the underlying explanation of the figures of ordinary statistics.[2] Ordinarily Statistics does not weigh; it only counts, and in its reckoning it includes nothing but acts, acts of manufacture and consumption, purchases, sales, crimes, prosecutions, etc. But it is only after it has reached a certain degree of intensity that growing desire becomes action, or that decreasing desire suddenly unmasks itself and gives way to some contrary and hitherto restrained desire. This is also true of belief. In looking over the work of statisticians, it is most important to remember that the things which are under calculation are essentially subjective qualities, desires and beliefs, and that very often the acts which they enumerate, although equal in number, give expression to very different *weights* among these things. At certain times during the last century, church attendance remained numerically the same, whereas religious faith was on the decline. When the prestige of a government has been injured, the devotion of its adherents may be half destroyed although their number may hardly have diminished. This fact is shown by the vote on the very eve of a sudden political downfall. It is a source of delusion to those who are unduly reassured or discouraged by electoral statistics.

Successful imitations are numerous indeed, but how few they are in comparison with those which are still unrealistic objects of desire! So-called popular wishes, the aspirations of a small town, for example, or of a single class, are composed exclusively, at a given moment, of tendencies, which, unfortunately, cannot at the time be realised, to ape in all particulars some richer town or some superior class. This body of simian proclivities constitutes the potential energy of a society. It takes only a commercial treaty, or a

[2]   According to the statistics of railroads, omnibuses, excursion steamers, etc., their receipts diminish regularly every *Friday*. This points to the very widespread, although much weakened, prejudice about the danger of undertaking anything at all on that day of the week. If we followed the variations in this periodic diminution from year to year, the gradual decline of the absurd belief in question might be easily calculated.

new discovery, or a political revolution, events which make certain luxuries and powers, which had before been reserved for the privileged ones of fortune or intellect, accessible to those possessing thinner purses or fewer abilities, to convert it into actual energy. This potential energy, then, is of great importance, and it would be well to bear its fluctuations in mind. And yet ordinary statistics seem to pay no attention to this force. The labour of making an approximate esimate of it would seem ridiculous, although it might be done by many indirect methods and might at times be of advantage to Statistics. In this respect, archaeology is superior in the information which it gives us about buried societies; for although it may teach us less about their activities in point of detail and precision, it pictures their aspirations more faithfully. A Pompeiian fresco reveals the psychological condition of a provincial town under the Roman Empire much more clearly than all the statistical volumes of one of the principal places of a French department can tell us about the actual wishes of its inhabitants.

Let me add that Statistics is of such recent origin that it has not yet shot out all its branches, whereas its older collaborator has ramified in all directions. There is an archaeology of language, comparative philology, which draws up separate *monographs* for us of the life of every root from its accidental origin in the mouth of some ancient speaker through its endless reproductions and multiplications by means of the remarkable uniformity of innumerable generations of men. There is in archaeology of religion, comparative mythology, which deals separately with every myth and with its endless imitative editions, just as philology treats every word. There is an archaeology of law, of politics, of ethnology, and, finally, of art and industry. They likewise devote a separate treatise to every legal idea or fiction, to every custom or institution, to every type or creation of art, to every industrial process, and, in addition, to the power of reproduction by example which is peculiar to each of these things. And we have a corresponding number of distinct and flourishing sciences. But, hitherto, in the matter of truly and exclusively sociological statistics, we have had to be content with statistics of commerce and industry, and with judicial statistics, not to speak of certain hybrid statistics which straddle

both the physiological and the social worlds, statistics of population, of births, marriages, deaths, medical statistics, etc. In tables
of election figures we have merely the germ of political statistics.
As to religious statistics, which should give us a graphic represen-
tation of the relative annual spread of different sects and of the
thermometric variations, so to speak, in the faith of their adherents; as to linguistic statistics, which should figure for us not only
upon the comparative expansion of different idioms, but upon the
vogue or decline, in each one of them, of every vocable, of every
form of speech, I fear that, if I should say anything more about
these hypothetical sciences, I might bring a smile to the lips of my
readers....

If this point of view is correct, if it is really the fittest from
which to elucidate social events on their regular, numerable, and
measurable sides, it follows that Statistics should adopt it, not partially and unconsciously, but knowingly and unreservedly, and
thus, like archaeology, be spared many fruitless investigations and
tribulations. I will enumerate the principal consequences that would
result from this. In the first place, sociological Statistics, having
acquired a touchstone for the knowledge of what did and what did
not belong to it, and having become convinced that the immense
field of human imitation, and only that field, was its exclusive possession, would leave to naturalists the care of tabulating statistics
so purely anthropological in their results as, for example, the statistics of exemption from military service in the different departments of France, or the task of constructing tables of mortality
(I do not include tables of birth rates, for, in this case, example is
a powerful factor in restraining or stimulating racial fecundity).
This is pure biology, just as much as the use of Mr. Marey's graphical method, or as the observation of disease through the myograph
and sphgymograph and pneumograph, mechanical statisticians, so
to speak, of contractions and pulsations and respiratory movements.

In the second place, the sociological statistician would never
forget that his proper task was the measurement of specific beliefs
and desires and the use of the most direct methods to grasp these
elusive quantities, and that an enumeration of acts which *resem-*

bled each other as much as possible (a condition which is badly fulfilled by criminal statistics among others), and, failing this, an enumeration of like products, of articles of commerce, for example, should always relate to the following, or, rather, to the two following ends: (1) through the tabulation of acts or products to trace out the curve of the successive increases, standstills, or decreases in every new or old want and in every new or old idea, as it spreads out and consolidates itself or as it is crushed back and uprooted; (2) through a skilful comparison between series that have been obtained in this way, and through emphasising their concomitant variations, to denote the various aids and hindrances which these different imitative propagations or consolidations of wants and ideas lend or oppose to one another (according to the varying degrees in which the more or less numerous and implicit propositions of which they always consist, more or less endorse or contradict one another). Nor should the sociological statistician neglect the influence, in these matters, of sex, age, temperament, climate, and seasons, natural causes whose force is measured, at any rate when it exists, by physical or biological statistics.

In other words, sociological statistics have: (1) to determine the imitative power which inheres in every invention at any given time and place; (2) to demonstrate the beneficial or harmful effects which result from the imitation of given inventions and, consequently, to influence those who are acquainted with such numerical results, in their tendencies towards following or disregarding the examples in question. In brief, the entire object of this kind of research is the knowledge and control of imitations. . . .

When the field of sociological statistics has been clearly defined, when the curves relating to the propagation, that is to say, to the consolidation as well, of every special want and opinion, for a certain number of years and over a certain stretch of country, have been plainly traced, the interpretation of these hieroglyphic curves, curves that are at times as strange and picturesque as mountain profiles, more often as sinuous and graceful as living forms, has still to be made. I am very much mistaken if our point of view will not prove very helpful here. The lines in question are always ascending or horizontal or descending, or, if they are irregular, they can always be decomposed in the same way into three kinds of linear elements, into inclines, plateaux, and declines. According to Quételet and his school, the plateaux would belong pre-eminently to the satistician; their discovery should be his finest triumph and the constant object of his ambition. According to this view, the most fitting foundation for a *social physics* would be the uniform reproduction, during a considerable period, of the same number, not only of births and marriages, but also of crimes and litigations. Hence the error (it no longer exists, to be sure, thanks, especially, to recent official statistics concerning the progressive criminality of the last half-century), of thinking that the latter figures have, in reality, been uniformly reproduced. But if the reader has taken the trouble to follow me, he will realise that, without detracting at all from the importance of the horizontal lines, the ascending lines, indicating as they do the regular spread of some kind of imitation, have a far higher theoretical value. The reason is this: The fact that a new taste or idea has taken root in a mind which is constituted in a certain fashion carries with it no reason why this innovation should not spread more or less rapidly through an indefinite number of supposedly like minds in communication with one another. It would spread *instantaneously* through *all* these minds if they were absolutely alike and if their intercommunication were perfect. It is this ideal, an ideal that is happily beyond realisation, that we are fast approaching. The rapid diffusion of telephones in America from the moment of their first appearance there is one proof in point. This ideal is almost reached already in the matter of legislative innovations. Laws or decrees which were once slowly and laboriously administered in one province after another are today executed from one end to the other of a state the very day of their passage or promulgation. This occurs because in this case there is no hindrance whatsoever. Lack of communication in *social physics* plays the same role as lack of elasticity in physics. The one hinders imitation as much as the other, vibration. But the imitative spread of certain well-known inventions (railroads, telegraphs, etc.), tends to diminish, to the benefit of every other invention, this insufficiency of mental contact. As for mental dissimilarity, it likewise tends to be effaced by the spread of wants and ideas which have arisen from past inventions and whose work of assimilation in this way facilitates the propagation of future inventions. I mean of future non-contradictory inventions.

When wants or ideas are once started, they always tend to continue to spread of themselves in a true geometric progression.[3] This is the ideal scheme to which their curve would conform if they could spread without mutual obstruction. But as such checks are, at one time or another, inevitable, and as they continue to increase, every one of these social forces must eventually run up against a wall which for the time being is insurmountable and must through accident, not at all through natural necessity, fall temporarily into that static condition whose meaning statisticians in general appear to so little understand. In this case, as in all others, a static condition means equilibrium, a joint standstill of concurrent forces. I am far from denying the theoretic interest of this state, because these equilibria are equivalent to equations. If, for example, I see that the consumption of coffee or chocolate has ceased to increase in a certain country at a certain date, I know that the strength of the desire there for coffee or chocolate is exactly equal to that of certain rival desires which would have to remain unsatisfied, considering the average fortune, by a more amble satisfaction of the former. The price of every article is determined in this way. But does not every one of the annual figures in progressive series or *slopes* also express an equation between the strength, at a certain date, of the desire in question and the strength of competing desires which hindered its further development at the same date? Moreover, if progression ceased at one point rather than at another, if the plateau is neither higher nor lower than it is, is it not because of a mere accident of history, that is to say, because of the fact that the opposing invention, from which arose the antagonistic wants that barred the progress in question, appeared at one time and place rather than at another, or because of the fact that it actually did appear instead of not appearing at all?

Plateaux, let me add, are always unstable equilibria. After an

---

[3]   At the same time, they tend to entrench themselves, and their progress extensively hastens their progress intensively. Let us note, incidentally, that there is no past or present enthusiasm or fanaticism of historic importance that cannot be explained through this interaction of the imitation of self with the imitation of others.

approximately horizontal position has been sustained for a more or less prolonged time, the curve begins to rise or fall, the series begins to grow or diminish with the appearance of new auxiliary and confirmatory or antagonistic and contradictory inventions. As for diminishing series, they are merely, as we see, the result of successful *growths* which have suppressed some declining public taste or opinion which was once in vogue; they do not deserve the attention of the theorist except as *the other side of the picture* of the growing series which they presuppose.

Let me also state that whenever the statistician is able to lay hold of the origin of an invention and to trace out year by year its numerical career, he shows us curves which, for a certain time, at least, are constantly rising, and rising, too, although for a much shorter period, with *great regularity*. If this perfect regularity fails to continue, it is for reasons which I will shortly indicate. But when very ancient inventions like monogamy or Christian marriage are under consideration, inventions which have had time to pass through their progressive period and which have rounded out, so to speak, their whole sphere of imitation, we ought not to be surprised if Statistics, in its ignorance of their beginnings, represents them by horizontal lines that show scarce a deviation. In view of this, there is nothing astonishing in the fact that the proportion of the annual number of marriages to the total population remains about constant (except in France, I may say, where there is a gradual diminution in this proportion) or even in the fact that the influence of marriage upon crime or suicide is expressed each year by pretty much the same figures. Here we are dealing with ancient institutions which have *passed into the blood of a people* just like the natural factors of climate, seasons, temperament, sex, and age, which influence the mass of human acts with such striking uniformity (which has been greatly exaggerated, however, as it is much more circumscribed than is generally supposed) and with a regularity that is also remarkable, in quite a different way, again, in connection with vital phenomena like death and disease. . . .

. . . These curves are now relegated to the last page, but they tend to encroach upon the others, and, perhaps, before long, at any rate, at some time in the future when people have been satiated with declamation and polemic, just as very well read minds begin to be with literature, and when they will read the papers merely for their multifarious statements of exact and ungarnished fact, they will usurp the place of honour. The public journals, then, will become socially what our sense organs are vitally. . . . The ideal newspaper of this kind would be one without political articles and full of graphical curves and succinct editorials.

13

QUANTIFICATION AND
SOCIAL INDICATORS

1897

THE QUANTITATIVE oppositions of societies merit our consideration for a moment. Whether simultaneous or successive, symmetrical or rhythmic—especially if rhythmic—they have a reality and an importance that need to be clearly defined and delimited. First of all, what are social quantities? What is their nature and their relationship to the psychological quantities of social beings and to the physical quantities these beings possess? From whatever angle it is considered, a society easily reveals things which increase or decrease, highs or lows, among which only a small number can successfully be measured by statistics. This does not mean to say that these measurable quantities are more pure or more real quantities than the others. Their privilege of being measurable usually derives from some external sign which is conveniently perceptible and which, despite their insufficient homogeneity, designates them for calculation, whereas others, much more homogeneous but less visible, elude the calculators.

Population advances or declines; a religion gains or loses followers; and a political party, adherents. A language is spoken by an increasing or decreasing number of individuals. Primary, secondary, and higher education expands or declines. Production and consumption of a commodity, a cloth, any industrial article, augments or diminishes.[1] A vice, such as drunkenness or alcohol-

---

From *L'Opposition universelle* (Paris: Alcan, 1897), pp. 332–60.

1   Economic life is full of the most precise quantitative oppositions. For example, paper is negotiated abroad sometimes above face value (face value here is zero), sometimes further and further below. The first effect

ism, a type of crime, such as indecent assault on children, becomes more frequent or more rare. These many things therefore can be called *dimensions*, since they are capable of augmentation or diminution and are measured by statistics; and there are a host of others which, while not statistically measurable, are no less certain. But these are derived and complex dimensions in which the physical and vital elements are mixed in with the social ones as heterogeneous elements are mixed with homogeneous ones: it is important to distinguish what there is in them that is truly quantitative and truly social. Shall we say that this something is one or the other of the two psychological quantities that we know about, belief and desire? No, because even though these two psychological quantities are always found combined and summed up in social quantities, the social quantities differ greatly from the psychological ones, precisely because they both derive from and are the sum and the combination of the psychological quantities—the sum, thanks to imitative propagation; the combination, thanks to logic. Properly speaking, social quantities do not exist because psychological quantities exist but because there exist mental things, either quantitative or even qualitative, which repeat themselves and accumulate by repeating themselves. Thus even if everything about each of us were affective and sensate, with nothing homogeneous, it would suffice for our minds to reflect one another and to communicate their states of being to one another in order for the imitative propagation of each of these states to become a dimension expressible in regularly increasing or decreasing numbers. And are we really ever sure, even in physics, that beneath the quantities we measure, such as the intensity of light or the pitch of a sound, there are not hidden realities, complicated and picturesque but more or less alike, which are repeated in such great numbers that their true discontinuity acquires the false air of continuity? In chemistry it is quite probable that the elements of a substance are small and different individual items, which are, however, similar in some respects, and it is these aspects that we consider when we confer

occurs when debts toward foreign countries are more numerous on the market than credits with foreigners; the second takes place in exactly the opposite case.

the name of quantity to them as a group, to the whole *mass* of them.

The same holds true for men. Statistically they are counted as similar—as French, English, Russian, farmers, merchants, industrialists, or criminal or reformatory recidivists. In these various enumerations, statistics treat truly social quantities. But if they indiscriminately enumerate Frenchmen, Chinese, Polynesians, and Negroes, or if they consider race only in the physiological and not the ethnic sense of the word and do not distinguish nationalities, classes, cults, or professions, they are looking at men only from the point of view of their vital similarities and are then dealing with vital, not social, quantities.

One essential observation must be added: if it is the similarity of beings or phenomena that allows us to enumerate them and treat them as dimensions, the numbers thus obtained will have quite a different meaning according to whether the similarity is a fortuitous one, produced by an unsolicited encounter of different causes, or is the direct and in some way intentional effect of a single cause —as for example elasticity, which is the cause of the repetition of light and sound waves, or generation, the cause of the hereditary repetition of living phenomena, or attraction,[2] the cause of the imitative repetition of the acts, thoughts or feelings of others. In the first case the number only expresses a subjective grouping; but in the second it grasps an objective reality distinct from the unities of which it is composed. Thus when a physicist gives us the number of light waves per second in the same ray from the same source or the number of sound waves emanating from the same chord of the same organ pipe, he knows that the optical number, or color, and the acoustical number, or note, are not pure entities. Similarly, when Malthus and Darwin speak of the geometric progression of individuals of a living species unhindered by the competition of neighboring species, they know that this *specific number*, however hypothetical, is real in the highest degree. And analogously, when a new idea such as Marxism or anarchism, when a new passion such as locomotion for the sake of locomotion, or

[2]   Attraction (*sympathie*) in the broadest sense of the word, in an abusive sense if you wish, in which one can say that there is an attraction of envy and not just of admiration, sometimes even one that is hateful.

change for the sake of change, or revolution for the sake of revolution, is advanced by some great theoretician, mechanic, or politician, no one doubts but that the spread of the idea among the masses, the number of examples of the idea projected into the heads and hearts of the people, is a social reality of the first order.

Therefore let no one reproach me any longer—and I am answering the criticism once and for all—for having absorbed sociology into psychology because, in order to find this newcomer science a place all its own, I do not feel obliged, as do other sociologists, to deny it every psychological element, to drain it of all substance in order to emphasize its originality. I have not had to hunt that philosopher's stone, the "purely social thing," which, by hypothesis, is pure and purged of all individual reality. It sufficed for me to see that with individual entities, with mental entities, men assembled together create a social entity by virtue of their animal or presocial attraction, and that *the* social thing is distinct from psychological *things*, precisely because it is composed of them, because it is the nonartificial synthesis of them, their true union, their objective number, and (which I have not yet shown) their logical aggregate. But let us return to the subject.

Thus, sociological quantities would or could exist even if there were no psychological ones; and in fact, with the imitative diffusion of certain aural and visual aesthetic predelictions, great artists are creating social forces just as worthy of the name force, just as capable of increasing and decreasing with regularity, as the energies of a living being. But it is no less true that the quantitative aspects of psychological phenomena are those which are by far the most easily and rapidly communicated from one mind to another, the most recognizable as identical in all minds, the most able to form logical and fruitful unions—fruitful in products—called ideas and needs, which spread and combine with the same facility, and so forth ad infinitum. There is nothing more contagious among men than faith, unless perhaps passion. Sensations are not contagious, and one is never certain that they are transmitted without considerable alteration; an image loses its special character when it passes from *visual* to *auditory* or *motor*. In an overexcited crowd it is not sensations themselves that are reciprocally aroused but rather beliefs and desires, which, through simple contact and reciprocal awareness, become exalted to such a degree that their whole is more their *product* than their *sum*. Consequently, however imperfect the mathematical expressions of such phenomena may be, it is above all because of the currents of belief and desire circulating among them that we can legitimately count men, their actions, their works, and that we can claim for these enumerations the measurement of incontestable social realities. . . .

From this follow those two great social quantities which could be called *truth* and *value*, in the broadest sense of these words, or more concretely, *enlightenment* (*les lumières*) and *wealth* (*les richesses*). Whether measured by statisticians or not, all types of dimensions flow from this fundamental duality[3] in which belief and desire are reflected though also transformed. As I have stated elsewhere, sociology is not just magnified psychology; it is above all a psychology exteriorized, transcendent, and exceptionally well used. The social quantities which I have just named are composed of psychological quantities but differ from them, first because they assume and affirm the homogeneity of beliefs and desires of the distinct individuals of which they are the living union, and second because they are characterized by the communicability of these beliefs and desires from one mind to another. *Truth* is none other than this. The psychological quantity is belief or desire as passed or capable of being passed without basic alteration from one group of sensations or images to another within the same individual. The social quantity is belief or desire as communicated or communicable without changing its nature from one individual to other individuals. As it accumulates in an individual, belief becomes conviction; as it is spread and intensified among the masses, it acquires the name of truth.[4] This name is justified if the idea adjudged to be true is not only the most widespread but also, despite all contradictions, the most apt to be universally accepted: because

3   *Power* is reducible to a combination of enlightenment and wealth with armed force at its disposal.
4   Remember that individual *conviction* comes from *truth* (a social thing) rather than vice versa. It is extremely rare that anyone is convinced by himself without knowing that others are also, or could be so.

this aptitude belongs solely to scientifically, experimentally demonstrated ideas. As it grows within an individual, the desire for a thing becomes a *special need for that thing*; as it spreads in an outside group, this desire becomes the *value of that thing*. Through the knowledge that this thing is desired or capable of being desired by someone else, or through the judgment on the capacity of this thing to satisfy a desire, there takes place a combination of belief and desire which, quite as much as the communicability of the belief and the desire, is essential to the idea of value. There is the idea of truth as well, but less visibly so, a combination of two psychological quantities. A belief is not judged true except insofar as it satisfies at least a curiosity of the mind, and even more often—if religious or moral "truths" are in question—certain elevated aspirations of the spirit or imperative needs of the heart.

The truth of an idea, in the social sense of the word, increases proportionately as the faith in this idea gains credence in a greater number of minds of equal social importance and becomes strengthened in each of them. It diminishes in the inverse case. The value, or more exactly, the utility of a product augments or diminishes insofar as the desire for this product, as well as faith in it, expands or contracts. Enlightenment thus is no less a quantity than wealth. How does it happen, then, that we commonly speak of the extent of the public wealth, that we are able to evaluate the national wealth of France at approximately 200 billions, and yet no one has thought of setting up even a very approximate inventory of national truth, the statistics of its growths and losses? Simply because there is a common measure of wealth—money, and there is no common measure of knowledge. But why does not this mental currency exist? Because the need for it has not made itself felt. Unlike wealth, which can only be exchanged at the cost of someone's sacrifice and which, consequently, requires some measure to regulate the extent of this sacrifice, the exchange of knowledge is an addition on both sides, not a subtraction, except when the knowledge exchanged is contradictory; but in this case there is no exchange but a duel to the death either in the enclosed field of an individual mind or on the battlefields of sects or parties or religious wars. And whereas advancement in wealth consists of multiplying costly exchanges, advancement of knowledge consists of diminishing the frequency of the duels just mentioned as well as multiplying truths which can be freely exchanged and be added together without contradiction. By truth we mean this agreement of knowledge, just as by utility and value we mean the adaptation of products to one another through their exchange, which renders each one appropriate not only for its corresponding need but also, in a different sense, for all the other products against which it can be exchanged. In certain respects, however, it is true to say that when faced with two partially contradictory hypotheses, the individual, after quietly hesitating in a manner comparable to bargaining, often makes a choice and exchanges one of these for the other, which he then renounces. Even when two ideas are in no way contradictory, are we not required to refrain from thinking of one in order to think of the other, hence to evaluate their relative importance? Yes, but these are individual hesitations and sacrifices, which require no more than an individual measure of truth or of the intellectual value of ideas. If one could learn something new from someone else only by forgetting a truth one already knows, which one gives up in favor of others, there would arise the necessity for a social measure of truth, of the *general credibility* of ideas, as there is a measure for utility—the *general desirability* of products.

It is therefore due to its eminently liberal character and to its obvious superiority that truth, in the sense I give it, was cast down from the sociological rank where it belonged and in the various attempts to construct a social science has played a role so much less important than that of value. No one, in fact, has tried to build sociology entirely upon it, when so many economists have thought to universalize the idea of value or wealth and to create a systematic social science on this foundation alone, thereby running the risk of mutilating the human spirit. Nonetheless it would have been easy to see that, despite the absence of a form of mental currency accepted by everyone, it is permissible to encompass several things under one point of view, to consider the knowledge of men, their most heterogeneous ideas—religious, linguistic, legal, scientific and others—all as beliefs; and that this synthesis is just as legitimate as to consider any satisfaction of human desire for food, love, luxury, the military, industry, etc., as a desire. It is distressing that the first of these two variously useful generalizations has been neglected, as it could have suggested interesting observations: that, for example, the proportion of the total truth represented by the various great areas of mental activity—language, religion, science, law—varies considerably from one century to another and that, among the Ancients, by far the most important capital of truth was of a linguistic and religious nature, which explains the particularly grammatical nature of Greek metaphysics. Language was the magic treasure where one dug for the key to all problems, as we dig the earth for the secrets of geology. Language retains this strength of fascination among children and absorbs the greatest proportion of belief attached to the meanings of words.

Is there a pattern to the secular displacements of major truth which is incarnated in turn in myths and poetry, in formulas of law, in moral maxims, in rules of art? It would seem so. And if the two syntheses that I drew are compared, it also seems that the progress of enlightenment precedes rather than follows the progress of wealth. But let us leave these questions aside. Elsewhere[5] I have shown, I believe, that social statistics must never lose sight of their special mission, which is to measure as exactly as possible, by all the direct or indirect means at their disposal, the imitative propagation of a belief or a desire, of an idea or a type of act. But social statistics have great gaps here, some of which will perhaps never be filled, which are explained either by the real or apparent practical inutility of certain records or by the practical difficulty of making them. It would be interesting to calculate, over ten-year periods, the highs and lows of religious faith as attested to by the number of people entering different places of worship or the number of confessions and communions. Similarly, it would be of the greatest interest to have good statistics on bookstores, which, from the number of copies sold, would tell us the rise and fall of curiosity about and public favor for a given type of publication—novels, travelogues, philosophical stories, poetry, newspapers of a par-

[5]   I refer the reader to *Laws of Imitation*, the chapter on archaeology and statistics ("What Is History"?). [Sections of the chapter are reprinted in this volume, pp. 210–21—Ed.]

ticular bent. We should then clearly observe the variations of public opinion and the direction of its transformations. But such indiscreet investigations would have great difficulty in achieving their goal. There are no statistics for morality, whereas those for criminality are already ancient and detailed. The reason for this lack is different from, though similar to, that which explains the absence of a common measure of enlightenment. If virtuous acts are not recorded, it is because such a record is less necessary than that of criminal acts; and it is less necessary, or has appeared to be so, because a contagion of virtuous acts is less to be hoped for than one of crimes is to be feared; and in any case it is less urgent to reward the perpetrators of good actions in order to incite others to imitate them than it is to punish the perpetrators of bad actions in order to discourage their potential imitators. In support of this distinction one may cite this factual observation: private charity is better than public charity, whereas public justice is better than private justice, at least as far as criminal justice is concerned.

Linguistically, statistics provide us with almost no information. They provide only approximate figures of the number of people who speak French, German, English, Spanish. But on the border between contiguous and rival languages, they ought at least to offer a careful record of the encroaching of one on the other. We would see if it is always the same language that encroaches in different areas, in the north as in the south, in the east as in the west, or if it is sometimes one, sometimes another. In the first case there would be reason to believe that the situation is due to some intrinsic advantage of the conquering idiom, in the second case, to external factors. We shall return to these language battles later in our discussion of dynamic oppositions. As for each language taken by itself, if we could note and record day by day the use of each word or of each turn of phrase by everyone who speaks a given language, we should obtain, in numerical columns of a truly staggering length, a most accurate picture of the internal transformations of the language in question. Between the old and the new expressions of the same idea we should discover the turns of fortune of their silent battle, how fast an innovation grows, how rapidly an archaic term becomes obsolete. But here again it is a dynamic opposition which appears as the cause of a quantitative opposition, of a decline succeeding a rise. This should not surprise us, for perhaps basically it is always like this. And this is what we shall soon see.

Industrial and commercial statistics, the basis for the instructive publications of the Office du Travail* and of several ministries, are treated in great detail, and this has produced the present-day passion for questions concerning labor. In their clearest form these statistics show us the imitative propagation, year by year, of industrial production and consumption, or of unemployment (strikes) or salaries, that is, the diffusion of an opinion or a resolution, a belief or a desire. In brief, the ideal of statistics would be to be able to trace the origin of every theoretical or practical innovation, of every minor or major discovery in matters of religion, science and language, just as for industry, and to follow it from its originator to the present, tracing the changing curve of the number of its adherents and explaining the variations in each one of those curves by similar or inverse variations in one or more other curves.

Having demonstrated, defined, classified, and explained social quantities, we must ask whether the oppositions that they present, their increases and decreases, are systematic or not, what their role is, and what law seems to govern them. There seems to be a general persuasion that through a sort of internal necessity all things which have grown to a certain point tend to diminish of their own accord, just as a living being, having climbed the hill of life, supposedly longs to descend it once again. I shall not have wasted my time if I manage to make evident the lack of basis for this popular prejudice, which has been adopted by the majority of systematic minds and which is all the more irresistable for being hasty. When Mme de Sévigné said, "Racine will pass as will coffee," she, like everyone else, was surely misled by the mirage of the idea of opposition. She was convinced that a regular and rapid success must necessarily terminate in a regular and rapid fall into disfavor. She was mistaken: after rising for a long time, Racine's literary

* A governmental bureau devoted to labor questions, which later became part of the Ministry of Labor.—Ed.

radiance reached its zenith, where it remains and whence it shows no signs whatever of dropping, any more than the reputations of Shakespeare or Corneille. As for coffee, its use like that of tobacco continues to spread in France, and our neighbors have shown it very unlikely that this tonic and this narcotic will revert to their point of departure after having achieved a certain limit of popularity. They will simply not exceed this point.

When a stone falls into a lake, the circular waves spread, multiply by enlarging, but never on their own do they fall back on themselves. If they retrogress, like the sound waves of an echo, it is because they have forcefully run into an obstacle or because the expansion of another series of waves has partially driven them back. A type or race of plant is born somewhere, progresses little by little, and tends to progress indefinitely until it has filled the entire region with the necessary conditions for its development; and this equilibrium, both stable and mobile, is destined by nature to endure forever. If some day this species retreats and disappears, it is because another rival species which is hostile to it has progressed to the point of expulsing the first from its territory. A species does not die, it is killed. A theory or a machine—for example, the theory of selection or a bicycle—appears one day in a human brain and arouses a new faith or need, which, like the theory or the machine, itself multiplies and spreads, tending to continue in this direction endlessly. If someday the theory or the machine is repressed and disappears, it is because a more powerful conception, a preferable invention has supplanted it by furnishing a more satisfactory solution to the same problem or need. The first bicycles died in this way, as did the later models with solid or inflated rubber wheels; the [pneumatic] "tire" now reigns and will reign forever unless some other type of velocipede succeeds in doing what this one has already done—conquer the world.

Thus no progression, whether social or natural, should be ranked symmetrically with regressions. A progression has an internal cause; a regression, when one does occur, has an external cause, which is one or more other progressions, and its entire reality consists of being the reverse, and ordinarily very inexact reverse image, of the progressions. The inverse never takes place or is only apparent and illusory. Progression is the initial, normal, positive, essential fact; regression is the secondary, abnormal, negative, and accidental fact.

This thesis is not without significance. Applying it to the question of population among other topics, one of the most poignant issues for France today, we note that our population has ceased to grow, and everyone seems convinced, in accordance with the prejudice that I am fighting, that it will inevitably begin to decline. And indeed I think a decline is quite possible; but I maintain that it is pushed toward growth by its natural causes and also by certain social causes in constant progression, such as the desire to perpetuate one's name, faith, memory, traditions; and that in order to paralyze the action of such powerful causes, there was needed a progression of other social forces, of certain false ideas, of certain disastrous needs, calculations of egotism, or needs of luxury.[6] It is irritating that statistics do not shed light on these causes. I admit that this remark is undoubtedly not sufficient consolation, but is it a matter of indifference to know that the anticipated decline which saddens us in advance is not inevitable and that if it does take place, it will be contrary to the nature of things? Then, instead of brooding on the discouraging idea that it is useless to seek to go against an irreversible current, we shall believe, we shall know that the nature of things is fighting in our favor and that if we fight, it will support us.

Have the causes which produce enlightenment and wealth, as well as population, health, vigor, intelligence, and character, a

[6]   Unfortunately, among the progressions which counteract that of population there are some which are excellent, *except for this counteraction.* For example, demographers have established an inverse relationship between the advance of births and the development of foresight: the French departments in which the number of children per family is decreasing most rapidly are those which stand out for their multiplying savings accounts and insurance policies. Note in this regard the preference of statisticians for *inverse relationships,* which are often imaginary. Italian criminologists imagined them between tendencies to suicide and to homocide, between the curve of crimes against persons and those against property. I shall not examine these more or less chimerical or exaggerated inversions, nor many other of the same type.

tendency to regress after having progressed, simply because they have progressed? This is the question—to which I answer no. I know that many peoples, at some turning point in their history, after having had abundant births, robust children, energetic characters, loyalty, morality, and prosperity, have seen a shadow cast from another people, the lethal influence of foreign vices and luxuries and fatal doctrines, sterilize their marriages, sap their courage, and paralyze their energies. But were they absolutely unable to avoid this fatal contact which killed them? The major reason here for our despair is the deceiving comparison of society with the individual (I do not say with the species, as we have seen). Does it not seem that the same internal cause makes an individual grow old after making him grow up? I am not even really sure of that, despite the apparent necessity of death among higher living beings. However necessary it may seem *in fact*, even the death we call natural is always *by rights* (*en droit*) a thing against nature, the object of obstinate protest by the living being up to his last breath (except perhaps in the very last minutes of life), which is made inevitable solely by the coalition of all other ambient and hostile phenomena, always victorious one day or another. *Violent death* signifies a death caused by the blow of a single being or a single hostile phenomenon; *natural death* is death caused by the conspiracy of anonymous hostile events that invade from all sides. But, even though an exception must be made for the living individual, let it be made for him alone: let us not hasten to generalize the necessity for growing decrepitude and death without good reason.

From this almost universal tendency of things to progress, not regress, to stop in an indefinite equilibrium, not to retrogress and die, it follows that when regression occurs (and this is not always the case), it is usually far less regular than the corresponding progression, which, as shown by statistical curves, it almost never resembles. In every country, look at the rise in taxes, public debts, public expenditures, and military troops. Is there anything more sadly and regularly on the increase? Does one ever see, and if so where, a similar regularity in the decrease of taxes, armies, debts? What is clear is that at certain times there occurs a military or financial crash, bankruptcy or voluntary or forced disarmament that is abrupt and general, as in 1815,[7] after which a new progression, analogous to the preceding one, begins to appear and soon grows. Or else, quite by chance, a small amount of wisdom appears in the government, and a sinking fund is set up, for example, which functions for a while but with great difficulty, since "the nature of things" here unfortunately runs in quite the opposite direction.

Sometimes a slow and gradual progression is followed by a brusque and rapid regression, as in the case of the majority of private fortunes, which, when destroyed (by dissipation or gambling), are destroyed much more quickly than they were formed (by saving and work, or even through a series of successful undertakings). On the whole, they continue to grow slowly up until they undergo a general collapse. Sometimes a rapid progression is succeeded by a slow regression. In about fifty years during the sixteenth century, the wealth, strength, and glory of the Spanish attained their apogee, and they have been declining now for two centuries. In Ireland, Britain, and rather generally, the Christian faith progressed with unbelievable speed from the first preachings of its missionaries to its peak, where it stayed for centuries; when it began to weaken on account of other, contradictory ideas which were beginning to spread, its decline was interspersed with aggressive recoveries, and in any case it has been and is remarkably slow. I could cite innumerable further examples.

This lack of similarity between progression and regression is due to the fact that regression is caused, not by a corresponding progression or progressions, but by alien and consequently different ones, whose rhythm it reproduces in reverse. If the retreat or rather the rout of the diligence by the train was much more rapid than had been its previous development, this was the effect of the

---

[7]   In his *Political and Social Europe*, which appeared in 1869, Mr. Maurice Block protests against the exaggeration of military forces, in France especially. "But," he adds, "the time has come when *it is not possible to go further*; we are thus forced to stop and to *think of reversing ourselves*." Alas, it can be seen that the learned economist shared the illusions of his time and spoke of European armies the way Mme de Sévigné spoke of coffee.

development of railroads, which advanced at quite a different pace than had the development of the diligence. If religious or general faith fades from and weakens among the masses much less quickly than it spread out and took root among them, if its ebb is much slower than was the sudden overflow of its rising tide, it is because the ebb is due to the antireligious elements in scientific or philosophical ideas whose propagation among the people is slow. If the sole reason or principal for regression lay in the corresponding progression, that is, if regression had an intrinsic cause, the dissimilarity I am pointing out would not occur.

From the above it follows that a regression can be as regular as a progression if it depends on a single progression of which it is the upside-down translation, as it were. Thus the decrease in the consumption of rye in certain countries shows about the same regularity as the increase in the consumption of wheat. In all countries having only two political parties electoral statistics indicate the same gradual character of gains by one and losses by the other. According to navigation statistics, sailing vessels decreased in fleet size and total tonnage carried just about as regularly as steamships increased. The marking of steel by the ancient process of tempering subsided after Bessemer's discovery quite as gradually as the making of steel by the new process increased, and so forth. But this case is exceptional because it assumes the direct and complete engagement of an old invention and a new one, a battle limited to these two adversaries, a battle to the death, with no other old or new invention intervening during the battle to give aid to the side that is attacked, to strengthen it or help it find refuge elsewhere. In general, an already established invention is only partially dislodged from its place, and after the relative upset of its departure, it finds somewhere else to flourish. Or else it retrenches and, impregnable, immures itself in a part of its old domain, like the art of the copyists, printing notwithstanding, or hand sewing despite the sewing machine. By confining itself to a more limited area, it sometimes regains in depth what it has lost in breadth; by shifting about (as perhaps will be the case with religious faith which moves more than it declines), it encounters new allies and new aggressors and, supported by the former, attacked by the latter, it seems to follow a fortuitous course, which visibly transcribes the picturesque statistical curves with their irregularity alternating *rises*, *plateaux* and *falls*.[8] In short, even where the conditions of the duel to the death indicated above seem to obtain, it is rare that the regression is as regular as the progression whose the sequel it is. No statistics have been compiled on this subject, but has the work of copyists decreased as regularly as that of typographers has increased? Has the work of seamstresses decreased as regularly as that of sewing machines has increased, or that of coachman decreased (if indeed it has decreased) as regularly as that of train conductors has increased?

We can see that the question we are treating touches on the much debated one concerning the competition of machines with men for jobs, and our solution may be not without usefulness in resolving this debate or in better understanding the problem as well as many other economic problems related to it. What is important to see clearly is that an old invention, represented by the workers who incarnate its imitation, tends to increase by itself, as does its corresponding need among the public; the fatal or wounding confrontation with a new invention, represented by a machine, is really a pure accident in the course of its destiny, an accident against which the old invention in legitimate possession of its domain should very naturally protest with all its forces, supported in this battle by the "nature of things," which has created the universal *desire to live* and *desire to grow*. It should not be said that "this profession now loses ground each day as it gained ground before; after all, one is as natural as the other." No, the natural destiny of an industry with its base in human nature is to progress or persist forever: its reversal is against nature. Hence, it is wrong to be surprised when it fights with such frenzy and prolongs its existence for longer than the often overwhelming superiority of its rival gave it reason to hope for—unless it commits suicide, so to speak, from despair when in fact it still had a chance for life and success.

[8]   I showed in *Laws of Imitation* (in the chapter indicated above) that the *rises*, which basically represent imitative propagation, were the essential part to consider, the key to all the rest.

For analogous reasons the outcry of workers when their salaries are reduced is understandable, for it is natural that salaries rise or stabilize, not that they descend, since social evolution effects an augmentation or a stabilization but never a diminution in the number of needs and forms of consumption imitated, a complication, not a simplification of the conditions for basic well-being. That is why, by virtue of imitative propagation, when salaries do decrease they do so much less regularly and much less continually than they increase; growth occurs because of an inherent and almost irreversible tendency. On the other hand, the rate of interest has an undeniable, historically demonstrated tendency to decrease constantly until it reaches a minimum from which it would probably never rise again were it not for some great catastrophe or an unanticipated influx of major revolutionary industrial inventions. This decrease only looks like a regression. Actually it is the mathematical expression of a true progression, and I leave it to Mr. Paul Leroy-Beaulieu to prove it, since, in his great treatise on political economy, he put his finger on the true causes of the age-old and normally necessary lowering of capital income: in the long run, these causes may be reduced to imitative propagations, particularly the decreasing productivity of industrial inventions as a consequence of their more extensive and general exploitation.[9]

9   Do we see in a series of oscillations the interest on capital rising and falling in turn? Yes, but these oscillations, very irregular and with no symmetry, are only secondary and as it were intermediary between the maximum interest, which is situated at the very beginning (not in the middle) of the economic evolution we are considering, and the minimum interest toward which this evolution incessantly tends. Here, as everywhere, opposition, inversion, rhythm, appear as middle terms. Are the causes producing these two inverse effects, the increase and the decrease in rates of interest, themselves inverse? No. Let us take an example: an industrial invention—railroads—appears as *the need for consumption*, to which the invention corresponds, spreads from the higher or richer levels to the lower ones, it is necessary for the price to decrease in order to be accessible to people with increasingly smaller fortunes—which results in a diminution in the proportional profit reaped by the exploiters of this invention and their backers. On the other hand, as the *desire to produce* railroads is itself spread, as much as and more than the need to use them, the competition of the various exploiters as well as their common necessity to conform to the

The number of insurance policies, of savings accounts, of members of mutual benefit societies* is always on the increase; it is to be presumed that it will stop; but will it retrogress, and with the same regularity? This is quite unlikely. A general panic could, one fine day, cause all deposits to be withdrawn at once, all insurance to be canceled, all mutual benefit societies to be dissolved; but unless new processes appear which are capable of responding to the same needs for security and protection and of satisfying them in a way deemed preferable, these old processes will not gradually and by themselves fall into disuse. And why not? Because the people who have a savings account, for instance, must choose between the example of those who followed this current of examples and those who did not; but the non-imitation of fact, a negative example, is always much less contagious than its imitation. Hence, I am inclined to think that if we ever see a decrease in criminality or divorces or suicides, their regression will be irregular, intermittent, and capricious, and will have none of the striking continuity that characterizes their progression.

The opposite of *opulence* is *indigence*, and the median state between these two extremes is *ease*, the level of which varies with the country and the period but which on the average rises. An urgent question is the economic and social role of this age-old opposition. Is it necessary, is it useful, and if so, what for? Note that it cannot be rigorously pushed to infinity except through one of its branches, indigence. To *lack everything* is the infinity of poverty, an ex-

---

ever more imperious demands of the ever more numerous public, forces them to lower prices and consequently to lower the return on the new capital engaged in the enterprise. Thus the spread of needs, either for consumption or for production, created by inventions tends to bring about a reduction in the rates of interest. What is needed to raise them? An influx of new inventions to unseat the old ones, following the same laws of imitative propagation, to conquer all or part of their domain. Now, between continuous and constant imitative phenomena and the intermittent eruption of inventions there is the same difference as there is between sedimentary and eruptive formations in geology.

*   Organizations of workers in France concerned with care of the unemployed, sick, etc., but often functioning as nascent labor unions (which were illegal until 1884).—Ed.

treme too often realized. To *possess everything* is an ideal that even billionaires do not achieve. But, practically speaking, one may say that when they have *too much of everything*, the plenitude of wealth and luxury is realized as, elsewhere, the plenitude of misery. In his economic career man tends to move from infinite misery to infinite luxury. If the prospect of this ideal were surpressed, if there were an attempt to limit his wishes to a precise degree of well-being, thereby showing him a barrier which would arouse either the imperative desire to cross it or the grief of knowing that he could not do so, his activity would be stifled. But, on the other hand, what a scandal that there is such a gap between the poorest and the richest. How can we be resigned to the fact that necessarily, inevitably, this gap must continue to increase in the course of increasing civilization and wealth![10] This cannot be: from the day it was measured, the day the knowledge of this disproportion gripped consciences and violated that highest of civilizing sentiments, that of justice, it was impossible that this inequality not decrease, not, it is true, by a diminution of the largest fortunes, but by the gradual elevation of average fortunes and the suppression of poverty.

And this is necessary according to our principles, owing to the laws of imitative propagation of civilizing inventions, which tend to cause the gradual leveling of needs and resources, combined with their common increase.

In short, in the social world at least, it is not true that, from the point of view of quantity as from any other, decline is the inevitable successor to progress, and that when it follows, it is of a comparable nature. Here again obsession with the idea of symmetry leads the human mind into error, among the elite as among the populace. John Stuart Mill was right in saying that the normal level for all men is the highest level that they can attain. Having mounted his own relative pinnacle, a man may fall precipitously from it, but he will not descend as he mounted rung by rung. When the Roman patrician had advanced from one dignity to another

[10]   "The progress of poverty is parallel and adequate to the progress of wealth," Proudhon used to say, only to contradict himself a moment later.

until he reached the summit of the *cursus honorum*, the anger of a prince was able to send him to prison, exile, torture, but did he ever rerun his career in reverse? It is the same with families and with societies, which are groups of families; it is the same with all things human, considered in all their aspects. To progress together, and I mean everything that survives, until they achieve an equilibrium like stars in the same solar system, a stable harmony, the theme and the theater necessary for modulations and infinite variations: this is their essential nature; against which even frequent accidents cannot triumph.

VI. Social Stratification

14

THE ORIGINS AND FUNCTIONS
OF ELITES

1899

WE HAVE seen that the true, basic sources of power are propagated discoveries or inventions. Now we must ask if the conditions necessary for the *creation* of some social institution or its reform, for the formation or transformation of a language, a religion, a science, a government, a law (*un droit*), an industry, an art, a morality, are the same conditions as those required for the *propagation* of this new thing? The answer is no. Modern Europe is well suited to the diffusion and rapid propagation of a language but is incapable of creating one. . . .

Similarly, with the exception of a few scoffing or skeptical nations, our modern world is rather favorable to the diffusion of an existing religion or at least to its preservation from father to son, but it is clear that the world has passed the age of religious creation. The imperial civilization of Rome was an excellent soil for the propagation of Christianity, but it could never have engendered that religion; creation needed the intense fermentation of the Jewish people. The sixteenth century was the last period in which this special creative force gave signs of life, and the Protestant sects which are its products are far from equal in richness, imagination, and profundity to the great religions of the past. In the same way Europe's last linguistic creation, English, with its grammatical poverty, is very far from attaining the original beauty of Greek or Sanscrit. A religion is only elaborated in the exalted consciousness of a man whose exaltation inflames the small band of disciples and apostles among whom he lives.

From *Les Transformations du pouvoir* (Paris: Alcan, 1899), pp. 70–78.

Likewise, in our own time, an ancient monarchical tree, such as the Hohenzollern dynasty or the House of Savoy, can be favored in its expansion and in the external diffusion of its prestige and system of government by those very democratic and equalizing revolutions which thereafter preclude the creation of new, viable, and lively monarchical roots.

We produce many laws at each session of parliament, but are they true legal creations? A law regarded as hereditary, held to be sacrosanct, and obeyed with a sort of loving fear, a national right, does not emerge to the light of day like Venus from the foam of parliamentary waves. It is formed in one of two ways: either little by little, mysteriously and through custom which is rooted first in a narrow area, like the right of Quirites,* and then slowly extends its roots to cover a vast empire; or else such a right develops *ex abrupto* but fostered by the prestigious glory which marks the legislative work of a Lycurgus, a Solon, a Justinien, a Theodosius, a Napoleon, with the obvious seal of superior wisdom. In times such as ours, when respect has been lost, what is there that can be established as respectable? But though no longer capable of creating viable new legislation, we are always able, in order to answer our need for civilizing assimilation, to use an established body of law and even propagate it to the outside. However, we repeat, this is only true of truly national law, which shares nothing but a name with those emphemeral laws voted into being by our legislatures.

Mr. Boutmy noted that the parliamentary and political institutions of which England is so proud could not have been born in the democratized England of today. "Democracy was able to appropriate the parliamentary regime and imitate it, with some difficulty, only after many perfect specimens of it had been fashioned and fixed by other hands. Only an aristocracy could create it, form its customs, and initiate its traditions." These English institutions which have traveled all around the world arose from a small nobility in the corner of an island.[1]

Will not a time come when, although more favorable to the

---

*   Those citizens of the Roman Empire living in Rome itself.—Ed.

[1]   Innovations destined to become the most widespread are like plants brought in from outside; they need to become acclimated at first in a re-

popularization of science, the conditions of our civilized life will be less compatible with the discovery of truly profound new scientific theories? Mr. de Candolle's *History of Science* enumerates the circumstances most propitious to the formation of true scholars and original creators. Will family life—austere, moral, self-contained, and traditionalist yet inspiring—will the peacefulness of the countryside, that half-solitude needed for the best development of scientific genius, be possible in the whirlpool of the ever busier and more dispersive urban life in which people seem to be turning? And what are the best conditions for the formation and growth of genius in all the paths of art? Certainly they are not the same as those which favor its success and glory after it has been born.[2]

Following these general considerations we should note the importance of those two acknowledged social superiorities, nobility

---

stricted culture in a hothouse or a small enclosure. Every civilization has begun thus, by flourishing in a garden before germinating in open earth. I have said in my *Laws of Imitation* that even that innovation which consists of admitting the equality of members of a society is not exempt from this law, and that, like most other styles, it owes its first steps to the example set by an aristocracy. And in fact it was among the highest nobility, peers in England and courtiers in France, that the habit of treating one another as equals became daily practice. Whatever their diversity of origin and rank, the English peerage equated all who achieved it. Court life was the same. Of it one could say, as Cicero did of friendship, *pares aut facit aut invenit* ["it either makes equals or finds them"]. It was of just this that Saint-Simon complained when, for the ducal rank of which he was a member, he so arrogantly claimed a prerogative of superior consideration and deference, which he saw slighted more and more around him. For the gradual assimilation produced by the intensity of court relationships was inevitably accompanied by a gradual equalization. Later the salons continued and generalized this assimilative and equalizing movement. The various levels of English society evidenced a similar movement to equalize each one despite the distance separating them from one another, a distance which changed a good deal from one period to another, sometimes diminishing, sometimes growing.

[2]   Without being the least inclined to abuse biological comparisons, I may add that perhaps in the animate world as well the creation of a new species requires a concurrence of unique and local circumstances that are reproduced at infrequent intervals (which explains why we never see them), whereas the habitual circumstances are well suited to the propagation of extant species.

and a capital—one or the other of which is dominant according to the times—in creating and propagating a form of government and as a breeding ground for governmental personnel. A nobility or a capital is a sometimes necessary, always useful agent of creation for a country's political and administrative institutions at the same time that it is an agent of propagation, a social fountain for literary, religious, moral, and even industrial novelties born outside it, in a foreign country or in the lower levels of the nation itself.[3] The English nobility is not alone in having made the constitution of England; in America the big Southern plantation owners made that of the United States. The French nobility made the Capetian monarchy, and after that, Paris completed France just as London did England after the lords. Let us first ask how a nobility is founded—a major problem in sociology, as is the question, to be examined later, of how a city is founded.

There are many different, often coexisting origins of the nobility: success in war, wealth, mysterious and transcendental saintliness or morality, aesthetic and civilized culture. But whatever the point of view, superiority always depends on the adaptation of one individual—and then of his children and family through presumed inheritance of aptitudes—to the state of knowledge and all the kinds of resources which enable a man to win, gain wealth, become saintly or heroic, and be reputed more civilized. It is always a question of a real or supposed relationship between the individual, and later his family, and the ideas or needs of his time in the various areas enumerated.

When no greater weapon has been invented than the club, no better means of making a fortune than the harpoon or the bow and arrow, no greater morality than fidelity to prescriptions of family vendettas or to the requirements of ritual fetishism, no greater

---

3   Among the faults from which the "honnête homme" is exempt, the Chevalier du Méri lists, besides "injustice, vanity, avarice, ingratitude, baseness, bad taste, an air of the law courts or the bourgeoisie, laziness, etc., and *behavior which is too attached to custom and [which] sees nothing better.*" Which proves that even in his time [the seventeenth century], the aristocracy—of which "l'honnêtêté" was the purest expression—was thought of as the class most open to innovations.

art or luxury than tattooing or rough sculptures from reindeer ant-
lers, then the most noble personnage can only be the one who has
the greatest muscular force and ability of an archer, who is the
most ferociously vindictive or madly superstitious, who has the
most complicated tattoo or the most beautiful club to command
with. Later, when animals have been domesticated and the art of
sewing and weaving has been invented as well as that of metallurgy, the most noble will be the one who is the best rider, has the
most herds, is the most faithful observer of domestic and ancestral
worship, and the wisest in divining the future, has the most reck-
less and bracelets of gold and the most purple garments woven by
the women. Still later, when the knowledge of cultivable plants,
the invention of farming implements, and the discovery of agricultural secrets and of masonry have rendered social groups seden-
tary and enabled small armies to withstand sieges, when the fine
arts have been perfected and religious ideas have become sublime,
nobility will be acquired through strategic ability, wealth in land
and domains cultivated by slaves conquered in war, through conformity of life to divine examples, the possession of sacred books,
sacrifices in the temples, through gladiatorial combat, and through
a luxurious life, especially the luxury of food, clothes, and housing,
though not yet furnishings. Finally, in the industrial era, when
inventions and discoveries have been accumulated, will nobility
be acquired at all? Yes, in the sense of an aristocracy having industrial distinction, which is not usually hereditary, but prestigious
nonetheless. Then one will become a *gentleman* if not a nobleman,
through the display of genius in the maneuvering of large armies, in the direction of battles, in audacious and successful commercial speculations, in large industrial enterprises, in scientific,
artistic, or literary works, or simply the genius of an enthusiastic
dilettante.

In should be noted that in this last period the various types of
aristocratic distinctions which are all individual though incessantly renewed and reproduced, transmitted neither truly nor fic-
tively by blood but by example aided by social selection—all these
distinctions will tend to be concentrated in the large cities, the
capitals. That is why I have elsewhere stated the idea that capitals

are destined to replace the nobility.[4] They are the impersonal aristocracies of democratic times and participate in the vices and qualities of the nobility, which they both amplify and reflect. There is the same pride fostered by the same smug admiration (in which a fairly justified recognition of services rendered plays a part). There is the same imitative dissemination of ideas, needs, styles, of immorality and superior morality, the same wear and rapid refinement of the race which comes there to be consummated and consumed.

In short, we have found four sources of nobility: a military source, an economic source, a religious source, and an aesthetic source. The mistake made by Fustel de Coulanges in his explanation of the Roman and Greek patriciate was to take account of the religious source alone. The insufficiency of his interpretation of facts has already been indicated.[5] If Fustel had thought of the plebeians' debts to the patricians and of the role that from the very beginning, the relationship of debtor to creditor played in Roman history, he could not have helped observing that one of the most salient traits of the patrician was to be rich and, more especially, capitalistic. According to Sumner-Maine, the Brehon law shows us that the same was true of the Irish nobles: this Celtic nobility was rich in herds, the capital of its time, and its means of subjugating the lower classes was to lend them cattle according to a singular cattle lease. The continental feudal *land* tenure in the Middle Ages marks a more advanced stage of economic relations

---

4   See *Laws of Imitation* pp. 225–33 of the second [English] edition, and *Penal Philosophy*, the chapter on crime, sec. 2.

5   According to him, the patrician families were those who alone had "the power to create gods, to institute a cult, to invent the hymn and the rhythm of prayer." Agreed, but if that were the true and unique cause of the patriciate, how could it be that the lesser families who were incapable of inventing a cult (an invention moreover, which probably not *all* the patrician families had a hand in) did not dream of ennobling themselves by imitating the patrician families, something which would have been very easy? Is there not cause to think that, having had fetishes originally like all savage families, the plebeian family lost theirs, eclipsed as they were by the strikingly superior domestic gods of the patrician families? Where then did this striking superiority come from?

between the nobility and the common people. But it is no less true that in not one country does becoming rich suffice for becoming noble, even though it can sometimes suffice *to be born rich*, which is not the same thing. We must add to this a certain degree of *respectability* and of *hereditary* respectability (since that is, strictly speaking, the defining characteristic of nobility), whose causes are military or religious. (I am leaving aside the aesthetic source as secondary and rather more *urbanizing* than *ennobling*.) Hence, among the Arabs, for example, there are Marabout families, in which saintliness is hereditary, next to warrior families, in which bravery is similarly hereditary.[6] Because of the celibacy of Christian priests, the same distinction could not be established in Europe. Here the ecclesiastical peers and the noble peers did not appear to belong to the same noble caste except to the extent that the priests were also noble by birth. But the duality in question appears in other forms: our *noblesse de robe* is midway between the religious and the military nobility among the Arabs, and is more like the latter than the former. There is something priestly about the *noblesse de robe* and something ambiguous as well. According to the period they seem to constitute a lay clergy or to imitate the *noblesse d'épée*.*

[6]   In antiquity we find the two nobilities almost mingled, but in Greece and Rome we see exclusively sacerdotal families.

*   The *noblesse d'épée* or nobility of the sword was ennobled for military services to the crown; the *noblesse de robe* or nobility of the gown (referring to the robes worn by judges) were bourgeois ennobled for their legal and juridical services.—Ed.

VII. Social Control and Deviance

15

CRIMINAL YOUTH

1897

LETTER TO Mr. Buisson, former general director of primary instruction and professor at the Sorbonne:

Dear Sir:

Moved by the very remarkable article by Mr. Alfred Fouillée on "Young Criminals, the Schools, and the Press," which appeared last January in the *Revue des Deux Mondes*, you honor me by requesting my opinion on this serious subject. The difficulty lies in dealing with it after such a master, whose conclusions on the whole cannot be denied; but the question is so complex that it calls for yet another examination.

Let us first of all specify the facts and figures, which here refer to a double increase, especially of criminality and also of suicide among minors.

The official report preceding the criminal statistics for 1880

Revue pédagogique, February 1897, reprinted in *Etudes de psychologie sociale* (Paris: Giard & Brière, 1898), pp. 195–204, 209–25.

[At the time this letter was written, Tarde was director of the criminal statistics section of the Ministry of Justice as well as an established criminologist and sociologist. He was thus able to draw from unpublished statistical materials collected by the Ministry of Justice to report the most recent figures on delinquency.

Buisson, who asked Tarde to comment, was one of the most influential men in France in reforming the educational system near the turn of the century. An ardent republican, he gave up his chair (in pedagogy) at the Sorbonne when he entered the National Assembly. Because of this vacancy, Durkheim was called to Paris in 1902 as a substitute for Buisson, and a few years later he was named as permanent incumbent of the chair, the title of which was later changed to sociology.—Ed.]

demonstrates that in the fifty years from 1830 to 1880, when adult criminality tripled, criminality among minors ages 16 to 21 quadrupled, at least for boys. In absolute numbers, the increase for boys was from 5,933 to 20,480, and for girls, from 1,046 to 2,839. The report adds, "This fact is saddening, but we are justified in hoping that in view of the combined efforts on all sides to give moral direction to childhood the future will show improvement"— wishful thinking unfortunately. In 1894 the number of accused male minors of the ages indicated rose to 28,701 and that of females to 3,616. The increase is primarily in vagrancy and stealing. So much for misdemeanors (*délits*). Will someone point out to me that true *crimes*, "court cases," decreased in absolute number among minors? Yes, an apparent decrease, which is due to the progress of legal and extralegal correctional measures. But if one looks only at those crimes really worthy of the name and therefore not capable of correction, and especially at murder (*assassinat*), there is no decrease in the figures. Judge from this, from 1856 to 1860 the annual average of young people 16 to 21 years of age accused of murder was 20; from 1876 to 1880 it rose to 30; and from 1890 to 1894 it had almost doubled, reaching 39.[1] Despite the exceptional and ever-increasing indulgence, legal or extralegal, shown to children under 16, the number of them charged with the same crime increased as well, and in greater proportion. In the first of the three periods compared it was 0.8 per year; in the second, 2.8; in the third, 2.2. The decrease from the second to the third period is certainly a delusion and is to be explained by the doubling of the quasi-paternal protection with which our society rightly covers the misdeeds of the young. It should be added that the augmentation would appear more rapid if one counted the crimes that were not tried because of lack of proof, for the proportion of such crimes is continually on the increase.

Even without including this hardly negligible element in our calculations, we see that the number of murders with which minors were charged has doubled in less than 40 years, while that with which adults were charged rose only slightly or not at all. In 1856–

[1]   In 1895, with only 32, there is a noticeable decrease.

60 the annual average number of those accused of murder was 234; in 1876–80 it was 239; in 1890–94, 280. Subtracting the fraction relating to youths from 16 to 21 and that of children under 16, we have, for adults in the first five year period, 213 or 214; in the second, 206 or 207; and in the third, 239. Considering the population increase in these 35 years, the proportion of adult murders, I do not say homicides of all types, seems to have diminished rather than increased while that of minors doubled.

And what crimes are involved! Mr. Guillot notes "the exaggeration of ferocity, the search for lewdness" among young miscreants. Still, it should be noted that this cynicism and cruelty is the exclusive privilege of an elite, and that on the whole this new generation distinguishes itself rather by its spinelessness. "Those who carefully observe the children in our prisons and reform schools are struck, rather, by the moral abandon, the ignorance, the weakness of character and instability of most of them," says Mr. Henri Joly in his review of Mr. Fouillée's study. This is perhaps more painful than the preceding idea; so they are not all *monsters*, these young miscreants, but just the sons of their fathers.

Let us turn now to the suicides. All those concerned with criminal archaeology know how rare suicide used to be in the France of old. In their interesting work on *retrospective criminality* in Brittany, Mr. Corre and Mr. Aubry noted the amazing rarity of this sad phenomenon up to the reign of Louis XV. It seems then to have appeared or to have been awakened under cover of the general demoralization. But what a rapid advance in our own century! We might at least have been able to hope that children would escape this contagion of despair; let us see whether such is the case.

For children under 16, the average annual number of suicides in the period 1836–40 was 19. In the five-year periods from then until 1876–80 it progressed as follows: 20, 24, 29, 26, 28, 31, 31, 51. We may note parenthetically that the only two decreases, which we underlined, correspond, remarkably enough, to the period 1856–65, during which French criminality showed an exceptional real decrease for both misdemeanors and crimes. It is clear what we should think of the supposed inverse relationship of suicide and homocide conceived by the Italian criminologists—here too, for children under 16, the progression continues and even speeds up. The annual average becomes:

1881–85 61
1886–90 70
1891–94 75[2]

For minors from ages 16 to 21 the curve of suicide rose still more rapidly. From 1836–40 to 1876–80 the average figures for this age group are: 128, 134, 126, 151, 161, 167, 174, 243, and then

1881–85 309
1886–90 366
1891–94 450[3]

Now, from 1836 to 1880 the advance in suicides for all ages combined went from 2,574 to 6,259, an increase of 243 percent, while that of suicides among minors (combining the two age groups above) was approximately 200 percent, thus slightly lower than the rate for the country as a whole. From 1881 to 1894, however, the overall suicide rate increased from 6,741 to 9,703,[4] in other words by 153 percent (in only 14 years) while the rate for minors increased 176 percent, thereby exceeding the already accelerated and frightening rate for adults.

These are the facts, but in order really to understand them and not to run the risk of explaining them by causes having no relation to the real extent of the problem, we must look beyond our own borders. For this malady is general. Every country has the same complaints about the growing perversity of youth. Mayr's work on the criminal statistics of the German empire shows that in six years, from 1888 to 1893, the number of those convicted of all ages rose 21 percent and that of children or adolescents 12 to 18 rose

2   The progression continues: in 1895 I find 90 suicides in children of this age of which 8 are 13-year-olds, 2 are 10, one is 9, and one is 8 years old.
3   In 1895 there were 474 suicides in this age group.
4   For the first time, in 1895, the figure decreased; that year there were *only* 9,963 [*sic*] suicides. But the advance continued for minors.

by 32 percent, a truly enormous jump. In absolute figures there were 33,069 in this age group in 1888 and 43,742 in 1893. According to another German source, from 1882 to 1892 "the total number of convicted of all types," says Mr. Louis Rivière,[5] "grew by 28 percent, whereas the special category of minors under 18 went up 51 percent."

On the basis of certain reputable evidence, I, like Mr. Albert Fouillée, had thought that in this respect England was an exception among the European states. Has it not been said that through perseverance it had managed to reduce youthful criminality by 70 percent in a few years? Well, we must revise our estimate. The last official report on British criminal statistics in 1894 recounts this compliment addressed to our neighbors across the Channel and regrets that it is not warranted. The evidence unfortunately is unimpeachable, and when by chance the English to speak ill of themselves, we may believe them. A table attached to the report shows that the annual number of minors under 16 condemned to either imprisonment or detention in a *reformatory* or *industrial school* or to being whipped increased from 11,064 (annual average) in 1864–68 to 13,710 in 1894. In particular, the category of young Englishmen *whipped*, lamentably enough, shows an increase from 585 to 3,194![6]

5   See the *Revue pénitentiaire* for March 1895. These are the absolute figures: "in 1882 the number convicted throughout the empire for crimes and misdemeanors was 329,968 of which *30,719 were minors* under 18 years of ago. In 1892 the total number of convicted went up to 422,127 and that of minors to *46,496*."

6   Despite these official figures, Mr. Henri Joly (in the May 1897 issue of the *Correspondant*) persists in affirming the real decrease of criminality among English minors. He bases his argument on the claim that *industrial schools* are not comparable to our reform schools). That may be, but the *reformatory schools* . . . and the whippings?

[There follows a lengthy footnote containing Tarde's translation into French of the passage he cited of *Judicial Statistics, England and Wales, 1894 (being criminal statistics presented to Parliament by command of Her Majesty, 1896)* in which the British officials acknowledge the exception made regarding England and state that it is unjustified, as shown by the following table (giving the annual average for five-year

The ever more frequent lapse of youth into vice and delinquency and even into crime is thus not exclusively a French malady at this time; it is also an English malady, a German malady,
an Italian malady, a European malady. . . . It is therefore not possible to cite as the *principal* cause of this phenomenon a purely
French law, an innovation, in education or elsewhere, restricted
to France alone. From the start it is advisable to note the secondary
and subordinate character of legislative and political considerations to which this sad subject may give rise. Most important, the
fundamental explanation must be sought in the social transformations of our time. To be more precise, we should note a point of
fact: the progress either of criminality or of suicide was at first
more rapid among adults than among minors, or rather it showed
up among adults before being disclosed in minors; but as soon as it
struck the latter, it progressed so rapidly that they were soon in the
lead. This simple observation suffices to show us that whatever the
germs causing this contagion, they did not come to the children
directly but after they had acted on their older contemporaries,
and, above all, on their parents. In other words, whatever the
causes of the transformations of which I am speaking, they acted
first on the fathers before working on the sons; if their efficacy ap-

---

periods 1864 to 1893 and the absolute figures for 1894). The totals show
a considerable increase.—Ed.]

	1864–68	1869–73	1874–78	1879–83	1884–88	1889–93	1894
Imprisoned	8,285	8,266	6,155	4,557	3,659	2,698	1,913
Sent to *re-form schools*	1,228	1,336	1,382	1,333	1,245	1,161	1,790
Sent to *indus-trial schools*	996	1,921	2,234	3,328	5,095	6,737	6,815
Whipped	585	839	1,225	2,723	3,152	3,208	3,162
Total	11,064	12,362	10,996	11,941	13,151	13,803	13,710

[The officials suggest that the false impression was the result of looking
only at the figures of youth condemned to prison.—Ed.]

[Tarde concludes:] "I may add that the question of criminality
among British minors has, since the appearance of our article, been studied
in great depth and with great impartiality by Mr. Brueyre in *Revue
pénitentiaire* (December 1897) and that the author reaches the same conclusion as we do."

pears greater on the latter, it is very easy to understand: a new wind shakes young branches much more forcefully than the old limbs through which it blows.

No one will doubt the truth of this observation if he thinks about making another, namely that the causes to which the progression of suicide and criminality may be attributed are partly the same as those that enable us to explain the diminution in births, the population decline. And what are these causes—intellectual, sentimental, economic, pathological? First of all, there is an increase of general irreligion through the propagation of doctrines which have destroyed the traditional principles of morality and the family before replacing them. This purely negative and critical de-Christianization results in both demoralization and depopulation, as will be seen by a statistical comparison from this triple point of view among French departments. In the second place, there is an increasing desire for social advancement, stimulated by the spread of new needs, which were luxuries not long ago and are now basic necessities. This is a very important factor whose strength was demonstrated by Mr. Arsène Dumont regarding the birth rate: the number of children is in inverse proportion to the needs which arise or tend to arise in each family. This factor is no less strong in criminality, explaining as it does, along with the internal exodus from rural areas to the cities and the detachment from land and home, the frequency of a demoralizing change of social class. In the third place, not the increase in misery but the insufficiency, felt more and more strongly, of progress toward wealth in response to the more rapid increase of covetousness, the multiple desires of which I have just spoken. Only thus can we understand the parallel progress of criminality, depopulation, and wealth as attested to by our comparative statistics. And, finally, there is the contagious scourge of alcoholism, the source of degeneration and disequilibrium, of sterility and perversity, of vital impotence and social harm. . . .

But is it really certain that these considerations are relevant here, that they have something to do with our subject? To read certain statistics, notably those on school attendance, one might doubt it. Mr. Bonzon[7] says there is a great gap between the number of children registered in primary schools and the number actually present. Of 250,000 children registered, "about 45,000 are not in regular attendance, 31,500 of them being in public schools. It is not surprising if attendance is lower in these schools. Its pupils are the least regulated and the most neglected of children." Now, is reform school population recruited from among the regularly attending students or from among those registered in school but not present? The registers of the reform schools tell us that, upon entering, the most delinquent are those who show a proportionally higher ignorance than honest children of the same age.

I read in the 1893 *Statistique pénitentiaire*, just published by the Minister of the Interior, that only 2 percent of the boys have had primary instruction and 36 percent are completely illiterate. Thus it could be said that criminality in children is inversely proportional to their regular attendance at school, and it has been proved that school, whether public or private, and *when attended*, keeps the students, to an insufficient degree, to be sure, but still to some degree, from slipping down the slope to delinquency. It is unfair to attribute to the school the least role, direct or indirect, in the progress of juvenile criminality. On the contrary, school checks this criminality as much as it can, if not as much as we might hope. Is it the teachers' fault if people have deluded themselves about the panacea of education? Here again there is an argument with members of the same sort. Careful study of our criminal statistics will reveal that, in the last few years at least, the progression in question only refers to youths from 16 to 21 years of age, that is, those who have already left primary school and are released without restraint to the suggestions of the street, the workshop, the family, the liquor store. As for minors under 16, "the statistics indicate no increase, either from the point of view of misdemeanors or from that of crime," according to the official report of 1893. "The number of accusations in this age group is even decreasing as long as we look back no farther than 1890. *These improvements apply to the most important forms of*

[7]   *Le Crime et l'Ecole* by Jacques Bonzon, lawyer at the Court of Appeals (published by Guillaumin, Paris, 1896).

misdemeanors such as stealing and fraud, not to violations of public decency, which have remained fairly constant in number, nor to
blows and wounds, which have increased slightly." The 1894 statistics did not invalidate this conclusion.[8] From 1889 to 1894, in
five years, the number of boys under 16 accused of theft declined
from 4,080 to 3,582 and that of girls of the same age from 728 to
620, while the number of youths of both sexes in the 16 to 21 age
group accused of the same misdemeanor increased in the same
time interval from 8,370 to 8,701 and from 1,613 to 1,773. It
should be noted that there is an exceptionally remarkable decrease in the total number of people, men and women of all ages
taken together, accused of theft in this period, a decline from
50,427 to 47,709.

It is thus certain that the schools have acted neither directly
nor indirectly to encourage crime, and to prolong this demonstration would be an insult indeed. But does it follow—and this is really
the question—that they have acted as a deterrent with all the
energy that we are entitled to expect of them? One would like to
be able to say of the schools what Mr. Fouillée has said of religion,
that it is "a moral brake, and still more a moral spur." Unfortunately, the school is worth not exactly what the teachers are worth,
but what the students' parents are worth. In those cases where
there is high morality among the parents whose children attend
the school, it can do much good; where the immorality of the
families is notorious, it can only produce more or less bad efforts.
To be convinced of this, consider not the whole of the student population, a heterogeneous mass which contains a confused array of
complex forces difficult for statistics to single out, but rather a special category of children on whom a sort of conclusive sociological
experiment, so to speak, is made every day—the children detained
in correctional educational establishments. They arrive in these
institutions guilty of various misdeeds, and we have just seen that
the majority of them did not attend school. But the official document which gives us this information also informs us that as soon
as they enter, these children are forced to become model students,
and a table shows us the rapid progress of their knowledge by the

[8]   Nor those of 1895.

time they leave: 70 percent know by then at least how to read, write, and do arithmetic, and the proportion of illiterates has fallen to 5 percent. But—the sad confession of penal statistics— despite their increased knowledge and with ever-increasing rapidity they fall back into delinquency.

Summarizing these statistics, the *Bulletin de la Société des prisons* says,[9] "In 1888 recidivists made up 11 percent of the imprisoned boys; in 1889, 13 percent; in 1890, 14 percent; in 1891, 15 percent; in 1892, 17 percent." We may add that in 1893, it was 19 percent. "The proportion of recidivist girls, which until 1890 did not rise much above 8 percent, rose rapidly to 12 percent in 1891, to 15 percent in 1892," and to the same total in 1893. The writer from whom I am borrowing this summary points out the correlation of this increase in recidivism among children with no family life or whose parents have the greatest frequency of negligence, immorality, and bad examples. For the girls there is no doubt on this point. "The proportion of orphan girls without one or both parents, which was only 49 percent in 1890, rose to 52 percent in 1891, and 56 percent in 1892; that of illegitimate girls from 21 percent in 1890 and 1891 to 25 percent in 1892; that of daughters of habitual criminals—39 percent in 1891—attained in 1892 a figure never before achieved or even approached: 51 percent. I must further add that the proportion of girls having no *formal* education upon entering penitentiary school, rose from 70 percent to 75 percent in 1892." As for the boys, the figures are perhaps less clear. It is nonetheless verified that "the departments with the largest number of children in correctional educational establishments are those with large centers of population, or those departments which produce alcohol and have the greatest amount of taxed alcohol—thus all the places where one can safely presume that, because of intemperance or vice, the parents habitually render themselves incapable of raising children properly. It is the same everywhere. At the congress of the *Union du Sauvetage de l'enfance*, which took place in Berlin in May 1896, two reporters[10] confessed that "the creation of houses of education and reform (in

9   See the issue for February 1895, the study by Mr. Astor.
10   Cited by the *Bulletin de la Société des prisons*.

Germany) have not brought about a noticeable decrease in criminality," a euphemism for saying that they did not prevent an increase in criminality even more alarming than in France. According to them, this was due to "the gaps in legislation. It would be necessary to be able to remove morally abandoned children more easily from the authority of unworthy parents." The same situation holds true for America; the statistics of the Elmira reformatory tell us that of the parents of youths detained in this reform school, 38 percent are alcoholics; 54 out of 100 times the "domestic environment is *very* bad"; 38 or 39 percent of the time it is bad. In brief, according to Mr. Alimena (*Imputabilitá*, vol. 2, p. 279) "a good domestic environment is found only 7 to 8 percent of the time." And, since the efficacy of the morally therapeutic methods put into practice in this celebrated penitentiary has been much vaunted, there is some merit in pointing out, with Mr. Garofalo, that "20 percent of those freed from Elmira are recidivists 6 months after their departure."

It is thus abundantly proved that as far as the world of potential small-time miscreants is concerned, schools have been neither a moral *brake*, since they do not prevent recidivism, nor a moral *spur*, since everyone agrees on delinquents' cowardice and weakness of character. But rising above this sad group to consider the whole of the child population, is there cause to think that school is a moral brake or spur of much strength? Alas, no. It is no more than an intellectual stimulus, a mental aperitif—and that is not enough.

It is something, however, and it would be a great deal if the appetite or curiosity it aroused found satisfaction in a select and healthy nourishment, in good popular libraries freely open everywhere, even in the smallest town, in places for respectable meetings, circles, artistic societies. But it is the trashy and malicious press, scandal-mongering, riddled with court cases, that awaits the student when he leaves school. The little newspaper, supplementing the little drink, alcoholizes his heart. Primary instruction is therefore no more than a tool which may be good or bad according to how it is used.

By a deplorable coincidence pointed out by Mr. Fouillée, the

laws concerning schools were contemporaneous with those of freedom of the press in 1881 and the law of 1880 concerning the retail
sale of liquor. Against the desires of their authors, undoubtedly,
these laws removed the last obstacles to the unleashing of journalism and alcoholism. In 1880 France consumed 18,000 hectoliters
of absinthe; in 1893, 108,000; in 1896, 125,000.[11] No less rapid
and no less frightening was the double progress of pornography
and slander, which have become the two breasts nourishing the
newspaper. The *Chronique judiciaire* alone has caused more crimes
through the "contagion of murder"[12] and of theft, which it insti-
gates, than the schools could ever prevent. For not a murder is
committed but the press becomes aroused—except when it is a
question of murdering two or three hundred thousand Armenians,
which it fails to tell us about. And parallel to this overflowing of
provocation to vice and hate, to lechery and murder, comes an
overflow of criminality in general and especially juvenile criminality (which, strikingly enough, overflows in atavistic forms of
violence more than of greed and thereby acquires the color of a
social retrogression). People are surprised at all this, stirred up,
and apt to blame it all on whom? On journalists? On the wine
merchants? On the leaders and falsifiers of opinion, and the poi-
soners of the public? No, on the schoolteachers! This joke has
really lasted too long.[13]

If to these gigantic bellows which stir up passions from below
we add the strong scientific or philosophical battering ram which
breaks down Christian beliefs and principles of traditional morality from above and, by dechristianizing the sons after the fathers

[11]   See the report read in February 1897 by Mr. Louis Rivière to the
Société des prisons.
[12]   Read the substantial and instructive work of Dr. Aubry: "La
Contagion du meutre," pp. 102ff.
[13]   It is true that these scapegoats have not done all the good that
they might. But why? Frankly speaking, politics have falsified the role of
the teacher just as they have that of the justice of the peace. So long as the
justice is not permanent and independent of the deputy, so long as the
teacher depends on the prefect and the deputy more than on the rector,
neither one nor the other will respond very well to the mission which falls
upon him.

(even the most religiously brought up), works to demoralize them, at least temporarily, perhaps permanently, then the only surprise should be that the crisis of morality is not more acute. It is certainly much less so than the ethical crisis.[14] The problem is an enormous one but may be exaggerated, and it is possible that we are mistaken about how exceptional it really is. If criminal statistics dated back for several centuries, they would, I believe, furnish unimpeachable proof of the fact that every period of a crisis of conscience, which lasts as long as there remains turmoil after a people's conversion to a new religion in combat with the old, has been marked by a dark flowering of crime, even when the perturbation caused by this internal contradiction was due to the advent of a purer and higher religion. I do not doubt that in many regions of the Roman empire the invasion of Christianity was accompanied by a temporary lowering of virtue and an increase in criminal audacity, not among the first Christians but among the last pagans, who were cut loose from their faith without finding a mooring on a new shore. The same thing happened in the sixteenth century during the cruel sundering of peoples spiritually torn between Rome and Geneva. In the fifteenth century the literary renewal of pagan ideas in de-Christianized hearts also caused very profound demoralization, although it was less bloody (or less generalized) and localized in a narrow circle of humanists. A Machiavelli can be born only in such times. Of an entirely different order, it is true, is the moral state achieved when, after this period of painful conflicts, a peace, even a patched up one, is established, and numerous different sects and philosophies coexist in the same territory; their coexistence at that time is not necessarily a moral malady, on condition that they agree on certain capital points. Independently of the moral emulation stimulated by their juxtaposition, their disagreement on all other points emphasizes and gives singular value to their unanimity on these particular points.

And such was the relationship of religious or philosophical doctrines (however little sanctioned) in Europe and even France un-

[14] The latter is attached to the *university crisis* about which one can read, in the *Revue bleue* of February 13, an interesting discussion between Mr. Maurice Spronck and Count de Mun.

til recently; and such it is still among peoples who have retained a relative integrity of character. To tell the truth, it is always a matter of different offshoots of the same Christian trunk, or of some schematic skeleton of Christianity called spiritualism, be it the vague spiritualism of Cousin or the original Spiritualism of Kant or his followers. So much so that when these people feel the need to take away the "confessional nature" from the official teaching of ethics, the intent is not to make it irreligious and certainly not antireligious. Everywhere that there is more than one distinct *credo*, the schools at all levels, primary, secondary, higher, try to base themselves either on one or on another, or on a combination of the others, or when they are varieties of the same species— Protestantism and Catholicism or various Protestant sects—on what they have in common. In certain provinces of Canada such as Manitoba and in England, the children are taught a *minimum* or rather an *extractum carnis* of Christian doctrine: the Ten Commandments and the Lord's Prayer. Thus they obtain what is believed to be a "natural religion," which is superimposed on the positive religions in the same way that legal philosophers think they have discovered a "natural law" over and above all legislation. But as those credos multiply, it becomes necessary—and the necessity makes itself felt first for higher education, then for secondary education, finally for primary education—to reduce more and more the extract that supposedly expresses their common ground. Thus emerges this vague spiritualism that I spoke of, which occurred in France during more than the first half of this century, a spiritualism that is really a schema of a simplified and rationalized Christianity. The misfortune is that even this has become too substantial since the appearance and unparalleled success of more radical philosophies: positivism and transformism. It is not that I consider positivist or even transformist morality in themselves irreconcilable with Christian morality except for what touches its sexual side. The first, in the form received from Comte, excellently bases the inner beauty achieved by the saints, and *maximized* by the best doctors, on social utility. But the second is still seeking its true form and has not found it. In the meantime it presents itself in deplorable counterfeit form as a type of social

Darwinism that Darwin himself would have rejected, which, since the catastrophe of the *Terrible Year*,* is the only aspect of moral evolutionism to have invaded hearts and minds and even the domain of facts.

This is the truly new, truly perilous side of present times; for the first time a great and popular philosophy, differing thereby from all those which have held sway until now and from all churches, logically and inevitably leads to maxims that are in absolute contradiction with age-old precepts. From improperly understood concepts of competition for life, which were wrongly deemed sufficient and necessary to explain living harmony, was deduced the necessity for the greatest universal good of battle and war. What kind of ethics can you construct on this basis if not one that is antireligious and not just irreligious? Goodness, modesty, respect, devotion: by what reason can we praise these virtues of the past if they are reputed to be a cause of the degeneracy of peoples and races? If you believe that all, even and especially the most violent, forms of battle are the sacred and bloody road to progress, then it is the hardness of heart called *character*, it is pride, ambition, scorn for others, and cruel combativeness that should be vaunted and cultivated in our children. Or rather, it is quite useless to tell them so since they will tell it to themselves often enough; they have already said it to themselves too often. And I ask you, when a civilized society has reached the point of convincing itself that social life is essentially a battle, a natural aggravation of overexcited egoisms, that it is good to be thus, that all good comes from this situation, and that it is proper to push to extremes these contradictory drives, to generalize this confusion and make it gigantic in order to attain a future Eden—when this aberration triumphs, is it surprising that crimes, suicides, insanity, sword-thrusts of the *struggle for life*, should multiply?

Again, how is it that this cause of depravation has not been more fruitful? Suppose that in some period of the past a similar doctrine had been spread about, legitimating the right of force, justifying the "claims" of highway robbers and the "propaganda through

*   The reference is to the events of 1870–71, the Franco-Prussian war and the Paris Commune.—Ed.

action" of assassins, and just imagine the trail of murders and pillaging that would have filled and dishonored our annals!

Make another hypothesis, somewhat related to the preceding one. Ask yourself what would have happened in the past if the criminal justice of the ancien régime, instead of being ferociously savage, had been as paternalistic, as lenient as our own. Because here is still another cause of criminality that I have not yet talked about, which is not at all insignificant—with all due respect for the Italian criminologist who excludes it from his list of "factors of delinquency." We all know, however, to what degree intimidation from fear of punishment is effective, especially among youths and children. Hence it is natural that with the progress of judiciary indulgence—and there is abundant proof of indulgence of judges and juries alike—youthful criminality grows even faster than that of adults. True, to this it is objected: "Is not this mollifying indulgence itself a symptom of increasing immorality?" No, say rather that it is the very expression of the Duty which gains credence as a logical consequence of the uncertainty of principles, thus of the contradiction of principles. Severity in a skeptic would be immoral and unnatural; legitimately it falls only to a man of faith to condemn to death. Indulgence is the moral grace of skepticism, no matter how pernicious its social effects from the standpoint of utility. Thus the same cause, doctrinal contradiction, favors both the multiplication of delinquency and the reduction of punishment. In the face of all this, how can you be surprised at the advance of criminality? It would be no paradox to maintain that even the increase in homicides in these conditions testifies by its slowness to the real and increased gentleness of our morality.

There is nothing more formidable for a society than a general change of *credo*, and we must marvel that this is even possible.[15] One must pity a poor teacher in charge of giving a course on ethics

15   Parenthetically, the possibility, even the frequency, of this event establishes between societies and organisms a clear-cut and truly intractable difference, which takes away any serious value from the famous metaphor of the *social organism*. A *credo* is to a society what a specific type is to a living body. Imagine an adult individual setting out to change his species!

at such a time. What ethics do you want him to teach? There are at least two clearly contradictory sets present: the ethics of war and those of love. Should he be inspired by one or by the other or by both indiscriminantly? Will he add the incoherence of his own precepts to that of existing examples in order to further confuse his pupils' consciences? Happy the school teacher in those times and countries where everyone, despite doctrinal differences, is in agreement that one Book—the Bible, the Gospel, the Koran—be regarded as the treasury of truth; he has this book read to the children, and all is said. But what is our sacred book? Not even the penal code. It leads one to think that the less talk of morals to school children, the better it will be for their morality. Ethics are a little like orthography, about which it is dangerous to reason. When someone undertakes to change spelling, he quickly perceives the impossibility of a limited and truly practical reform. Once started on this course, one is pushed much farther than intended, as if by a spring, and comes up against the problem, logically insoluble, of a rational spelling. Ethics also has archaisms and oddities, which are as respectable as they are cumbersome, its useless letters, which must be maintained until it becomes impossible to do so.

I know very well that in the social world, as in the universe as a whole, there are a host of apparently insoluble problems which end up by solving themselves. Some time ago, Mr. Berthelot wrote about chemistry and crystallography as follows:[16] "Organic nature, as well as mineral nature, operates like human industry, by which I mean that it harmonizes irreconcilable effects in absolute geometry. These approximate arrangements yield different degrees and multiple solutions in the series of crystals as well as in the series of living beings." And recalling that he was a statesman, he added: "This is also the necessary rule for human societies." There is nothing sounder than this view; social logic excels at these harmonies of antinomies, the squaring of the circle, which individual logic judges absurd. Religions and factions, sects and philosophies, races and classes—no matter how irreconcilable all these adversaries, it is only a game for social logic to make them

[16]   See the *Revue scientifique* for December 26, 1893.

272 SOCIAL CONTROL AND DEVIANCE

embrace each other. What is needed for this? The apparition of a great man or a great idea which touches our heart; an apparition followed by a great emotion. When a star of the first magnitude rises before the nervous, discouraged, broken-down little Frenchman, the energy of the great days will reappear, the law of Duty will be known again, and all the difficulties of Reason will vanish.

But where do we see shining this great collective goal capable of raising up all souls? This is the stumbling block of a *civic* ethics at the present time in our history. The strength that patriotism lends to ethics might be sufficient in the small republics of antiquity because the walls of the city were dearer to their citizens than the frontiers of our modern states are to ours. Hence the purely civic education of the Spartans and the Athenians, of the early Romans, gave results with which we ourselves could not be content and in which we could not take pride in our time of imperceptibly emerging international federation. Yet it is certain that even in its modern form, considerably broadened and toned down, patriotism is capable of being highly moralizing when the country is progressing, gaining greater prosperity, and when the prospect of its future success, population, wealth, and great strength electrifies the citizens. But when it seems that the hour of fatal decline has struck, what good is it to try, so why should one? Discouragement takes hold of every heart.

The fact is that in its greatest difficulties the city of antiquity remained not only dear to its children like the country of today but also capable of rising again through their own sufficiently devoted efforts, whereas the defeat of modern states in the battle of European life, whether peaceful or bellicose, seems somehow impersonal and predetermined, like the movement of stars. We see, for example, that our population is going to decrease and we suffer from this, but can the individual efforts of each of us noticeably impede this current? We can do so little! By marrying young and having many children we shall be working for posterity or the prosperity of our families, for which we have sacrificed our personal well-being; but to us the service we might render our country appears infinitesimal and an inadequate recompense for our sacrifice. This is true in appearance at least; but we are wrong, nonetheless, to forget about the dissemination of our example through each of our acts and its unperceived social effectiveness, often of long duration. It seems, therefore, that in the present situation the morality of the French would gain by leaning more heavily on *family sentiment*; but unfortunately this sentiment is declining even faster than patriotism, though for a very different reason. Patriotism is subsiding because the patriotic future appears—now, and falsely, I believe—discouraging; family feeling is waning because both the individualism and the increasing socialization of contemporary life are killing it.

Is it true, then, that we do not know what to base Duty on? Religion, country, family—everything—is on the way out? Not at all. Say, rather, that everything is being transformed. And who knows but we are approaching the time when the true and powerful major attraction will be not the absorption, but the sublimation of all this into a higher *federalism*, where it will be rejuvenated and reforged into that transcendant and international patriotism which, in the highest levels of modern nations, tends to become the dominant feeling and is perhaps destined to replace "the immense hope" of the past? There is something in the cult and the love of our European civilization to propagate, spread, purify, establish peacefully, something that is really more attractive and fascinating than the socialist ideal, which will, I hope, have served to pave the way.

I shall stop here. I have already, kind sir, abused the hospitality you offered me, and for which I thank you.

VIII. Collective Behavior

16

THE PUBLIC AND THE CROWD

1901

NOT ONLY does a crowd attract and exert an irresistible pull
on the spectator, but its very name has a prestigious attraction for
the contemporary reader, encouraging certain writers to use this
ambiguous word to designate all sorts of human groupings. It is
important to put an end to this confusion, and notably not to confuse the crowd with the *public*, a word in itself subject to various
interpretations but which I shall attempt to define precisely. We
speak of the public at a theater, the public at some assembly, and
here public means crowd. But this is neither the sole nor even the
primary meaning, and while the importance of this type of public
has declined or remains static, the invention of printing has caused
a very different type of public to appear, one which never ceases
to grow and whose indefinite extension is one of the most clearly
marked traits of our period. There is a psychology of crowds;*
there remains to be developed a psychology of the public, understood in this other sense as a purely spiritual collectivity, a dispersion of individuals who are physically separated and whose cohesion is entirely mental. Where the public comes from, how it arises
and develops; its varieties and relationships with those who are its
directors; its relationships to the crowd, to corporations, to states;
its strength for good or evil, and its ways of acting and feeling—
this is what we plan to investigate in this study.

From *L'Opinion et la foule* (Paris: Alcan, 1922; originally published
1901), pt. 1, "Le Public et la foule," pp. 1–62, with elisions.

*   "Psychologie des foules," which Tarde uses here, is usually rendered as mass or mob psychology; in keeping with Tarde's thought in this
essay, we have given the more literal translation.—Ed.

In the lowest animal societies, associations are above all material aggregates. As one goes up the tree of life, social relations become more spiritual. But if the individual members separate to the point of no longer seeing each other or remain so separated beyond a certain short period of time, they cease to be associates. Now, in this respect the crowd has something animal about it, for is it not a collection of psychic connections produced essentially by physical contacts? However, not all communications from mind to mind, from soul to soul, are necessarily based on physical proximity. This condition is fulfilled less and less often in our civilized societies when *currents of opinion* take shape. It is not the meetings of men on the public street or in the public square that witness the birth and development of these kinds of social rivers,[1] these great impulses which are presently overwhelming the hardest hearts and the most resistant minds, and which are now being consecrated as laws or decrees enacted by governments and parliaments. The strange thing about it is that these men who are swept along in this way, who persuade each other, or rather who transmit to one another suggestions from above—these men do not come in contact, do not meet or hear each other; they are all sitting in their own homes scattered over a vast territory, reading the same newspaper. What then is the bond between them? This bond lies in their simultaneous conviction or passion and in their awareness of sharing at the same time an idea or a wish with a great number of other men. It suffices for a man to know this, even without seeing these others, to be influenced by them *en masse* and not just by the journalist, who is the common inspiration of them all and is himself all the more fascinating for being invisible and unknown. . . .

Neither in Latin nor Greek is there any word which is the

---

1   We should note that these *hydraulic* comparisons naturally come to mind every time we speak of crowds as well as publics. For in this respect they resemble each other: a crowd in action on the evening of a public celebration circulates with a slowness and numerous eddies reminiscent of a river having no specific bed. A public is even less comparable to an organism than is a crowd. They are both rather like streams with a poorly defined channel.

equivalent of what we mean by public. There are words to designate the masses, the gathering of armed or unarmed citizens, the
electoral body, and all types of crowds. But what writer of antiquity thought of talking about his public? None of them ever knew
anything other than his *audience* in rooms rented for public read-
ings, at which the poets contemporary to Pliny the Younger gathered a small sympathetic crowd. As for the few scattered readers
of manuscripts copied by hand and existing in perhaps a dozen
copies, they, unlike the present-day readers of a newspaper or even,
sometimes, of a popular novel, were not aware of forming a social
aggregate. Was there a public in the Middle Ages? No, but there
were fairs, pilgrimages, tumultuous multitudes dominated by pious
or belligerent emotions, angers or panics. The public could begin
to arise only after the first great development in the invention of
printing, in the sixteenth century. The transportation of force over
distance is nothing compared to this transportation of thought
across distance. Is not thought the social force *par excellence?*—
think of Mr. Fouillée's *idées-forces*. Then appeared, as a profound
innovation with incalculable effects, the daily and simultaneous
reading of a single book, the Bible, produced for the first time
in thousands of copies, and to the united mass of its readers this
gave the sensation of forming a new social body, detached from
the Church. But this nascent public itself was not yet anything
more than a church apart, coinciding with that church, and
it is the weakness of Protestantism to have been a public and a
church at the same time, two aggregates ruled by different and
irreconcilable principles. The public as such only began to assume
a definite form under Louis XIV. But although at that time there
were crowds as torrential as at present, and as sizable, at royal
coronations, the great holidays, and the demonstrations provoked
by periodic famine, the public was scarcely anything beyond a narrow elite of "gentlefolk" (*honnêtes gens*) reading their monthly
gazette, reading books, a small number of books written for a small
number of readers. And the majority of these readers were in
Paris, if not at court.

In the eighteenth century, this public grew rapidly and became
fragmented. I do not think that there was a philosophical public

distinct from the general literary public before Bayle, because I do not apply the term public to a group of scholars—united, it is true, despite their dispersion in various provinces or countries, by their preoccupation with similar investigations and the reading of the same writings, but so few in number that they can keep up an active correspondence and draw from these personal relationships the principal sustenance for their scientific communion. A special public does not take shape until that time—difficult to specify—when men given to the same study were too numerous to know each other personally and felt themselves bound only by impersonal communications of sufficient frequency and regularity. In the second half of the eighteenth century, a political public arose, grew, and soon overflowed and absorbed all the other publics—literary, philosophical, and scientific—just as a river absorbs its tributaries. Until the Revolution, however, the life of the public has little intensity of its own and only acquires importance through the life of the crowd, to which it is still connected, and through the very lively activity of the salons and cafés.

The true advent of journalism, hence that of the public, dates from the Revolution, which was one of the growing pains of the public. . . .

The revolutionary public was above all Parisian; outside Paris its influence was weak. Arthur Young, in his famous journey, was struck by seeing the public newspapers so little circulated even in the cities. Of course, this observation applies to the beginning of the Revolution; a little later it would be much less true. Until the end of the Revolution, however, the absence of rapid communication posed an insurmountable obstacle to the intensity and propagation of the life of the public. How could newspapers, arriving only two or three times a week and then a week after their publication in Paris, give readers in the south of France that feeling of immediacy and awareness of simultaneous unanimity without which the reading of a newspaper does not differ essentially from the reading of a book? It remained for our century, through its perfected means of locomotion and instantaneous transmission of thought from any distance, to give all publics the indefinite extension of which they are capable and which contrasts them so sharply with crowds. The crowd is the social group of the past; after the family it is the oldest of all social groups. Whatever its form, standing or seated, immobile or on the march, it is incapable of extension beyond a limited area; when its leaders cease to keep it in hand, when the crowd no longer hears their voices, it breaks loose. The biggest audience ever seen was in the Coliseum, and even that did not exceed 100,000 persons. . . .

But the public can be extended indefinitely, and since its particular life becomes more intense as it extends, one cannot deny that it is the social group of the future. Thus three mutually auxiliary inventions—printing, the railroad, and the telegraph—combined to create the formidable power of the press, that prodigious telephone which has so inordinately enlarged the former audiences of orators and preachers. I therefore cannot agree with that vigorous writer, Dr. LeBon, that our age is the "era of crowds." It is the era of the public or of publics, and that is a very different thing. . . .

Up to a certain point, a public is confused with what we call a *world*, "the literary world," "the political world," and so forth, except that this idea implies personal contact such as an exchange of visits or receptions among those who are part of this world; this contact need not exist among the members of the same public. From the crowd to the public is an enormous leap, as we have already seen, even though the public comes in part from a type of crowd, from the orators' audience.

Between the two there are many other instructive differences which I have not yet pointed out. One can belong—and in fact one always does belong—simultaneously to several publics, as to several corporations or sects; one can only be part of one crowd at a time. From this follows the far greater intolerance of crowds, and consequently of nations dominated by the spirit of crowds, because one is completely taken over, irresistibly drawn along by a force with no counterbalance; hence the advantage of the gradual substitution of publics for crowds, a transformation which is always accompanied by progress in tolerance, if not in skepticism. Admittedly, it often happens, that an overexcited public produces fanatical crowds which run around in the streets crying "long live" or "death" to anything at all. In this sense the public could be defined as a potential crowd. But this fall from public to crowd, though extremely dangerous, is fairly rare; and without questioning whether or not these crowds which have arisen from publics are a little less brutal, on the whole, than crowds preceding any public, it remains evident that the opposition of two publics, always ready to fuse along their indistinct boundaries, is a lesser danger to social peace than the encounter of two opposing crowds. . . .

It has been contested, wrongly but not without a deceptive appearance of reason, that every crowd has a leader and that in fact it is often the crowd that leads its chief. But who will contest the fact that every public has someone who inspires it and is sometimes its creator? What Sainte-Beuve said of genius, that "genius is a king who creates his people," is especially true of the great journalist. How often one sees publicists create their own public![2] For Edouard Drumont to resuscitate antisemitism it was necessary that his initial attempts at agitation respond to a certain state of mind among the population; but as long as no voice made itself heard, echoed and expressed this state of mind, it remained purely individual, with little intensity and even less contagion, unaware of itself. He who expressed it created it as a collective force, artificial perhaps, yet nonetheless real. I know of areas in France where the fact that no one has ever seen a single Jew does not prevent antisemitism from flowering, because people there read antisemitic papers. Nor did the socialist state of mind or the anarchist state of mind amount to anything before a few famous publicists, Karl Marx, Kropotkin, and others, expressed them and put them into circulation. Accordingly it is quite understandable that the individual stamp of its promoter's genius is more marked on a public than the genius of its nationality, and that the opposite is true of the crowd. . . .

It may be objected that a newspaper reader is much more in

---

[2]   Will it be said that if every publicist creates his public every sizable public creates its publicist? This second proposition is much less true than the first; there are large groups which for many years do not succeed in bringing forward the writer adapted to their true orientation. Such is the case with the Catholic world at present.

control of his intellectual freedom than a lost individual swept up in a crowd. He can think about what he reads, in silence, and despite his ordinary passivity he may change newspapers until he finds the one that suits him or that he thinks will suit him. On the other hand, the journalist seeks to please him and to keep him. Statistics of circulation and subscriptions are excellent thermometers, which are often consulted and which warn the editors of the lines of behavior and thought to follow. An indication of this nature motivated the sudden about-face of a well-known paper in a famous affair, and such a recantation is not unusual. The public, then, sometimes reacts on the journalist, but he is continually acting on his public. After a few trial runs, the reader has chosen his paper, the paper has selected its readers, there has been mutual selection, hence mutual adaptation. The one has a paper which pleases him and flatters his prejudices and passions; the other has hold of a reader to his liking, docile and credulous, whom he can easily direct with a few concessions to his positions, analogous to the oratorical precautions of the ancient orators. The man of one book is to be feared, it has been said; but what is he beside the man of one newspaper! This man is each one of us at heart, or nearly so, and therein lies the danger of modern times. Therefore, far from preventing the action of the publicist from being finally decisive on his public, the double selection, the double adaptation, which makes the public a homogeneous group, pliable and well-known to the writer, enables him to act with more force and certainty. A crowd is, in general, much less homogeneous than a public; it always swells with many bystanders—simply curious or semi-involved—who are momentarily caught up and assimilated but succeed in making it difficult for the incoherent elements to achieve a common direction. . . .

As every supplier has two sorts of clientele, one fixed and the other floating, there are also two sorts of publics for newspapers and journals: a consolidated stable public and a floating, unstable public. The proportion of these two is very unequal from one newspaper to the next; for the older newspapers, organs of old parties, the second group does not count, or scarcely so, and I agree that here the action of the publicist is singularly hindered by the intolerance of the organization he has entered and from which he will be driven by a manifest dissidence. On the other hand, when it does occur in such a situation, his action is extremely durable and penetrating. Note, finally, that faithful publics traditionally loyal to a paper tend to disappear, being increasingly replaced by more mobile publics on which the talented journalist often has a more effective, if not more lasting, hold. This evolution of journalism can rightly be lamented, because firm publics make for honest and convinced publicists, just as capricious publics make for light, versatile, unsettling publicists; but this evolution certainly seems irresistible at present and not easily reversible, and one can see the growing resources of social power it opens up for writers. It may be that this evolution results in increasing subservience of mediocre publicists to the whims of their public, but it certainly subjugates the public more and more to the despotism of important publicists. Far more than statesmen, even the most elevated, these men make opinion and lead the world. And when they have become indispensable, what a solid throne is theirs! . . .

Indeed, one has only to open one's eyes to see that the division of a society into publics, an entirely psychological division which corresponds to differences in states of mind, tends not to substitute itself for, but to superimpose itself more and more visibly and effectively on, divisions along economic, religious, aesthetic, political lines, and divisions into corporations, sects, professions, schools or parties. It is not uniquely the crowds of old, the audiences of orators and preachers, that are dominated or enlarged by their corresponding publics—the parliamentary and religious publics; there is not one sect that does not wish to have its own newspaper in order to surround itself with a public extending far beyond it, causing a sort of mobile atmosphere in which it will be bathed, a collective awareness by which it will be illuminated. And we cannot say of this awareness that it is a simple *epiphenomenon*, in itself inefficacious and inactive. Nor is there any profession, be it small or large, that does not want its own newspaper or review as well, as each corporation in the Middle Ages had its chaplain or its habitual preacher, and each class in ancient Greece its regular orator. Is not the first concern of a new literary or artistic school to have its newspaper, and would it think itself complete without one? . . .

This transformation of any and all groups into publics can be explained by an increasing need for sociability, which necessitates the regular communication of the associates by a continual current of common information and enthusiasms. It is therefore inevitable, and it is important to seek the consequences that it has, or in all probability will have, on the destiny of the groups thus transformed, on their duration, their solidity and strength, their battles and alliances. . . .

The relative force of existing social aggregates is also singularly modified by the intervention of the press. First of all, note that the press is far from favoring a preponderance of professional classifications. The professional press, the one dedicated to the interests of the judicial, industrial, or agricultural worlds, is the least read, the least interesting, the least active, except when dealing with strikes or politics in the guise of work. What does visibly emphasize and give preponderance to the press is social division into groups by theoretical ideas, aspirations, and feelings. Interests are only expressed—and this is to its credit—when disguised or sublimated into theories and passions; even when it arouses excitement over these ideas, the press spiritualizes and idealizes them; and however dangerous this transformation may sometimes be, it is basically a fortunate one. Ideas and passions may foam up when they clash, they are still less irreconcilable than interests.

Religious or political parties are those social groups over which the newspapers have the greatest hold and to which they give the most prominence. Mobilized into publics, parties come apart, reform and transform themselves with a rapidity that would have stupefied our ancestors. And it must be agreed that their mobilization and mutual interlacing are hardly compatible with the regular functioning of English-type parliamentarianism. This is a small misfortune, but one which forces a profound modification of the parliamentary system. Sometimes the parties are reabsorbed and destroyed in a few years. Sometimes they grow to unheard-of proportions, in which case they acquire enormous, but only temporary, force. They take on two characteristics not previously seen in them: they become capable of interpenetration and internationalization. They interpenetrate easily because, as we said above, each of us does or can belong to several publics at once. They become international because the winged words of the papers easily cross borders which were never crossed by the voice of the famous orator or party leader.[3]

Thus, whatever the nature of the groups into which a society is fragmented, be they religious, economic, political, or even national, the public is in some way their final state and, so to speak, their common denominator. Everything is reduced to this entirely psychological group of states of mind in the process of perpetual mutation. It is remarkable that the professional aggregate, based on the mutual exploitation and adaptation of desires and interests, has been affected most deeply by this civilizing transformation. In spite of all the dissimilarities that we have noted, the crowd and the public, those two extremes of social evolution,[4] have in common the bond between the diverse individuals making them up, which consists not in *harmonizing* through their very diversities, through their mutually useful specialties, but rather in reflecting, fusing through their innate or acquired similarities into a simple and powerful *unison* (but with how much more force in the public than in the crowd!), in a communion of ideas and passions which, moreover, leaves free play to their individual differences. . . .

After having shown the birth and growth of the public, noted its characteristics, similar or not to those of a crowd, and indicated its genealogical relationship with the different social groups, we shall now delineate a classification of its varieties compared with those of a crowd.

3   Certain large newspapers, the *Times*, the *Figaro*, and certain journals have their public spread throughout the entire world. The religious, scientific, economic, and aesthetic *publics* are essentially and constantly international; religious, scientific, etc. crowds are so only rarely, in the form of a congress. And the congresses could only become international because they were preceded in this direction by their respective publics.

4   The family and the horde are the two points of departure of this evolution. But the horde, the gross, pillaging band, is only the crowd in motion.

Publics, like crowds, can be classified from different points of view. From that of sex, we see masculine and feminine publics as well as masculine and feminine crowds. But feminine publics made up of readers of popular novels or fashionable poetry, fashion magazines, feminist journals, and the like, scarcely resemble crowds of the same sex. They have quite a different numerical importance and a more inoffensive nature. I am not speaking of a female audience in church; but when women assemble in the streets, they are always appalling in their extraordinary excitability and ferocity.

From the point of view of age, juvenile crowds—processions or demonstrations by students or Paris urchins—have much greater importance than juvenile publics, even the literary ones, which have nexer exercised any serious influence. On the other hand, elderly publics conduct the world of business while elderly crowds have no effect. This unperceived *gerontocracy* establishes a counterbalance to the *ephebocracy* of electoral crowds, in which the dominant element is young and has not yet had time to become disgusted with the right to vote. Elderly crowds are, moreover, extremely rare. One could cite a few tumultuous councils of old bishops in the days of the early Church or a few stormy sessions of ancient and modern senates as examples of the excesses into which assembled old men may be drawn and of the collective juvenility which they sometimes manifest when they meet. . . .

Crowds can be distinguished according to the temper of the times, the season, the latitude. . . . We have said why this distinction is inapplicable to publics. The action of physical agents on the formation and development of a public is almost nil, whereas it is supreme in the formation and behavior of crowds. The sun is a great tonic to crowds; summer crowds are much more feverish than winter ones. Perhaps if Charles X had waited until December or January to publish his famous ordinances,* the result would have been different. But the influence of race, taken in the national sense of the word, on the public as well as on the crowd is not negli-

* Of July 25, 1830, which, dissolving the Chamber of Deputies and modifying the Constitution, provoked the July Revolution.—Ed.

gible, and the "enthusiasms" characteristic of the French public bespeak the effects of the *furia francese.**

In spite of everything, the most important distinction to make between various publics, as between various crowds, lies in the nature of their *goal* or their *faith*. Passers-by in the streets, each one going about his own business, peasants assembled at a fairground, people out walking, may form a dense mass, but they are merely a throng until they have a common faith or a common goal that moves them, and moves them as one group. As soon as a new spectacle demands their attention, an unforeseen danger or sudden indignation orients their hearts toward the same desire, they begin to aggregate docilely, and this first degree of the social aggregate is the crowd. A parallel statement can be made: so long as they read only notices and practical information relevant to their private affairs, even the habitual readers of a newspaper do not form a public; and if I could believe, as is sometimes claimed, that notices will grow at the expense of the news, I should hasten to erase all that I said above about the social transformations caused by journalism. But this is not true, even in America.[5] It is from the moment when the readers of a newspaper are seized by the idea or the passion which provoked it that they truly become a public.

We must therefore classify crowds, as well as publics, before all else according to the nature of the goal or the faith which animates them. But first of all, let us distinguish them according to the extent to which the faith—the idea—or else the goal—the desire—dominates. There are believing crowds and desirous crowds,

---

* Expression used by the Italians after losing the battle of Fornova (1495) to characterize the impetuosity of the French in combat.—Ed.
5 In his fine work on the *Principles of Sociology*, the American, Giddings, speaks incidentally of the major role played by the newspapers in the Civil War. In this regard he goes against the popular opinion according to which "the papers have suppressed all individual influence under the daily deluge of their *impersonal* opinions. . . ." The press, he says, "produced its maximum impression on public opinion when it was the voice of a remarkable personality, a Garrisson [*sic*] or a Greeley. Furthermore, the public is not really aware that in the newspaper offices, the idea-man, unknown to the public, is known by his co-workers and stamps his individuality on their minds and their work."

believing publics and desirous publics; or rather (since men assembled or united from afar rapidly push all thought and desire to extremes) there are crowds and publics which are convinced and fanatic and those which are impassioned and despotic. There is scarcely ever a choice of more than these two categories. Let us agree nonetheless that publics are less extremist than crowds, less despotic and dogmatic too, but that on the other hand their despotism or dogmatism is far more tenacious and chronic than that of crowds.

Believing or desiring, crowds differ according to the nature of the corporation or the sect with which they are connected; and the same distinction, as we know, applies to publics, which always come from organized social groups of which they are the *inorganic* transformation.[6]

Though more difficult to activate originally, rural crowds are more to be feared once they are roused; there is no Parisian riot with ravages comparable to those of a peasant uprising. Religious crowds are the most inoffensive of all; they do not become capable of crimes until a dissident or opposition crowd offends their intolerance, which is not greater than, but only equal to, that of any other crowd. Individuals can be liberal and tolerant when each is alone, but once assembled together they become authoritarian and tyrannical. This is because beliefs become heightened through mutual contact, and no strong convictions withstand contradiction. Hence, for example, the massacre of the Arians by the Catholics and that of the Catholics by the Arians, which bloodied the streets of Alexandria in the fourth century. Political crowds, mostly urban, are the most impassioned and the most furious; fortunately they are versatile, passing from execration to adoration, from excessive anger to excessive joy with extreme facility. Economic or industrial crowds, like rural ones, are much more homogeneous than the others, much more unanimous and persistent in their wishes, more massive and stronger, but all in all less inclined, when they become exasperated, to murder than to material destruction.

Aesthetic crowds (which along with religious crowds are the

[6]   This is a new proof that the organic bond and the social bond are different and that the progress of the latter in no way implies the progress of the former.

only crowds based on belief) have been neglected, why I do not know. I use this term for those crowds that are aroused by a new or old school of literature or art in favor of or against a drama or a musical work, for example. These crowds are perhaps the most intolerant, just because of the arbitrariness and subjectiveness of the judgment of taste that they proclaim. Their need to see the spread of their enthusiasm for such and such an artist, for Victor Hugo, Wagner, or Zola, or the opposite, their horror of Zola, Wagner, or Victor Hugo, is all the more imperative because this propagation of artistic faith is almost their only justification. Hence, when they find themselves face to face with an opposition which is itself forming ranks, their anger can at times become sanguinary. Did not blood run in the eighteenth century in the battles between the partisans and the adversaries of Italian music? . . .

Whether they are formed principally by a communion of beliefs or by one of wishes, crowds can show four stages of being, which mark the various degrees of their passivity or activity. They are either *expectant, attentive, demonstrating* or *active*. Publics show the same diversity.

Expectant crowds are those which, gathered in a theater before the curtain goes up or around a guillotine before the arrival of the condemned man, await the rise of the curtain or the arrival of the prisoner; or else those which, having run to meet a king, an imperial visitor, or a train carrying a popular leader, orator or victorious general, await the royal cortege of the train. The collective curiosity of such crowds attains unparalleled proportions without the slightest relation to the sometimes insignificant object of that curiosity. It is even more intense and exaggerated than among expectant publics, where it nonetheless runs so high when millions of readers, overexcited by a sensational affair, await a verdict, an arrest, or any new development. The least curious, the most serious of men, upon entering one of these feverish gatherings, asks himself what is keeping him there despite his urgent business, what strange need he, like all those around him, is now experiencing to see an emperor's carriages or a general's black horse. Note that expectant crowds are always much more patient than individuals in similar circumstances. During the Franco-Russian festivals, mul-

titudes of Parisians stationed themselves along the route that the
Czar was to follow, three to four hours in advance, and remained
immobile, pressed together, with no sign of discontent. From time
to time some carriage was taken for the beginning of the cortege,
but once the error was recognized, people returned to their waiting
without the occurrence of those repeated illusions and disappoint-
ments that usually create exasperation. Well-known too is the indefinite amount of time spent in the rain, even at night, by curious
crowds awaiting a big military review. Inversely, it often happens
at the theater that the same public which calmly resigned to an
excessive delay suddenly becomes exasperated and will not suffer
another minute's delay. Why is a crowd thus always more patient
or more impatient than an individual? The same psychological
cause explains both cases: the mutual contagion of sentiments
among the assembled individuals. So long as no manifestation of
impatience, foot stamping, catcalling, sound of canes or of feet
is produced in a group (and they never occur when it would do no
good, such as before an execution or a review), each individual
is impressed by the sight of his neighbors' resigned or cheerful
attitude, and unconsciously reflects their gaiety or resignation. But
if someone (when, as at the theater, it can help reduce the delay)
takes the initiative and becomes impatient, he is soon imitated by
degrees, and the impatience of each individual is redoubled by
that of the others. Individuals in a crowd have achieved both the
highest degree of mutual moral attraction and mutual physical
repulsion (an antithesis which does not exist for publics). They
elbow each other aside, but at the same time they visibly wish to
to express only those sentiments which are in agreement with those
of their neighbors, and in the conversations which sometimes occur
between them they seek to please each other without distinction for
rank or class.

Attentive crowds are those who crowd around the pulpit of a
preacher or lecturer, a lectern, a platform, or in front of the stage
where a moving drama is being performed. Their attention—and
also their inattention—is always stronger and more constant than
would be that of each individual in the group if he were alone.
On the subject of the crowds in question, a professor made a re-

mark to me that seemed accurate. He said that "an audience of young people at the Law Faculty or in any other faculty is always attentive and respectful when it is not large; but if instead of being 20 or 30, there are 100, 200, 300, they often cease to respect and listen to the professor, whereupon foot-tapping is frequent. Divide them into four groups of 25, and from these 100 rebellious and turbulent students you will get four audiences full of attention and respect." The arrogant sensation of their numbers intoxicates men when they are assembled and makes them scorn the isolated man who is speaking to them, unless he manages to dazzle or "charm" them. But it must be added that when a large audience is captured by a speaker, size makes it all the more respectful and attentive.

In a crowd of people fascinated by a spectacle or a speech, only a small number of spectators or listeners can hear very well, many only see or hear partially or almost not at all, and nonetheless, however poorly seated they may be, no matter how expensive their seat, they are satisfied and regret neither their time nor their money. Those people waited two hours for the Czar, who did finally pass by, but, crowded together behind several rows of people, they saw nothing; at most they could have heard the noise of the carriages—or sometimes only a deceptive noise. Yet when they went home they recounted the spectacle in all good faith as if they had been witnesses, for, in truth, they had seen it through the eyes of others. They would have been astonished had they been told that the man in the provinces, 200 leagues from Paris, looking at a picture of the imperial procession in his illustrated paper, was more truly a spectator than they. Why are they convinced of the contrary? Because the crowd itself on such occasions serves as its own spectacle. The crowd draws and admires the crowd.

Halfway between the more or less passive crowds of which we have just spoken and the active ones lie the demonstrating crowds. Whether they demonstrate with love or with hate, with joy or with sorrow, with conviction or with passion, it is always with their own particular excesses. Two somewhat feminine characteristics may be noted in them: a remarkably expressive symbolism related to a great poverty of imagination in inventing of these symbols, which are always the same, repeated to the point of satiety. Marching in procession carrying banners and flags, statues, relics, sometimes heads cut off and stuck on pikes, shouting *vivas* or slogans, hymns or songs: that is about all they have been able to invent to express their sentiments. But if they have few ideas, they hold on to them and do not tire of shouting the same slogans, starting again on the same march. Publics too, when brought to a certain point of excitement, can become demonstrative, not only indirectly through the crowds arising from them, but especially, and directly, through the contagious influence that they exert on the very people who stirred them up in the first place and who can no longer control them, through torrents of lyricism or imprecations, adulation or defamation, Utopian delirium or bloody fury called forth from the pens of their obedient publicists, the masters who have become slaves. Their manifestations are therefore more varied and more dangerous than those of crowds, and we must deplore the inventive genius expended on clever lies, specious fables, all continually contradicted, continually revived, for the simple pleasure of serving each public the dishes it desires, of expressing what they think to be true, or what they wish to be true.

We come now to active crowds. But what can crowds do? We see what they can undo, destroy—but what can they produce with their essential incoherence and the lack of coordination in their efforts? Corporations, sects, organized associations are productive as well as destructive. The *pontifical brothers* of the Middle Ages built bridges, the monks of the Occident cleared land and built villages; the Jesuits in Paraguay made the most interesting attempt at phalansteries that has ever been successfully undertaken; and groups of masons put up the majority of our cathedrals. But can we cite a single house built by a crowd, any land cleared and worked by a crowd, or any industry created by a crowd? For the few trees of liberty that they planted, how many forests have been burned, homes pillaged, chateaux demolished by them. . . .

The danger for new democracies is the growing difficulty for thoughtful men to escape the obsession and fascination of turmoil. It is difficult to descend in a diving bell into a very rough sea. The guiding individuals whom contemporary society brings into prominence are more and more often writers living in continual contact with society; the powerful action that they exercise, though preferable to the blindness of leaderless crowds, is still a refutation of the theory of creative masses. But this is not enough, and since to spread average culture everywhere is not enough, and since we must carry high culture still higher, we could, like Summer Maine, already be concerned with what will be the lot of the last *intellectuals*, whose long-term services do not stand out. What keeps mountain populations from razing and transforming the mountains into workable land, vineyards, or grasslands is certainly not the gratitude for the services of these natural water-towers; it is simply the solidity of their peaks, the durability of their substance, which is too expensive to dynamite. What will preserve the intellectual and artistic summits of humanity from democratic leveling will not, I fear, be recognition of the good that the world owes them, the just esteem for their discoveries. What then? I should like to think that it will be their force of resistance. Let them beware if they should separate!

IX. Public Opinion, Mass Communications, and Personal Influence

17

OPINION AND CONVERSATION

1898

Opinion

OPINION is to the modern public what the soul is to the body, and the study of one leads us naturally to the other. Might one object that public opinion has always existed whereas the public, as defined here, is fairly recent? This is certainly true, but we shall soon see how little this objection amounts to. What is opinion? How is it born? What are its various sources? While growing, how is it articulated, and by being articulated, how does it grow still further—a phenomenon illustrated by its contemporary modes of expression, universal suffrage and journalism? What is its productivity and its social significance? How is it transformed? And toward what common outlet, if there is one, do its multiple currents converge? It is to these questions that we shall essay a few answers.

Let us first say that in the word *opinion* two things are generally confused which are intermingled in practice, but which a careful analysis must distinguish: opinion proper, a totality of judgments; and the general will, a totality of desires. It is primarily but not exclusively opinion taken in the first sense that will concern us here.

However great the importance of opinion and despite its present excesses, its role must not be exaggerated. Let us try to circum-

---

From *L'Opinion et la foule* (Paris: Alcan, 1922), pp. 62–158, with elisions. First published in the *Revue de Paris*, 1898.

scribe its domain. Opinion should not be confused with two other parts of the social mind, which both feed and limit it, and which are in perpetual border disputes with it. One is Tradition, a condensed and accumulated extract of what was the opinion of those now dead, a heritage of necessary and salutatory prejudices frequently onerous to the living. The other is what I take the liberty of calling by the collective and abbreviated name Reason. This I understand to be the relatively rational although often unreasonable personal judgments of an elite which isolates itself, reflects, and emerges from the popular stream of thought in order to dam it up or direct it. Originally priests, then philosophers, scholars, lawyers—councils, universities, law courts—are successively or simultaneously the incarnation of these resistant and directive judgments, which are clearly differentiated both from the passionate and sheeplike enthusiasms of the multitudes and from their own innermost motives or age-old principles. I should like to be able to add to this listing parliaments, whether assemblies or senates. Are not their members elected specifically to deliberate in perfect independence and to serve as a brake to the public train? But it is a long way from the ideal to reality. Well before an opinion is experienced as such, the individuals who comprise a nation are aware of possessing a common tradition and knowingly submit to the decisions of judgments deemed superior. Thus of the three branches of the public mind, Opinion is the last to develop but also the most apt to grow after a certain time; and it grows at the expense of the two others. No national institution can resist its intermittent assaults; there is not one individual judgment that does not tremble and stutter in the face of its threats or demands. Which of its two rivals does Opinion most impair? This depends on who is in control of Opinion. When those in control are part of the reasoning elite, they sometimes raise up Opinion like a battering ram to breach the ramparts of tradition, enlarging them through destruction, an act not without danger. But when the direction of the multitude is left to the firstcomers, it is easier for them, leaning on tradition, to rouse opinion against reason, which nevertheless triumphs in the end.

All would be for the best if opinion limited itself to popularizing reason in order to consecrate it in tradition. Today's reason would thus become tomorrow's opinion and the day after tomorrow's tradition. But instead of serving as a link between its neighbors, Opinion likes to take part in their squabbles and sometimes, becoming intoxicated with new and fashionable doctrines, it pillages established ideas or institutions before it is able to replace them; sometimes, under the authority of Custom, it expulses or oppresses rational innovators, or forces them to don the hypocritical disguise of traditionalist livery.

These three forces differ as much in their causes and effects as in their natures. They work together, but very unequally and variably, to create the *value* of things; and value is very different according to whether it is primarily a question of custom, or of style, or of reasoning. Later we shall affirm that conversation at all times, and the press, which at present is the principal source of conversation, are the major factors in opinion, without counting, of course, tradition and reason, which never cease to have part in it and to leave their stamp on it. The factors[1] of tradition, besides opinion itself, are family education, professional apprenticeship, and academic instruction, at least on an elementary level. In all the judicial, philosophical, scientific, and even ecclesiastical coteries where it develops, reason has as its characteristic sources observation, experience, inquiry, or in any case reasoning, deduction based on subject matter.

The battles or the alliances of these three forces, their clashes, their reciprocal trespassing, their mutual action, their multiple and varied relations are one of the keen interests of history. Social life has nothing more intestine but also nothing more productive than this long travail of often bloody opposition and adaptation. Tradition, which is always national, is more restricted between fixed limits than Opinion, but infinitely more profound and stable, for opinion is something as light, as transitory, as expansive as the wind, and always striving to become international, like reason. It can be said, in

---

[1]   This word *factor* (*facteur*) is ambiguous; it means *channel* or *source*. Here it means channel, because conversation and education only transmit the ideas which constitute opinion or tradition. *Sources* are always individual initiatives, small or great inventions.

general, that the cliffs of tradition are endlessly eroded by the flow of opinion's unebbing tide. Opinion is all the stronger because tradition is weaker, which is not to say that then reason too is weaker. In the Middle Ages reason, represented by the universities, the councils, and the courts of justice, had much more strength than today to resist and repress popular opinion; it had much less strength, it is true, to fight and reform tradition. The misfortune is that contemporary Opinion has become omnipotent not only against tradition (which is serious enough) but also against reason —judicial reason, scientific reason, legislative or political reason, as the opportunity occurs. If Opinion has not invaded the laboratories of scholars—the only inviolable asylum up to now—it overwhelms tribunes of the judiciary, it submerges parliaments, and there is nothing more alarming than this deluge, whose end is not in sight.

Now that we have delimited Opinion, let us essay a better definition.

Opinion, as we define it, is a momentary, more or less logical cluster of judgments which, responding to current problems, is reproduced many times over in people of the same country, at the same time, in the same society.

All these conditions are essential. It is also essential that each of these individuals be more or less aware of the similarity of his judgments with those of others; for if each one thought himself isolated in his evaluation, none of them would feel himself to be (and hence would not be) bound in close association with others like himself (unconsciously like himself). Now, in order for the consciousness of this similarity of ideas to exist among the members of a society, must not the cause of this similarity be the manifestations in words, in writing, or in the Press, of an idea that was individual at first, then gradually little by little generalized? The transformation of an individual opinion into a social opinion, into Opinion, is due to public discourse in classical times and in the Middle Ages, to the press of our own time, and at all times, most particularly, to those private conversations which we shall soon be discussing.

We say Opinion, but for every problem there are always two

opinions. One of the two, however, manages to eclipse the other fairly quickly by its more rapid and striking brilliance or else because, even though less widespread, it is the more clamorous of the two.[2]

Every age, even the most barbaric, has had an opinion, but it has differed profoundly from what we call by that name. In the clan, in the tribe, even in the classical or medieval city everyone knew everyone else personally, and when, in private discussion or the speeches of orators, a common idea was established, it did not appear like a stone fallen from heaven, of impersonal and hence so much more prestigious origin; for each person the idea was linked to the tone of voice, the face, of the person from whom it had come, a person who lent it a living visage. For the same reason it served as a link only between people who, seeing and speaking to each other every day, were never deceived about each other.

For as long as the state did not extend beyond the ramparts of the city or, at most, the borders of a small canton, opinion thus formed, original, and strong, strong sometimes against tradition itself but especially against individual judgments, played in men's government the preponderant role of the chorus in Greek tragedy, a role often assumed by modern opinion, which is of quite another origin, in our large states or in our immense and growing federations. But in the enormously long interval separating these two historical phases, the importance of opinion underwent an enormous depression, which can be explained by its disintegration into local opinions unaware of each other and without liaison.

In a feudal state, such as medieval England or France, each village, each town had its internal dissentions, its own politics. And the currents of ideas, or rather the eddies of ideas which whirled around inside these enclaves, were as different from one

---

[2]   However widespread an opinion may be, it is never *manifest* if it is moderate; but however narrowly held a violent opinion may be, it is very *manifest*. Now the "manifestations," expressions which are at once all-inclusive and very clear, play an immense role in the fusion and interpenetration of opinions of various groups and in their propagation. It is the most violent opinions which, through manifestation, are soonest and most clearly aware of their coëxistence, and thus their expansion is strangely favored.

place to another as they were alien and indifferent to one another, at least in normal times. Not only were local politics absorbing in these places, but to the extent, the small extent, that there was interest in national politics, it was only among acquaintances, and there was only the vaguest notion of the way in which the same questions were resolved in neighboring villages. It was not Opinion that existed but thousands of separate opinions with no continuous link between them.

This link was not provided until the advent, first, of books, and then (and with greater efficacy) newspapers. The periodical press enabled these primary groups of similar individuals to form a secondary and far superior aggregate, whose units were closely bound without personal contact. From this situation arose important differences—among others, this one: in the primary groups the voices *ponderantur* rather than *numerantur*, while in the secondary and much larger group, adhered to blindly by individuals who cannot see one another, voices can only be counted and not weighed. Unconsciously the press thus worked to create the strength of numbers and to reduce that of character, if not of intelligence.

At the same time it suppressed the conditions which made possible the absolute power of the governing group. This power was greatly favored, in actuality, by the local splitting of opinion: even more, it found here its raison d'être and justification. What kind of a country is it whose various regions, cities, towns are not linked by a collective consciousness of their unity of views? Is it really a nation? Is it anything more than a geographical or, at most, political expression? Yes, it is a nation but only in the sense that political submission of these various factions of a realm to the same chief is already nationalism. In the France of Philip the Fair,* for example, with the exception of a few rare occasions when a common danger preoccupied all the cities and fiefs, there was no *public mind (esprit public)*, there were only local minds aroused separately by their own fixed ideas or passions. But through his administrators the king was aware of these diverse states of mind; he assembled them in his person, as it were, and in

---

* 1268–1314, king of France who convoked the first Estates-General (1302).—Ed.

his own summary knowledge of them, which served as a basis for his plans, he thus unified them.

It was a fragile unification, an imperfect one, to be sure, which gave to the king only a vague awareness of what was general in local preoccupations. His person was the only area of their mutual penetration. When the Estates-General were convened, a new step was taken toward the nationalization of regional and local opinion. In the mind of each deputy these opinions met, and found themselves similar or dissimilar; and the entire country, its eyes on its deputies, interested to a small (infinitely smaller than today) degree in their work, then created the unusual (at that time) spectacle of a nation aware of itself. And this intermittent, exceptional consciousness was very vague, as well as slow and obscure. The meetings of the Estates-General were not public. In any case, for want of a press the discussions were not published, and, lacking even postal service, letters could not make up for this absence of newspapers. In short, it became known through sometimes distorted news passed from mouth to mouth, after weeks and months, from travelers on horseback and on foot, wandering monks and merchants, that the Estates-General had met, and that they had considered such and such a subject—and that was all.

Note that the members of these assemblies, during their short and infrequent meetings, themselves formed a local group, the site of an intense local opinion, born contagiously from meeting man to man, from personal relationships, from reciprocal influences. And it was owing to this superior, temporary, elective local group that the inferior, permanent hereditary local groups composed of relatives or traditional friends in the towns and fiefs felt themselves united in transitory alliance.

The development of the mails by multiplying first public then private correspondence, the development of highways by multiplying new contacts between people, the development of permanent armies by making soldiers from all the provinces fraternize with each other, and finally the development of courts by drawing the aristocratic elite from all corners of the earth to the monarchical center of the nation—all had the effect of gradually developing the public mind (*l'esprit public*). But it remained for the printing press to extend this great work to the fullest. It was for the press, once it had reached the stage of newspaper, to make national, European, even cosmic, anything local which, despite its possible intrinsic interest, formerly would have remained unknown beyond a limited range. . . .

Let us try to be more precise. In a large society divided into nations, subdivided into provinces, fiefs, and cities, international opinion, arising every now and then, has always existed, even before the press: beneath international opinion are national opinions, still intermittent but already more frequent; beneath national opinions are the almost continuous regional and local opinions. These are the superimposed strata of the public mind. But the proportions of these diverse layers have varied considerably with regard to importance and depth, and it is easy to see how. The farther back one goes into the past, the more local opinion is predominant. The work of journalism has been to nationalize more and more, and even to internationalize, the public mind.

Journalism both sucks in and pumps out information, which, coming in from all corners of the earth in the morning, is directed, the same day, back out to all the corners of the earth, insofar as the journalist defines what is or appears to be interesting about it, given the goals he is pursuing and the party for which he speaks. His information is in reality a force which little by little becomes irresistible. Newspapers began by expressing opinion, first the completely local opinion of privileged groups, a court, a parliament, a capital, whose gossip, discussions, or debates they reproduced; they ended up directing opinion almost as they wished, modeling it, and imposing the majority of their daily topics upon conversation.

We shall never know and can never imagine to what degree newspapers have transformed, both enriched and leveled, *unified in space* and *diversified in time*, the conversations of individuals, even those who do not read papers but who, talking to those who do, are forced to follow the groove of their borrowed thoughts. One pen suffices to set off a million tongues.

Parliaments *before the press* differed so profoundly from those *after the press* that they seem only to have their name in common. They differ in their origins, the nature of their mandates, their functioning, the extent and the efficacy of their action. Before the press, the deputies to the Cortès, to the Diets, to the Estates-General could not express opinion, which did not yet exist; they only expressed local opinions of a very different nature, as we well know, or national traditions. . . .

The old parliaments were groups with heterogeneous mandates, each organized around distinct interests, rights, and principles; the new parliaments are groups with homogeneous mandates (even if contradictory ones), concerned with identical preoccupations and conscious of their identity. Besides, the dissimilarity of the old deputies was due to the peculiarities of their original modes of election, which were all based on the principle of the inequality and the electoral dissimilarity of various individuals, on the eminently personal nature of the right to vote. Strength of numbers was not yet known or recognized as legitimate; and for this very reason, in the deliberations of assemblies thus elected, no one considered a simple numerical majority as having the force of law. . . .

Universal suffrage and the omnipotence of parliamentary majorities were only made possible by the prolonged and accumulated action of the press, the sine qua non of a great leveling democracy (I am not speaking of a democracy limited to the ramparts of a Greek city or a Swiss canton).

The differences just indicated explain another, namely the sovereignty inherent in parliaments *after the press*, which those *before the press* never had thought of claiming. . . .

The monarchies before the press could and were supposed to be more or less absolute, intangible and sacred because they embodied national unity as a whole; after the press, they can no longer be so, because national unity is created outside them, and better than it was created by them. They can subsist, however, but they are as different from the old monarchies as present-day parliaments are from former ones. The monarch of old had the supreme merit of *constituting* the unity and the conscience of the nation;

the monarch of today can no longer have any justification except in expressing the unity created by the continuity of a national opinion conscious of itself, in conforming to this opinion and bending with it without submitting to it.

To complete our discussion of the social role of the press, is it not to the great progress of the periodical press that we owe the broader and clearer delimitation, the new and more prominent sentiment of nationality that is the political characteristic of our present period? Is it not the press that has caused the growth of our internationalism at the same time as that of our nationalism, which seems to be its opposite but may only be its complement? If growing nationalism has replaced decreasing loyalty to become the new form of patriotism, should we not credit this change to the same terrible and productive power? It is surprising to see that as nations intermingle and imitate one another, assimilate, and morally unite, the demarcation of nationalities becomes deeper, and their oppositions appear more irreconcilable. At first glance one cannot understand this contrast of the nationalistic nineteenth century with the cosmopolitanism of the previous century. But this result, however paradoxical, is actually very logical. While between neighboring or distant peoples the exchange of merchandise, ideas, all kinds of items multiplied, the exchange of ideas, in particular, between people speaking the same language progressed even more rapidly, thanks to newspapers. Therefore, even though the *absolute* difference between nations diminished, their relative and conscious differences grew. Note that geographic limits of nationalities tend at present to be confused more and more with those of the principal languages. There are countries in which the language battle and the nationality battle are one and the same. The reason for this is that national sentiment was revived by journalism and that the truly effective influence of newspapers stops at the frontiers of the language in which they are written.

The influence of books, which preceded that of newspapers and was dominant in both the seventeenth and eighteenth centuries, could not produce the same effects; for even if the book made

all who read it in the same language feel their philological identity, it was not concerned with questions both current and simultaneously exciting to everybody. National existence is well attested
by literatures, but by their great daily fluctuations it is the newspapers that fire national *life*, stir up united movements of minds
and wills. Instead of drawing its interest from the concrete facts
it presents, as a newspaper does, a book seeks to interest the reader
primarily by the *general* and abstract character of the ideas it
contains. It is thus more apt to arouse a humanitarian current,
like our literature of the eighteenth century, than a national or
even international current.

Conversation

We have just cast a rapid first glance on our subject to
give an idea of its complexity. After defining opinion we concentrated in particular on showing its relations to the press, but
the press is only one of the sources of opinion, and one of the most
recent. We studied it first because it is the most clearly visible.
But now it is advisable to study in greater depth an unexplored
domain, that factor of opinion that we have already recognized
as the most continuous and the most universal, its invisible source,
flowing everywhere and at all time in unequal waves: conversation.
First, the conversation of an elite. In a letter of Diderot to Necker,
in 1775, I find this very accurate definition: "Opinion, that motive (*mobile*) whose force for good or evil is well known to all
of us, is originally no more than the effect of a small number of men
who speak after having thought and who continuously form centers
of instruction, in different parts of society, from which errors and
well-reasoned truths flow by degrees until they reach the outer
confines of the city, where they become established as articles of
faith." If no one conversed, the newspapers would appear to no
avail—in which case one cannot conceive of their publication—
because they would exercise no profound influence on any minds.
They would be like a string vibrating without a sounding board.
On the other hand, without papers or even speeches, if conversa-

tion did succeed in making progress without these nutriments—
hard to believe—it would in the long run take over to a certain
extent the social role of public oratory or the press as formers of
opinion.

By conversation I mean any dialogue without direct and immediate utility, in which one talks primarily to talk, for pleasure, as
a game, out of politeness. This definition excludes judicial inquir-
ies, diplomatic or commercial negotiations or councils, and even
scientific congresses, although the latter abound in superfluous
chatter. It does not exclude flirtations or amorous exchanges generally, despite the frequent transparence of their goals, which does
not keep them from being pleasing in themselves. It includes all
nonessential discussions (*entretiens de luxe*), even among barbarians and savages. If I were only concerned with polite and cultivated conversation as a special art, I could not trace it back farther
(at least since classical antiquity) than the fifteenth century in
Italy, the sixteenth or seventeenth in France and then in England,
and the eighteenth in Germany. But long before this aesthetic flower
of civilizations began to bloom, its first buds appeared on the tree
of languages; and although less fruitful in visible results than the
discourse of an elite, the elementary discussions (*entretiens terre
à terre*) between primitive people are not lacking in great social
importance.

Never, except in a duel, does one observe an individual with
all the force of one's attention unless one is talking with him, and
that is the most constant, the most important, and the least observed
effect of conversation. It marks the apogee of the *spontaneous attention* that men lend each other,[3] by which they interpenetrate to
a much greater depth than in any other social relationship. By
making them confer, conversation makes them communicate via an
action as irresistible as it is unconscious. It is, consequently, the
strongest agent of imitation, of the propagation of sentiments,
ideas, and modes of action. A captivating and much applauded
discussion is often less suggestive because it avows the intention of

[3]   Mr. Ribot, in his clear and penetrating studies, has shown the importance of "spontaneous attention."

being so. Interlocutors act on each other from close at hand,[4] not by language alone but by the tone of their voices, glances, physiognomy, magnetic gestures. It is rightly said of a good conversationalist that he is a *charmer* in the magical sense of the word. Telephone conversations, which lack the majority of these interesting elements, tend to be boring unless they are purely utilitarian.

Let us sketch as briefly as possible the psychology or rather the sociology of conversation: What are its varieties? What have been its successful stages, its history, its evolution? What are its causes and its effects? What are its relations to social peace, to love, to transformations of language, customs, and literatures? Each of these aspects of so vast a subject would require an entire volume, and we cannot claim to exhaust them here.

Conversations differ greatly according to the natures of those talking, their degree of culture, their social situation, their rural or urban origin, their professional habits, their religion. They differ in subjects treated, in tone, in ceremony, in rapidity of delivery, in length. The average speed of pedestrians in various world capitals has been measured, and the published statistics show quite great variation in these speeds, as well as the constancy of each one of them. I am convinced that, if it were judged relevant, the rapidity of speech in each city could be measured just as well and that it would be found to be very different from one town to another, as from one sex to another.

It seems that as people become more civilized, they walk and speak faster. In his *Voyage to Japan* Mr. Bellessort notes "the slowness of Japanese conversations, the shaking of the head, the immobile bodies kneeling around a brazier." All travelers have also noted

---

[4]   Despots are well aware of this. Hence they keep a close and wary eye on talk between their subjects and prevent them as much as possible from conversing. Authoritarian housekeepers do not like to see their servants talk with those from elsewhere, because they know that it is this way that they "get ideas into their heads." From the time of Cato the Elder the Roman ladies got together to gossip, and the fierce censor looked askance at these feminine circles, these *feminist* sprees of the salons. Cato himself advised his successor, saying that he should see to it that his wife "fear you, that she not care too much for luxury, that she see as little as possible of her neighbors or other women."

the slowness of speech of the Arabs and other primitive peoples. Does the future lie with the peoples who speak fast or with those who speak slowly? Probably with the former, but I think it would be well worth the effort to treat this aspect of our subject with numerical precision; for such a study would be amenable to a sort of social psycho-physics. At the moment, the elements for this are lacking.

Conversation takes on an entirely different tone, even a different rapidity between inferior and superior than between equals, between relatives or than between strangers, between persons of the same sex than between men and women. Conversations in small towns between citizens linked to one another by hereditary friendships are and must be quite different from conversations in large cities between educated people who hardly know each other. Both talk about what they know best and what they have in common in the realm of ideas. However, since the latter do not know each other personally, what they have in common with each other they also have in common with a great many other people—whence their penchant for general subjects, for discussing ideas of general interest. But small town citizens have no ideas more common and at the same time better known than the peculiarities of the lives and characters of the people they know—whence their propensity for gossip and slander. If there is less gossip in the cultivated circles of the capitals, it is not because there is less meanness or nastiness but because this meanness has more difficulty finding subject matter, unless it is exercised on prominent political personages or stage celebrities. These *public gossips* are no better than the private ones, which they replace, except insofar as they unfortunately interest a greater number of people.

Leaving aside many secondary distinctions, let us differentiate first of all between the conversation-battle (*conversation-lutte*) and the conversation-exchange (*conversation-échange*), between discussion and mutual informing. There is no doubt, as we shall see, that the second develops at the cost of the first. It is the same in the course of life for the individual who, inclined to argue as well as fight during his adolescence and youth, avoids contradiction and seeks accord among ideas as he grows older.

Let us also distinguish obligatory conversation—regulated and ritual ceremony—from voluntary (*facultatif*) conversation. The latter generally takes place only between equals, and the equality of men fosters its progress as much as it contributes to shrinking the domain of the first. Unless explained historically, there is nothing more grotesque than the obligation imposed on civil servants by decrees and on private individuals by social convention to make or receive periodic visits to and from one another during which, seated together, they are forced for a half hour or an entire hour to torture their minds in order to talk without saying anything or to say what they do not think and not say what they do think. The universal acceptance of such a constraint can only be understood if one goes back to its origins. The main purpose of the first visits made to the leaders and chiefs by their inferiors, to the suzerains by their vassals, was to bring presents, which at first were spontaneous and irregular presents and later became customary and regular, as has been abundantly demonstrated by Herbert Spencer. At the same time it was natural that they also be the occasion of a long or short conversation between the two, consisting of excessive compliments on the one hand and protective thanks on the other.[5] Here conversation was only the accessory of the gift, and it is still understood in this way by many peasants in regions that are the most backward in their relations with people of the higher classes. Little by little, these two elements of the archaic visits became dissociated, the present becoming the tax and the conversation developing separately, but not without keeping, even between equals, something of its past ceremonial form—from which we derive the formulas and sacramental formalities with which all conversation starts and finishes. Despite their variations, all conversations agree

[5]   The customs of visits and gifts are tied together: it seems probable that the visit was only the necessary consequence of the gift. The visit is, in short, a relic: the gift was its original raison d'être, which the visit outlived. Nonetheless something of this remains and in many visits to the country, when one goes to see people who have children, it is still the custom in many countries to bring candy or treats. Compliments must once have been simple accompaniments of gifts in the same way as visits. And in the same way, after gifts became obsolete, the compliments continued, but little by little became more *mutual*, and in the form of *conversation*.

in evincing great interest in the precious existence of the one who is being talked to and an intense desire to see him again. These formulas and formalities, which are becoming briefer but which nonetheless remain the permanent frame for conversation, stamp it with the seal of a true social institution.

Another origin of obligatory conversation must have been the profound boredom that solitude creates for primitive peoples, and illiterate peoples in general, when they have leisure time. The social inferior then makes it a duty to go, even without a gift in hand, to keep his superior company, talking with him in order to relieve his boredom. This origin and the one above easily explain the ritual frame of obligatory conversations.

As for the source of voluntary conversations, it is to be found in human sociability, which at all times has been apparent in free discussions with peers or comrades.

. . . At all times people speak of what their priests or their teachers, their parents or their masters, their orators or the journalists have taught them. Thus the monologues pronounced by superiors feed the dialogues between equals. Let us add that between interlocutors it is rare that the roles are perfectly equal. Most often, one speaks much more than the other. . . .

. . . The greatest force governing modern conversation is books and newspapers. Before the deluge of these two, nothing varied more from one town to another, from one country to another, than conversational subjects, tone, and style, nor was anything more monotonous. At present the reverse is true. The press unifies and invigorates conversations, makes them uniform in space and diversified in time. Every morning the papers give their publics the conversations for the day. One can be almost certain at any moment of the subject of conversation between men talking at a club, in a smoking room, in a lobby. But this subject changes every day and every week, except in the case, fortunately very rare, of a national or international *obsession* with a fixed subject. This increasing similarity of simultaneous conversations in an ever more vast geographic domain is one of the most important characteristics of our time. . . .

Having spoken of the varieties of conversation, its transformations and causes, let us say something about its effects, a subject we have barely touched upon. In order not to omit any, we shall classify these effects according to the well-known broad categories of social relationships. From the linguistic point of view, conversation conserves and enriches languages as long as it does not extend their territorial domain. It stimulates literature, drama in particular. From the religious point of view, it is the most fruitful means of proselytizing, spreading dogmas and skepticism in turn. Religions are established or weakened not so much by preaching as by conversation. From the political point of view, conversation is, before the press, the only brake on governments, the unassailable fortress of liberty. It creates reputations and prestige, determines glory and therefore power. It tends to equate the speakers by assimilating them to one another and destroys hierarchies by expressing them. From the economic point of view, it standardizes judgments of the utility of various riches, creates and specifies the idea of value, and establishes a scale and system of values. Thus, superfluous chatter, a simple waste of time in the eyes of utilitarian economics, is actually the most indispensable of economic agents, since without it there would be no opinion, and without opinion there would be no value, which is in turn the fundamental notion of political economy and of many other social sciences.

From the point of view of ethics, conversation battles constantly and with frequent success against egoism, against the tendency of behavior to follow entirely individual ends. It traces and lays out the precise opposite of this individual teleology, an entirely social teleology whose salutary illusions or conventional conversations give credit to lies by means of appropriate praise and blame which spreads contagiously. By its mutual penetration of hearts and minds, conversation contributes to the germination and progress of a psychology which is not exactly individual, but primarily social and moral. From the aesthetic point of view, conversation engenders politeness first by unilateral, then by mutual flattery. It tends to bring judgments of taste into agreement, eventually succeeds in doing so, and thus elaborates a poetic art, an aesthetic code which is sovereign and obeyed in each era and in each country. Conversation thus works powerfully for civilization, of which politeness and art are the primary conditions. . . .

There is a tight bond between the functioning of conversation and changes of opinion, and on this depend the vicissitudes of power. . . .

If a man of state, a Mirabeau or a Napoleon, could be *personally* known by all Frenchmen, he would have no need of conversation to establish his authority; the French might be mute, but the majority would still be fascinated by him. But since this cannot be, as soon as the extent of the state has exceeded the limits of a small town, it is necessary for men to talk among themselves to create the prestige which must rule them. After all, three-quarters of the time we obey a man because we see him obeyed by others. The first people who obeyed this man had, or thought they had, reasons for doing so: they had faith in his protective and guiding capabilities or his advanced age, high birth, his physical force, or his eloquence, or his genius. But this faith, which arose in them spontaneously, was communicated by their remarks to others who had faith in their turn. It is by talking of a man's acts that we make him notorious, celebrated, illustrious, or glorious; and once he has achieved power via glory, it is in discussions of his campaign plans or his decrees, his battles or his governmental actions, that we make his power grow or decrease.

In economic life especially, conversation has a fundamental importance that the economists do not seem to have noticed. Is not conversation, the exchange of ideas—or rather a reciprocal or unilateral gift of ideas—the preamble to the exchange of services? It is by words at first, by talking, that men of the same society communicate to each other their needs and desires concerning consumption or production. It is extremely rare that the desire to buy a new object arises simply by our seeing it, without its having been suggested in conversation. . . .

. . . The first mails began as a university and ecclesiastical privilege, or, to go back even farther, a royal privilege.

Of this important institution I shall say only a word to note that its development conforms to the law of propagation of examples from *top to bottom*. First the kings and popes, then the princes and prelates, had their own mail, before the ordinary lords, then their vassals, then successively all the layers of the nation all the way down to the last also yielded to the temptation to write. . . .

[The number of letters] increased from two and one-half million in 1700 to ten million in 1777: it quadrupled. At present postal statistics enable us to measure the rapid and continuous increase in the number of letters in various countries,[6] and to measure the unequal but still regular rise in the general need to which it responds. It is able to instruct us on the unequal degrees and the progress of sociability.

But this very statistic is also a good specimen of the fact that there are always qualities hidden beneath social quantities of which statistics in general are the approximate measure.[7] In fact, from the outside there is nothing more similar than letters of one period and one country, and it would seem that the condition of homogeneous units necessary for the statisticians' calculations could not be better fulfilled. Letters have just about the same format, the same type of envelope and seal, the same type of address. They are now covered with identical stamps. Criminal and civil statistics are far from counting units as similar as these. But open the letters, and what characteristic differences, profound and substantial, you find, despite the constant element of the ritual formulas at the beginning and the end! Adding up such heterogeneous things is therefore not doing very much. We know their number, but not even their length. It would be interesting to find out, at least, if as they become more numerous they become shorter, which seems likely, and more prosaic as well. And if sta-

[6]   In France, for example, from 1830 to 1892 the number of letters grew regularly from year to year (except in 1848 and 1870) from 63 million to 773 million. From 1858 to 1892 the number of telegrams rose, in round numbers, from 32 to 463 million.

[7]   If this were the place, I would show the qualitative elements that are hidden beneath the physical quantities measured by scientific procedures, which are basically analogous to and no less specious than statistics even though they seem more solid.

tistics existed for conversations,[8] which would be just as legitimate, one would wish, likewise, to know their length, which in our busy century could be in inverse relationship to their frequency. The cities in which it rains the most, in which the most water falls from the sky—please excuse the analogy—are quite often those where it rains the least often. It would be especially interesting to know the innermost substantive transformations of letters as well as of conversations, and here statistics give us no information at all.

In this regard, there is no doubt that the coming of journalism gave a decided stimulus to epistolary transformation. The press, which activated and nourished conversation with so many new stimulants and foods, exhausted, on the other hand, many of the sources of correspondence, which it used for its own benefit. . . .

Will it be said that the press, by liberating and freeing private correspondence from the burden of reporting the news, did epistolary literature the service of pushing it into its true path, narrow but deep, entirely psychological and cordial? I am afraid it would be a delusion to think so. Owing to the increasingly urban nature of our civilization and because the number of our friends and acquaintances does not cease to grow while their degree of intimacy decreases, what we have to say or write is addressed less and less to isolated individuals, and more and more to ever larger groups. Our real interlocuter, our real correspondent is, and more so each day, the Public.[9] It is, therefore, not completely surprising that printed announcements,[10] and advertisements in newspapers,

---

[8]   It would be possible if each of us regularly kept a diary analogous to that of the Goncourt brothers. Up to now the only types of conversations recorded are the numbers of meetings of Congress or of learned societies, and the statistics affirm a constant progression.

[9]   The need to speak to a public is fairly recent. Even the kings of the ancien régime never spoke to the public: they spoke to bodies, such as Parliament, the clergy, never to the nation taken *en masse*, and certainly not to particular individuals.

[10]   Printed announcements of marriages, births, and deaths deprived private correspondence of one of its most fruitful topics. In a volume of Voltaire's correspondence is a series of letters dedicated to announcing to the friends of Mme du Châtelet, with ingenious and laborious variations of style, the birth of the child she had just produced.

increase much more rapidly than private letters. Perhaps we even have the right to think it probable that these latter, the familiar, chatty letters, which must be distinguished from business letters, continue to diminish in number and still more in length, to judge by the extraordinary simplification and abbreviation even of love letters appearing in the "personal correspondence" section of certain newspapers.[11] The utilitarian terseness of telegrams and telephone conversations, which are trespassing on the domains of correspondence, has repercussions on the style of even the most intimate letters. Invaded by the press from one side, by the telegraph and the telephone from the other, preyed upon on both sides at once, if correspondence still lives and even, according to postal statistics, gives illusory signs of prosperity, it can only be because of the increase in business letters.

The personal letter, familiar and well developed, was killed by the newspaper. This is understandable, since the newspaper is the superior equivalent of the letter, or rather its extension and amplification, its universal dissemination. The newspaper does not have the same origins as the book. Books come from speeches, from monologues, and especially from poems and songs. The book of poetry preceded the book of prose; the sacred book preceded the profane. The origin of books is lyrical and religious. But the origin of the newspaper is secular and familiar. It comes from the private letter, which itself comes from conversation. Hence newspapers began as private letters addressed to individuals and copied a certain number of times. . . .

The newspaper, in short, is a public letter, a public conversation, which is derived from private letters and conversation and is becoming their great regulator and their most abundant nourishment, uniform for everyone in the whole world, changing pro-

[11]   What is undeniably decreasing and becoming simplified in letters of all types is their ceremony. Compare "yours sincerely" of the present with the closing formalities of the sixteenth and seventeenth century. The change in ritual conversational formulas in this same direction is not to be doubted, but since they never left a durable trace it is easier to study this progression or regression in the correspondence of the past and the present.

foundly for everyone from one day to the next. It began as only a prolonged echo of chats and correspondences and ended up as their almost exclusive source. Correspondence still lives, more than ever, and especially in the most concentrated and modern of its forms, the telegram. A private telegram addressed to the editor-in-chief results in a sensational new story of intense immediacy, which will instantaneously arouse crowds in all the great cities of the continent; from these dispersed crowds, in intimate though distant contact through their consciousness of their simultaneity and their mutual action born of the action of the news story, the newspaper will create an immense, abstract, and sovereign crowd, which it will name opinion. The newspaper has thus finished the age-old work that conversation began, that correspondence extended, but that always remained in a state of a sparse and scattered outline— the fusion of personal opinions into local opinions, and this into national and *world* opinion, the grandiose unification of the public mind. I say the *public* mind, not the national or the traditional mind, which remain basically distinct despite the double invasion of this *rational*, serious internationalism, of which the national mind is often no more than the popular echo and repercussion. This is an enormous power, one that can only increase, because the need to agree with the public of which one is a part, to think and act in agreement with opinion, becomes all the more strong and irresistible as the public becomes more numerous, the opinion more imposing, and the need itself more often satisfied. One should thus not be surprised to see our contemporaries so pliant before the wind of passing opinion, nor should one conclude from this that characters have necessarily weakened. When poplars and oaks are brought down by a storm, it is not because they grew weaker but because the wind grew stronger.

The Bibliography of Gabriel Tarde

Gabriel Tarde published some five thousand pages of books and articles. This bibliography contains his major serious works as well as a few more light-hearted contributions. Book reviews are not included. In compiling the bibliography, we have been greatly assisted by the work of Michael M. Davis, Jr., *Psychological Interpretations of Society* (New York: Columbia University Studies in History, Economics, and Public Law, 1909).

I. Books

La criminalité comparée. Paris, 1886; 2d ed., revised, 1890.

Les lois de l'imitation. Paris, 1890; 3d ed., revised and enlarged, 1900.

The Laws of Imitation. Translated by Elsie Clews Parsons, with an introduction by Franklin H. Giddings. New York, 1903.

La philosophie pénale. Paris, 1890; 2d ed., 1891.

Penal Philosophy. Translated by Rapelje Howell, with an editorial preface by Edward Lindsey. Boston, 1912.

Etudes pénales et sociales. Paris, 1892.

Les transformations du droit. Paris, 1893.

La logique sociale. Paris, 1895.

Essais et mélanges sociologiques. Paris, 1895.

L'opposition universelle. Paris, 1897.

Les lois sociales. Esquisse d'une sociologie. Paris, 1898.

Social Laws. An Outline of Sociology. Translated by Howard C. Warren, with a preface by James Mark Baldwin. New York, 1899.

Etudes de psychologie sociale. Paris, 1898.

Les transformations du pouvoir. Paris, 1899.

L'opinion et la foule. Paris, 1901.

Psychologie économique. 2 vols. Paris, 1902.

Fragment d'histoire future. Paris, 1905. Reprinted from the article in the *Revue internationale de sociologie*, IV: 603. Translated into English by Cloudesley Brereton and published (London, 1905) as *Underground Man*, with preface by H. G. Wells. This preface, translated, appears in *Archives de l'anthropologie criminelle*, XXI (1906): 233–40.

II. *Literary and Historical Works*

Contes et poèmes. Paris, 1879.

"La Roque de Gajac, monographie archéologique." *Bulletin de la Société historique et archéologique de Périgord-Périgueux,* 1881.

Introduction aux Chroniques de Jean Tarde, aumônier de Henri IV, pour servir à l'histoire de Périgord. Paris, 1888.

Les deux Statues. Brochure. Paris, 1892.

III. *Articles*

Revue philosophique.

X (1880) : 150, 264. "La croyance et le désir: possibilité de leur mésure."

XII (1881) : 232, 401. "La psychologie en économie politique."

XIV (1882) : 270. "Les traits communs de la nature et de l'histoire."

XV (1883) : 49. "La statistique criminelle du dernier demi-siècle." 658. "Quelques criminalistes italiens de la nouvelle école."

XVI (1883) : 363, 492. "L'archéologie et la statistique."

XVII (1884) : 607. "Darwinisme naturel et Darwinisme social."

XVIII (1884) : 173. "Travaux sur le socialisme contemporain." 489. "Qu'est-ce qu'une société?"

XIX (1885) : 593. "Le type criminel."

XXI (1886) : 1, 122. "Problèmes de criminalité."

XXII (1886) : 400. "Avenir de la moralité."

XXIV (1887) : 625. "Publications récentes sur la psychologie criminelle."

XXVI (1888) : 18, 148. "La dialectique sociale." 379. "La crise de la morale et la crise du droit pénal."

XXVIII (1889) : 113, 292. "Catégories logiques et institutions sociales." 449. "Le crime et l'épilepsie."

XXIX (1890) : 505. "La misère et la criminalité."

XXX (1890) : 337. "Le délit politique."

XXXI (1891) : 123, 289. "L'art et la logique."

XXXII (1891) : 482. "Etudes criminelles et pénales."

XXXV (1893) : 618. "Questions sociales."

XXXVI (1893) : 561. "La logique sociale des sentiments."

XXXIX (1895) : 148. "Criminalité et santé sociale."

XL (1895) : 26. "Le transformisme sociale."

XLI   (1896) : 637. "Sur l'idée de l'organisme social."
XLIII (1897) : 1, 160. "L'idée de l'opposition."
XLIV (1897) : 337. "La graphologie."
XLVI (1898) : 337. "Qu'est-ce que le crime?"
 LI   (1901) : 661. "Lettre à M. Espinas."
 LII (1901) : 457. "La réalité sociale."
Congrès internationale d'anthropologie criminelle: Comptes rendus.
Session 1885. *Rome:* p. 40. Discussion.
Session 1889. *Paris:* p. 92. "Les anciens et les nouveaux fondements de responsabilité morale."pp. 165, 183, 199, 284, 346, 374, 391. Discussion.
Session 1892. *Bruxelles:* p. 73. "Les crimes des foules." pp. 253, 335, 380, 384. Discussion.
Session 1896. *Genève:* p. 76. "La criminalité professionelle."
Archives de l'anthropologie criminelle, de criminologie, et de psychologie normale et pathologique.
 II (1887) : 32. "Positivisme et pénalité." 407. "La statistique criminelle pour 1885."
 III (1888) : 66. "Les actes du Congrès du Rome."
 IV: 92. "L'affaire Chambige." 237. "L'atavisme morale."
 V: 585. "L'amour morbide."
 VI: 453. "A propos de deux beaux crimes." 569. "L'archéologie criminelle en Périgord."
 VII: 353. "Les crimes des foules."
 VIII: 7. "Biologie et sociologie, résponse au Dr. Bianchi." 258. *"Pro domo mea,* réponse à M. Ferri."
 IX: 241. "Les crimes de haine." 641. "Les délits impoursuivis."
 XI (1896) : 418. "L'idée de l'organisme social."
 XII: 452. "La jeunesse criminelle."
 XIII: 369. "Problèmes de criminalité." 615. "Les transformations de l'impunité."
 XV (1900) : 5. "L'esprit de groupe." 233. "Leçon d'ouverture d'un cours de philosophie moderne au Collège de France." 644. "Du chantage."
 XVI: 168. "L'action inter-mentale." 565. "La criminalité et les problèmes économiques."
 XVIII (1903) : 162. "La criminalité en France dans les vingt dernières années."
 XIX (1904) : 537. "L'interpsychologie." 561. "Fragment d'histoire future."

Revue d'économie politique.
    1888: 526, 561. "Les deux sens de la valeur."
Revue d'anthropologie.
    3d series, vol. III (1888) : 521. "La criminologie."
Revue scientifique (Revue rose).
    3d series, vol. XVIII (1889) : 684. "Le deuxième Congrès international d'anthropologie criminelle."
      XIX (1890) : 737. "Les maladies de l'imitation" (concluded in vol. *XX* [1890]:6).
Revue des deux mondes.
    317 (1891) : 849. "L'idée de culpabilité."
    332 (1893) : 349. "Foules et sectes au point de vue criminel."
Revue politique et littéraire (Revue bleue).
    3d series, V. 23 (1892) : 611. "Les géants chauves, conte."
    4th series, V. 2 (1894) : 435. "La religion, étude de logique sociale."
          V. 6 (1896) : 636, 702, 828. "Brins d'idées."
          V. 8 (1897) : 331. "Les oppositions sociales: la guerre."
          V. 16 (1901) : 545. "L'idée de valeur."
          V. 19 (1903) : 33. "Rôle social de la joie."
    5th series, V. 1 (1904) : 673. "L'élite intellectuelle et la démocratie."
          769, 801. "L'avenir latin."
Revue internationale de sociologie.
      I (1893) : 157, 231. "Les monades et les sciences sociales."
      II (1894) : 34. "La série historique des états logiques."
      IV (1896) : 603. "Fragment d'histoire future."
     VII (1899) : 177. "Les transformations du pouvoir" (opening pages).
    VIII (1900) : 50. "L'hérédité des professions." 309, 450. Discussions. Reports of Tarde's words. 165. "Leçon d'ouverture d'un cours de philosophie moderne."
      IX (1901) : 1. "La psychologie intermentale." Translated as: Inter-Psychology: the Interplay of Human Minds, by C .H. Page, in *International Quarterly*, VII (1903) : 59. 38, 214, 377, 453, 940. Discussions.
      X (1902) : 562. "L'invention considerée comme moteur de l'évolution sociale." 139, 219, 386, 911. Discussions.
      XI (1903) : 125. "Les classes sociales." Discussion.
     XII (1904) : 83. "La sociologie et les sciences sociales." 52. Discussion.
Revue pénitentiaire.
    XVII (1893) : 750. "Considérations sur l'indétermination des peines."

XVIII   (1894) : 981. "Les longues peines." Discussion.
XIX   (1895) : 115. "La diminution du crime en Angleterre."
XX   (1896) : 1237. "Le Congrès d'anthropologie criminelle de Genève."
XXI   (1897) : 282. "L'alcoölisme et la loi pénale." Discussion.
867. "Les aliénés criminels." Discussion.
XXII   (1898) : 202. "Le recouvrement des frais de justice, etc." Discussion. 479. "Repression du vagabondage." Discussion. 618. "L'indemnité due à la partie lésée." Discussion. 1206. "La défense dans l'instruction préparatoire." Discussion.
XXIII   (1899) : 783. "Les sentences indéterminées." Discussion. 945. "Le droit de grace." Discussion. 1190. "Le jury et l'échevinage." Discussion.
XXIV   (1900) : 254. "La réforme des maisons de correction." Discussion. 1444. "L'état de nécessité et le délit nécessaire." Discussion.
XXV   (1901) : 829. "Les facteurs psychiques et les effets materiels." Discussion. 1467. "Congrès d'anthropologie criminelle d' Amsterdam."
XXVI   (1902) : 198. "La loi de pardon." Discussion. 1146. "Les résultats de sursis." Discussion.
XXVII   (1903) : 158, 293, 684. "La criminalité de 1880 à 1900." 1322, 1340. "Juges de paix." Discussion.

Annales de l'Institut internationale de sociologie.
I   (1894) : 209. "La sociologie élémentaire."
II   (1895) : 338. "Observations."
III   (1896) : 189. "Note sur les rapports de la biologie et de la sociologie."
IV   (1897) : 83, 237, 311. Discussion upon the "organic theory of society."
VIII   (1900–1901) : 283. "Quelques mots sur le matérialisme historique."
IX   (1902) : 87. "Augustin Cournot."
X   (1903) : 67. "La psychologie et la sociologie." 120, 242, 264, 412. Discussions.

La Réforme sociale.
4th series. Vol. VI (1898) : 709. "Les transformations de l'impunité."
Revue de Métaphysique et de morale.
6 (1898) : 14, 202, 329. "Les lois sociales."
9 (1901) : 119. "L'action des faits futurs."
13 (1905) : 319. "L'accident et le rationnel en histoire d'après Cournot."

La Revue de Paris.

    1898 (vol. 4) : 287, 615. "Le public et la foule."

    1899 (vol. 4) : 689. "L'opinion et la conversation" (concluded in vol. 5 of same year, pp. 91 seq.).

Bulletin de l'Institut internationale de statistique.

    XII (1900) : 306. "Notes sur quelques cartes et diagrammes de statistique judiciaire." 112. Discussion.

Revue de philosophie.

    V (1904) : 497. "La notion de hasard chez Cournot."

Séances et travaux de l'Académie des sciences morales et politiques.

    LXII (1904) : 5. "Notice sur la vie et les travaux de Charles Levêque."

R. Saleilles, *L'individualisation de la peine.* Paris, 1898. pp. i–vi: Préface (by Tarde).